THE HOUSTON SYMPHONY ORCHESTRA, 1913–1971

Miss Ima Hogg, founder of the Houston Symphony Orchestra.
(Conway Studios)

HUBERT ROUSSEL

The Houston Symphony
Orchestra, 1913–1971

UNIVERSITY OF TEXAS PRESS, AUSTIN & LONDON

Library of Congress Cataloging in Publication Data

Roussel, Hubert.
  The Houston Symphony Orchestra, 1913–1971.
  1. Houston Symphony Orchestra.
ML200.8.H72R7   785'.06'27641411   74-38924
ISBN 0-292-73000-4

Composition by G&S Typesetters, Austin
Printing by The University of Texas Printing Division, Austin
Binding by Universal Bookbinding, Inc., San Antonio

73 - 19561

This book is dedicated to the spirit of all those who have worked in many ways to make the Houston Symphony Orchestra what it is.

CONTENTS

ILLUSTRATIONS

PREFACE

The history of a symphony orchestra is in no small measure recorded by the daily reviewers of its music, whose product goes piecemeal into the files of newspapers and is there left to investigators of exceptional patience or to inquisitive mice. I was at different times over a period of more than thirty years a reviewer of music for publications in Houston —the *Gargoyle*, a weekly magazine, and two daily newspapers, the *Press* and the *Post*. The many reviews and incidental reports I wrote about affairs of the Symphony Society from the Houston orchestra's reorganization in 1928 through the season of 1965–1966 form a sort of historical record. But in this effort to provide the orchestra's story in a more connected and convenient arrangement, I have naturally needed and have had assistance of various kinds that I would like to acknowledge.

Primarily my thanks go to Miss Ima Hogg, founder of the orchestra, both for reflections about the movement given to me at intervals over more than three decades, and for certain information concerning the society's initial period (1913–1918), of which scant records remain. Most of the organization's earliest documents were destroyed, through the carelessness of a servant in the home of one of its officers. After the reorganization the record becomes more ample, but even so it requires at times the assistance of memory. Some of its gaps are tantalizing.

I have had the full and resourceful help of the symphony's executive staff, beginning with that of Tom M. Johnson, the orchestra's exceptional manager since 1948. Invaluable aid has been given by Mrs. Alice Bruce Currlin, the society's former public relations director—an assistance that has carried the added gratification of warm friendship.

Special thanks also are extended to Mrs. Anita Rall, a senior and most considerate member of the office organization. The late Will Houston, a true Mercury of the symphony cause, is likewise fondly remembered for his help as a courier.

To Gen. Maurice Hirsch, president of the Symphony Society from 1956 to 1970, I am grateful for the kindest understanding and patience during the preparation of this book. To other dear friends, Roy and Genevieve Demme, I owe thanks for having placed in my hands certain records, not otherwise available, of the first Summer Symphony operations. I am also especially obligated to Dr. Clifford J. Hoffmann of Tucson, Arizona, son of the orchestra's fifth conductor and its longest in service.

From the outset the orchestra has enjoyed excellent program annotators, and the studious writings of Dr. H. L. Bartlett, Harriet Rowe, William E. Rice, Bradley Lewis, Jack H. Ossewaade, Dr. Alfred R. Neumann, Elmer Schoettle, Robert P. Morgan, and Robert Jobe have been of assistance in this effort. Particular thanks are extended to Mrs. Marian Orgain, curator of special collections in the library of the University of Houston, and her assistant, Mrs. Sally Jurgensen, for having made available the full assortment of memorabilia given the library by Miss Hogg. A short history of the orchestra begun in 1963 by Mrs. Ralph Ellis Gunn has stimulated recollections, as have other historical digests representing the work of Mrs. Currlin.

Most of all, I owe gratitude to D. H. R., who shared with me the labor of this endeavor, as of so many others, searched out and organized much of the documentary matter, typed the manuscript, and suffered her household to be disarranged and her own activities unsettled for many months while the writing was done. For the spirit of that support there can be no sufficient acknowledgment.

THE HOUSTON SYMPHONY ORCHESTRA, 1913–1971

Chapter 1

It is not strange that the first men to set foot on the moon should have been guided to their destination from Houston. The city itself is an unlikely occurrence and it does the improbable naturally. Many observers have found their imaginations both stimulated and baffled by the contrasts of this springing metropolis, and in their efforts to explain Houston have written some rather curious things.

They are entitled to sympathy. In appearance and impact Houston is apt to be more than a little confusing, and its history is a welter of paradox. The city occupies what has been termed an impossible site. When this tract on the upper reaches of Buffalo Bayou was selected in 1836, some apathetic Indians and small game were not loath to surrender the ground, which was little more than a swamp with an extraordinary abundance of magnolias and snakes. During most of the year it steamed under a sweltering tropical heat; the winters, though short, were chilling and treacherous because of a penetrating damp.

Few spots in the new Republic of Texas could have offered less tempting conditions to the settlement-makers. But this one lay only a few miles from the battlefield, bordered by the same stream, where Texas had won its independence of Mexico short months before, and the brothers Augustus C. and John K. Allen, who established the town, were opportunists and clever promoters. They named it for the hero of that decisive engagement, declared it a salubrious garden spot and a beacon of destiny, and by other stratagems brought about its selection as the first capital of the nascent republic.

This was brash confidence, for the town was hardly more than a camp. When the Congress met for the first time in Houston, it was given as a forum a building that had no roof. But it is not known whether this was due to inability to get the roof on, or to a sudden decision that it might be better to go on up with the structure.

For Houston was booming in 1837 and has continued to grow by a series of spectacular booms. During the past forty-five years, in particular, these surges have been highly dramatic; they have made Houston the sixth largest of the nation's cities in population, and there has been much fanciful writing about them. It is true that the city today is a wonderland of modernity and thus gives an impression of newness. But its graces of living were not acquired with the floating towers and other marvels of building that so distinguish it now. Houston has furnished itself with the instruments of cultural pleasure by extended and orderly process, and the Houston Symphony Orchestra, one of the finest of the nation's musical organizations, is a beautiful illustration in point. With the start of its 1971–1972 season, the orchestra entered its fifty-eighth year. It is thus nearly half the age of the city itself.

In order to understand the cultivation and present position of the orchestra, it is useful to glance further at the earliest history of Houston. One thing to be noticed is that Houston seems never to have had the attitudes typical of a village. It never thought of itself as isolated or rustic, and whatever the living conditions of its first years may have been, the town offered the manners and interests of a well-settled and prosperous community. The Allen brothers, who were New York speculators, insisted from the first that they were founding a city, and had their wilderness tract (6,642 acres) laid out on a grandiose plan.

Fortune must have accepted their argument, for she sent them a cosmopolitan company of settlers, with strong representation from the older cities of the northern and eastern United States and a generous immigration from Europe, especially from Germany.

Accordingly there was never a time when the town's entertainment was altogether that of a rude outpost. One of the first Germans to arrive on the scene was Gustav Dresel, a cultivated spirit and luckily an industrious diarist, who left note that in 1837, little more than a year after its founding and long before any visitor could be sure of a bed, Houston had a musical theater in operation. This surprised Dresel (since the town had neither a church nor a jail), but struck no one else as an oddity. "There was lively activity going on in Houston at that time," Dresel wrote in his journal. "Varied entertainment was never lacking; we had billiard rooms and also a theatre; even concerts were successfully organized." It is recorded that Mme Louise Thieleman, a German singer-actress of some note in her day, made the journey by water from New Orleans to Houston in 1837 to take part in "the first theatre season in Texas." She seems to have been one of the concert performers to whom Dresel referred, and other evidence of the period indicates that these occasions were considerably different, in spirit and style, from the callithumps that any American frontier village might then have been expected to furnish.

The German element, with its strong tradition of social music, was quick to establish old habits in new surroundings by grouping itself into *Saengerbunds* and *Vereins*. These undoubtedly played a considerable part in the rather precocious establishment of the town's musical atmosphere. By 1844 the Houston Saengerbund was a formally chartered and flourishing venture, the community's largest organized musical body. To the early settlement had come also a sizeable Belgian immigration—sufficient in number to regard itself as a colony—a condition to be noted in view of a certain connection it was to have with the later musical development of Houston.

At any rate, and whatever the precise reasons may have been, an inclination to accept musical entertainment as a natural community aim is reflected in the very earliest records of the city. As the settlement rapidly changed from a straggle of rough cabins and tents to a trading center of more solid constructions, its art groups mounted in number. Another theater and several halls at least partly given over to music (Kessler's Arcade, in particular) were soon standing among the houses of trade; and as Houston began gathering the transportation facilities that would make it by the mid-1870's the chief railroad center of Texas, it ordered for its stages an ever-increasing volume and variety of entertainment, musical and dramatic, offering every style of the day.

Midway of the 1880's, three theater establishments were serving a population of perhaps twenty thousand or so. These elected to call themselves opera houses, which in measure they actually were, but a study of their fare is enlightening. They presented most of the great concert virtuosos then touring the land and a surprising variety of other matter. A Gilbert and Sullivan repertory was among the traveling attractions offered the public of Houston in 1886; and when a Sullivan of another strain, the mighty John L., was theatricalizing the power of his fists as an entertainer at about that time, his appearance in Houston was promptly counterbalanced by the presentation of Edwin Booth's *Hamlet*. Such a town was no cultural wilderness.

One further note properly closes this summary. In 1901 Houston imported the young Metropolitan Opera Company of New York City to perform in its Winnie Davis Auditorium, a great wooden structure that stood at the corner of Main Street and McGowen Avenue. In 1905 the Metropolitan Opera was brought again, this time to appear in the new downtown Prince Theater. The opera chosen for the initial occasion was *Lohengrin* (with Schumann-Heink as Ortrud); the second was *Parsifal*. Considering the challenge offered to the general audience of that day by the later music of Wagner, such choices were not those of a city just finding its way into the art. They were knowledgeable and, for their time, sophisticated. Because the copyright of the opera had been "jumped" by the Met, Houston heard *Parsifal* six years before London and most other European cities west of the Rhine had a chance to satisfy their curiosity concerning this ultimate work of the German master.

The new century began with the promise of all good things. It was a time of peace, contentment and prosperity. The religion of Progress had captured the world's imagination; its effect was to stimulate and give life a fresh edge of excitement. Progress of every kind, scientific, industrial, and social, was expected to make over the human condition very swiftly in a pattern of order, abundance, and beauty. The first decade of the twentieth century, despite evils enough, was a period of high hope and endeavor.

Nowhere was the new spirit more easily assumed than in Houston. As the calendar turned, dramatic changes took place in the town. It expanded in all ways; business of every kind flourished. The striking development of this epoch was the springing up in the Gulf Coast region, not far distant, of the new empire of petroleum. Houston was in a splendid position to benefit as a headquarters and radiation point for this industry of tremendous potential.

By 1912 the population of the city had risen above eighty thousand; its whole picture was rapidly altering. More and more handsome and commodious buildings, which reached upward for space, began throwing their shadows across those of a homelier cut which belonged to the ways of a large town. New conveniences made their appearance, to everyone's fascination and profit; luxury was the note of the moment. Yet life was in no way hurried, the comfortable habits were not changed, and there was time for the savoring of all good things that were novel. Houston's sense of well-being had never before been as pronounced. And in that genial air, the seed of its musical interest, well planted for some seventy years, found the elements needed for germination.

As to their beginnings, at any rate, the better American symphony orchestras have had very similar histories. The stories differ only in time. Otherwise three typical factors appear. The cities represented, already of some musical leaning, discovered themselves to have considerable numbers of professional musicians, of whose presence they were often reminded. Second, these cities, enjoying times of prosperity and apparent security, were at points in their social development when large portions of their wealth had come into the hands of the cultivated and leisured. The third and most important condition was that individual leaders appeared who were able, by intuitive strokes, to present the argument for musical culture to their own cities with peculiar attraction and force. There was such a conjunction in Houston in 1912, and it brought about a proposal that the city establish its own orchestra. The idea had been mentioned before in the town, but not with the same sort of persuasion. The person who now gave it a different measure of interest, a logic fashioned especially for Houston, was a quiet, modest, and greatly attractive young teacher of music. She was fondly known to her pupils and friends as Miss Ima.

Today it is understood, not only within the borders of Texas, that the appellation refers to Miss Ima Hogg, one of the state's most distinguished and resolute women. Her story has been that of a greatly conscientious and intelligent citizenship. Descendant of a pioneer family, the daughter of an illustrious governor of Texas, a judicious but passionate lover of art, an exemplar of true taste as opposed to the sham and wheedle of dilettante culture, she has indeed played a vital and unique role in the cultural development of the Southwest. Other volumes will be needed to tell that story completely. But in 1912 Ima Hogg was newly settled in Houston as a teacher of music, imparting the art she loved most.

The second child and only daughter of James Stephen Hogg was born July 10, 1882, in the village of Mineola in northeast Texas, while her father was serving as district attorney of Wood County. Three days later he wrote to his brother John: "Our cup of joy is now overflowing! We have a daughter of as fine proportions and of as angelic a mien as ever gracious nature favored a man with, and her name is Ima!" The name had a family significance; it was the one of the heroine in a highly romantic novel, *The Fate of Marvin*, which Thomas Elisha Hogg, the older brother of Jim, had written some years before. Its selection now was Jim's token of admiration for the avocational *litterateur*.

The Hogg family, of Scottish origin, had played a part in American Revolutionary history, and Joseph Lewis Hogg migrated from Alabama to Texas in 1839. His son, James Stephen, had striking gifts of intellect and personality, enabling him to capture the interest, respect, and affection of the state's people as few political figures have done. Jim Hogg rose from the soil through sharecropping, became a publisher of country newspapers and holder of minor governmental positions, educated himself in the law, and eventually served with distinction as attorney general of Texas. He was elected governor in 1890, the first native of Texas to hold that office, in which he remained for two terms. Jim Hogg was a progressive democrat who combined a talent for statesmanship with a rustic plainness of manner that much endeared him to the masses of voters. Their intuitive sense of kinship and affection was not ungrounded. After his retirement from politics, Jim Hogg went on to amass one of the state's oil fortunes, which has now largely been placed, in the form of educational and other benefactions, at the service of the people he represented and whose trust and esteem he enjoyed.

Strains of modest musical talent existed in the families of both James Hogg, who was himself something of a violinist, and Sally Stinson, whom he married in 1874. With the birth of their second child, these inclinations appeared in another measure. Ima showed a precocious musical gift. At three she was picking out tunes for herself on the piano; at five she was placed under the tutelage of Professor Edmund Ludwig in Austin, whose claim was that he had himself been a pupil of Anton Rubinstein. Very soon Ima delighted her father by being able to join him at the keyboard in the playing of hymns on Sunday evenings, Jim Hogg singing the burdens in a voice that favored falsetto effects. They were the very best of companions.

Ima continued her studies with piano teachers in Austin for ten years. Then in 1899, when she was seventeen, after two years at the University of Texas, she was sent to finishing school in New York, and in that city began her truly serious study of music. The piano was now the one interest that absorbed her completely; the other subjects were a bother or tedium. She had heard her first symphony orchestra in Madison Square Garden when as an eight-year-old she was taken by her father to an oratorio performance. ("It was the most beautiful thing I had ever heard in my life.") At the University of Texas, in 1902, she had been enthralled by a sinfonietta from Mexico brought there to perform, "which made me determine to try to do something of that kind." Now, as a free agent, choosing her own entertainment, she gloried in the musical atmosphere of a great city.

Seeking further instruction, and with no lack of conviction, she applied directly to one of New York's most celebrated authorities of the instrument, Rafael Joseffy, the Hungarian virtuoso, who was then on the threshhold of his sixties. Joseffy was no little surprised. He listened with interest to his young caller in the piece he gave her to play, but after looking at her hands, he refused her. "I had wormy fingers," Miss Ima explains. She was accepted, however, by another noted pedagogue of the art, Adele Margulies, and under her guidance worked intensively for two years and at intervals for more than a decade thereafter.

Meanwhile the family residence had changed. Home had become Varner Plantation, a short distance southwest of Houston in Brazoria County, which James Hogg had acquired and begun to develop soon after his retirement from state office. Its chief structure was a simple, rambling, and comfortable farmhouse, overlooking quiet fields, and in that setting he spent his last years with his children around him. It was Ima who apparently gave him the most comfort; since the death of her mother, in 1895, he had especially depended upon her. This meant that her New York musical studies were interrupted by longer and longer stays at Varner. It was not at Varner, however, but in Houston that James Hogg died on March 2, 1906. And it was for the purpose of settling his estate that Ima and her older brother, Will, established residence in Houston in 1908.

Meanwhile, she had had a significant experience. She made a visit to Europe. She went in 1907, as a tourist interested in observing the cultural riches and habits of other lands, but her stay became longer than she had expected. The reason lay in her fascination with one of the great musical capitals of the world, Berlin. She was intoxicated and thrilled by the feeling it gave her of having entered the very penetralia of the art she adored. With wide eyes she went to the imperial opera and to sumptuous concerts in the other halls. And as the time to take leave of the city approached, the thought of it gave her distress. The next question she put to herself was inevitable: "Why should I not study here?" An exchange of letters with her brother arranged it. Will Hogg, like his father, could be expected to see the point of a case.

As soon as she had his agreement, Ima enrolled at a favored musical academy of Berlin, that of the Scharwenkas, Franz Xaver and Ludwig

Philip. The first of the brothers was at this time pianist to the Austrian court of Franz Joseph, an office he apparently bore with no little sense of afflatus. It was under Franz Xaver that the student from Texas began; they did not hit it off very well. After three or four months, Miss Ima dropped the Herr Doktor Scharwenka "for personal reasons"— she seemed to have had enough of the pseudoimperial airs. She transferred to another renowned German authority, Martin Krause, who less ceremoniously put her to work on the preludes and fugues of Bach's *Das Wohltemperirte Klavier*. He was a taskmaster, but a teacher more after her heart.

"I think Bach meant these pieces to be played with much feeling," she said to him.

"Ah, yes," agreed the fatherly Krause. "And so—?"

He listened with increasing attentiveness to the player's expressive ideas, and sometimes smiled in a way that rewarded her fully. She remained with him a year and a half, completely immersed in her work.[1]

When she saw Houston again the town wore its most cheerful countenance. The time was sunny and Houston society, astir with all manner of innovations and widening pleasures, was at its brightest and keyed to the mood of expectancy. There had never been so many interesting things to be done; it was a wonderful time to be alive.

But Ima Hogg was a realistic young person. During the crossing from Europe, with a chance to think carefully over her life and ambitions, she had made an important decision. It had not been easy, but it was characteristic and final. She had made up her mind that she lacked the natural equipment for a concert career at the first level. Any other kind she would not want to attempt, and so she had accepted the alternative way to remain close to the art of her choice. She would make her offering through the service of teaching.

---

[1] An evidence of her effort, during this period in Germany, is to be found in the Hogg Archives of the University of Houston Library. It is a well-thumbed score of Wagner's *Die Walküre*, in a piano reduction, containing her markings and annotation. The opera's leitmotifs are all carefully identified in her neat script, the harmony analyzed at various moments of expressive power, and portions of the text are translated. She was indeed the diligent Wagnerite, as further shown by her notation of programs heard at Bayreuth and other shrines of this master.

Accordingly, as soon as she was settled in Houston again, she opened a studio, and there she worked until 1919, when a critical illness made her an invalid for more than a year. She had been very successful, and her choice of pupils was sharp. The first two she accepted went on to distinguish themselves—Bessie Griffiths as a teacher in her own right and Jacques Abram as an illustrious concert artist. But as she took her position in the town's musical life, Miss Ima had other dreams too. The skies above Houston invited them.

Chapter 2

During the winter of 1912–1913 there
was more touring of theatrical entertainment, both musical and dramatic, than the nation had ever before known. Indeed the record would
prove to be lasting. There has never again been a time when that system afforded such a wealth of magnetic and often illustrious names. Attractions of every kind reached the theaters of Houston. Among them
was a Russian symphony orchestra—so called at least—which arrived
with a stagger and found itself stranded after its concert. The conductor, one Altshculer, decamped, but there was an effort by the concertmaster, Nikolai Sokoloff,[1] to assume the command and settle the
company in town. He offered Houston the theoretical glories of his
orchestra in return for a modest support. The concert, however, had
convinced nobody of the magnanimous nature of that bargain, and
there were few interested listeners to his proposition.

[1] Later to become first conductor of the Cleveland Symphony Orchestra.

Yet, except for the hungry musicians themselves, the attempt was not an unlucky occurrence. Sokoloff's proposal, urged for a month or so, became a topic of discussion at dinner parties and other gatherings where musical and theatrical matters were talked of. Ima Hogg was present at many of these; as a bright musical spirit with fresh impressions of the European scene, her opinions were especially solicited.

Although it was casual, she welcomed this interest in orchestra conditions. Perhaps its direction could be changed. Her first dream had been that of a Texas Symphony Orchestra, to be supported in part by state grants; she now altered that original concept. She believed in the doctrine of self-sufficiency and saw no reason why it shouldn't apply to the art of music as to other affairs. Since her return she had been struck by the many good musical talents in Houston. The professional body was a large one (the Houston union had been chartered by the American Federation of Musicians in 1897), and there were amateur organizations that did work of exceptional standard. The city's musical culture was lively, and Miss Hogg began asking why Houston should not set about forming an orchestra of its own. Would there ever be a better time to begin?

The reactions to her question, though generally cautious, were promising. She discovered that a number of other women who held prominent places in the town's music had also been turning over the thought. A leader among these was Mrs. Edwin B. Parker, then president of the excellent Choral Club; her close associates in that organization included Mmes. H. M. Garwood, William Abbey, Gentry Waldo, and Jules Hirsch. All were discriminating judges of the art, and all finally agreed with the idea that fascinated Miss Hogg and with her sense of an opportune moment.

Consequently, these ladies, with certain others of vision, set out to exploit such interest as the Russian proposition had stirred. Together they operated a clever diversion of the party-talk. Suddenly Maestro Sokoloff and his troubles were taken out of the picture, and the comfortable, well-fixed diners found themselves caught in discussions of another musical matter entirely, the question of whether Houston should not furnish itself, from its own resources, with a symphony orchestra, and whether a movement of that aim would not be the most reasonable and exhilarating adventure in culture to which the city could now possibly turn.

But though the times were so good, the idea encountered some very skeptical listeners. They felt it to be decidedly premature. After all, Houston was having a quite bountiful theater season, and more of the same kind were assured. Enough was enough. Let elaborate entertainment—especially elaborate musical entertainment—continue to be supplied by other places afar, which had gone to all the trouble and cost of producing it. Let Houston be satisfied to attend. That was also exciting, and far less risky and bothersome.

So the winter wore on, and though the ladies in question did much to win over these doubters (Miss Hogg, in particular, using a gift of cool suasion inherited from her father), nothing definite came of their idea. As spring approached, however, there was an unexpected development. It came from the professional quarter.

Most of Houston's professional musicians were employed in its theater orchestras, either those of the standard theaters or those of the luxury cinema houses that had lately come into vogue. The music they dealt with in these jobs was not often a challenge to serious interest, but there were places in town where the players found themselves handling a more varied and gratifying repertoire. One of these, the most widely noted and favored, was Sauter's Restaurant. Occupying two floors of a building at the northeast corner of Preston Avenue and Travis Street, Gus Sauter's establishment had for many years been Houston's most excellent public dining facility. It appealed to a dignified clientele. The atmosphere it afforded was Viennese; the decorations and service were models of Victorian comfort and elegance. And Sauter's completed its Old World charm with another attraction. In its principal dining room on the second floor, thickly carpeted and discreetly lighted, was an alcove bordered by potted palms, and in this niche, at the luncheon and dinner hours, there was always to be found a small orchestra.

That fact in itself was no novelty; other quality restaurants in town supplied music. The difference at Sauter's was that people were apt to listen a good deal more closely, if their epicureanism was not limited to delights of the table. The typical ensemble was a string quartette; sometimes it consisted of a piano trio or quartette, and sometimes a small serenade group with woodwind. In any case and whatever the instrumental group, the fare presented was never the chowder customarily offered as "Viennese music" in restaurants.

The provider and leader of these units in 1913 was Julien Paul Blitz, a musician of taste and an excellent cellist. He was of Belgian extraction and drew his associates chiefly from what he described as the Belgian colony of Houston. They were chosen with care, and at Sauter's they played the quartettes, trios, sonatas, suites, and other music of Haydn, Mozart, Beethoven, Brahms, and Franz Schubert quite as much as they did the waltzes of Johann Strauss and Lehar. Thus they manifested the tradition of chamber music as it had existed in Houston through all the vicissitudes of the town's growth.

Julien Paul Blitz was a leader of Houston's musical life and had the normal professional jealousy. He had been one of the strongest opponents of Sokoloff's effort to move in with the Russian organization. That threat out of the way, Blitz had been toying with the idea of organizing a Houston symphony orchestra of his own. He had been unable to find enough backing among his immediate friends, and in late winter, having heard of the ladies' committee, he went to Miss Hogg, asking her to help furnish support. She was surprised, and with a quick eye saw an interesting chance. She respected the musical qualities of Julien Paul Blitz; he had his obvious following in the city; he stood in position to recruit a body of players with ease. Ima Hogg thought of a plan. She took it first to the ladies of the informal committee, and they in turn took it to others. A few days later their efforts resulted in an interesting item for the papers. It announced the creation of a new society of music lovers, to test the question of whether Houston could be expected to support a symphony orchestra of its own. The test would consist of a trial concert, with Julien Paul Blitz as conductor of a provisional organization; if this succeeded, the association would attempt to continue the movement and establish regular concerts. The announcement contained no mention of underwriting. The ensemble would not cost much, and Mr. Blitz, for his own part, was not thinking of money matters at this point. He wanted only to be sure that sufficient time would be allowed for rehearsing the band.

As it turned out, the preparation of the concert took longer than anyone had expected. This was due less to the conductor's fine scruple, however, than to the lasting abundance of the theater season, which showed no signs of ending as the winter wore off, but went on into April and May. Glamor thrust glamor aside with a haste that was somewhat rude. Was it Otis Skinner in *Kismet* tonight? Or was it *The Pink Lady* or *The Count of Luxembourg*, or Nazimova's *Bella Donna*, or *The Merry Countess* with the Dolly Sisters in bloom? Or was it irresistible Ethel Barrymore, with her cello voice, or Gaby Deslys, or Valli-Valli, or Vaudeville suddenly flashing such magnets as Bernhardt, Eva Tanguay, Lillian Russell, and Valeska Suratt? The town scurried about to theater affairs and gay parties, imitating the fashions and manners of the medium. Irene Castle had divided the nation by bobbing her hair. But regardless of how one felt about that, learning the Castle Walk was obligatory if one wished to keep up with the current in 1913. The year itself was a hit.

Thus Houston's professional musicians, serving both the theater pits and the parties, were kept "jobbing" about at a great rate, and Mr. Blitz found difficulty in forming an ensemble that could get together for practice. There was too much in the air. He fretted over the problem, and the ladies of the concert committee, caught up in the prevalent quickstep, had never supposed they would have such a flutter about finding a spot for their enterprise. When the concert finally took place, it defied seasonal odds. It was given on June 21 in the new Majestic Theater, at the unlikely hour of five o'clock in the afternoon.

The Majestic, on Texas Avenue between Travis and Milam streets, was the city's principal vaudeville house. It belonged to the upper, or "two-a-day," rank of that popular form and was quite charming in design and appointment. There were loge boxes, and fat cherubs made sport on the auditorium ceiling. The theater was operated by Karl Hoblitzelle's Interstate circuit of Dallas, and Mr. Hoblitzelle had donated its use for the concert, which had to be given between the regular matinee and evening performances. That was taking a serious risk. Full summer had come, and no proper theater in Houston then attempted to operate all year round. The Majestic itself was about to shut down for two months. Meanwhile, five o'clock in the afternoon of a baking June day was a strange time to ask people to gather in a little theater that seated six hundred, without cooling arrangements excepting a few wall fans, for the purpose of hearing an experiment in the making of serious music. As the committeewomen waited in the lobby to see the results of their propaganda, they must have prayed quietly. There was a gratifying response. When the doors closed for the start of the concert, the Majestic was very well filled. Houstonians were still thirty years from the realization that in hot weather humanity could expect to be other than physically miserable.

A charming memento of this occasion exists in the form of a photograph, which shows the orchestra seated in front of that standard and fondly recalled horror of American vaudeville houses, the "palace drop." Mr. Blitz had a company of thirty-five instrumental performers, with B. J. Steinfeldt as the concertmaster;[2] the band had been carefully chosen and rehearsed in a program that was modest enough. It began with its main item, a Mozart symphony in E-flat (which of the four in that key is not clear, since no catalogue number was given); the other orchestral selections were a *Carmen* fantasia and the "Waltz of the Flowers" from Tchaikovsky's *Nutcracker* Suite, to which Lacombe's *Aubade Printemps* was added as an encore. And there was a soloist, Miss Blanche Foley, an excellent Houston soprano, who sang a substantial and beautiful repertory item, the *Divinités du Styx* from Gluck's *Alceste*. It seems that "Dixie" was played as a wind-up, after an address by Dr. Henry Barnstein, explaining the aims of the movement.

Press reports of this affair as a social occasion were suitably glowing and politely omitted reference to the perspiration exacted of the devotees. Mrs. Wille Hutcheson, the critic attending, wrote a plainer account in the *Houston Post* of the following morning; she said it had been "intensely warm," as she elected to put it, and went on to deliver an estimate: "The concert in many ways was a revelation to Houstonians, who, while realizing in a sort of offhand way that there is much musical talent in Houston, were yet unaware of the intensity of music study and the breadth of understanding and artistic conception of the

2 For other participants, see appendix.

majority of Houston musicians. If any want to criticize, the criticism must at least have become tempered with sympathy and appreciation; for while none would claim an afternoon of perfected offerings, there was far more to enjoy and admire than to condemn or sharply criticize."

Mrs. Hutcheson's feelings appear to have been those of the audience. There was much talk after the concert, and the sponsoring committee heard little but encouraging comment. The good attendance was a solid and gratifying fact; so was the work of Mr. Blitz as an organizer and leader. The enthusiasm appeared to be real. When the ladies again met to consider the total results, it seemed to them that the public had given its authorization for the orchestra scheme to proceed.

Another souvenir of the little victory is found in Mr. Blitz's payroll for the concert. Made out in neat script and methodically checked, it shows that his players, professional and amateur, received $5.00 each for the service—a total expenditure for talent of $165.00.[3] Such was the innocent age.

With this small buzz of excitement, however, the season's cultural gusto was exhausted. Summer pressed down with a grim, stultifying heat. After their habit, the privileged fled Houston for distant retreats, favoring the mountains or waterside, and those bound to remain in the city were no more active than duty demanded. Theaters were shuttered and formal entertainment suspended. The town became socially desolate.

Three months passed before the concert had its definite aftermath. October at last came, with its blessed recharging of the air, the annual miracle of revival in South Texas; and suddenly everbody was home again. The lights were full on, it seemed there were greatly interesting things to be said, and the quickened spirit was ready for adventure. Choosing her moment, Miss Hogg arranged for a meeting of those who had helped produce the experimental performance or had shown particular interest in its outcome. The gathering took place in the home of Mrs. Edwin B. Parker; the records of it are a testimonial—often to

[3] They had received three dollars apiece for rehearsals.

be repeated over more than half a century—of Ima Hogg's vision, dedication, and peculiar genius for expressing the cultural ideal to her native region.

On this day her cool logic was felt with unusual force. She and Mrs. Parker presented the meeting with a modest, well-considered, and thoroughly businesslike plan. They made no flowery predictions in support of the idea; they argued simply that the way to begin is to begin. The meeting agreed, and without further delay there was organized, and announced through the papers, the Houston Symphony Association, for the purpose of establishing a permanent orchestra and giving regular seasons of concerts. Mrs. Parker was elected president;[4] Miss Hogg, first vice-president; Frantz Brogniez, second vice-president; H. F. MacGregor, treasurer; Mrs. Z. F. Lillard, recording secretary; Mrs. William Abbey, corresponding secretary. Signers of the charter petition, in addition to Mrs. Parker, Miss Hogg, and Mrs. Abbey, were Mrs. Gentry Waldo and Mr. Blitz.

Twenty-two others were elected to a board of directors. They were Mmes. R. C. Duff, E. A. Peden, Gentry Waldo, Joseph Mullen, Will Jones, Turner Williamson, James Schuyler Stewart, Jules Hirsch, J. Lewis Thompson; Misses Laura Rice, Blanche Foley, and Ella Smith; and Messrs. H. F. MacGregor, Ike Harris, Henry Stude, Abe Levy, Will Kendall, Jesse H. Jones, D. B. Cherry, J. B. Bowles, J. S. Cullinan, and Dr. Edgar Odell Lovett. There was also appointed an advisory committee, consisting of Dr. Henry Barnstein, Dr. William S. Jacobs, Mrs. W. B. Sharp, Mrs. C. C. Wenzel, Mrs. Harris Masterson, Mrs. J. O. Carr, and P. W. Horn.

Most of these original officers gave long service to the symphony cause, and this tradition of service has been carried on by their descendants, to the second and third generations. The orchestra's present magnificent hall is the gift of Mr. and Mrs. Jesse H. Jones, through their heirs. Miss Nina Cullinan, daughter of J. S. Cullinan, has been one of the symphony's most imaginative and generous benefactors. Mrs. Jules Hirsch was the mother of Gen. Maurice Hirsch, who became president of the Symphony Society in 1956 (after serving on its board since

---

4 Over her objections, for she had been very skeptical before the trial concert and continued to have some doubts. "But she was the natural selection," says Miss Hogg.

1937), officiated during the orchestra's Golden Anniversary season, and has in all ways been a distinguished administrator of the movement. These are cases among many that illustrate how fully the welfare and advance of this instrument have been matters of family concern.

But that is to run ahead of the story. In October, 1913, with the charter secured, the question was how to set up a new cultural venture and make the most of the opportunities offered. It was a beautiful autumn, and the town was engaged with a host of distractions. Social conventions and dress fashions were changing in remarkable ways (teddybears were the current astonishment), and all the new customs, representing an escape from Victorian trammels, were delightful. This season the rage, just over from Paris, was *thé dansant*, which everyone felt bound to embrace. The favored places for this were the dining quarters of the new Rice Hotel; there was dancing by candlelight in its main salon at five o'clock in the afternoon or, when the weather allowed, in its colorful, open-air roof garden, eighteen stories above. This pinnacle commanded a view of the whole town; and far out to the south, as daintily fantastic as the towers in a Watteau painting, one saw the new buildings of Rice Institute, the city's first university of major endowment, which had also just opened its doors. Dr. Lovett of the symphony board was its first president. Everywhere there were signs of a new age. Already some people were riding in glass-enclosed automobiles, the ladies no longer required to lash down their coiffures or wear goggles. It was all very alluring.

Against this panorama the Symphony Association announced its arrival and plan. The scheme for the first season was again of a modesty scarce to be challenged; it called for a series of three "twilight" concerts to be given in the Majestic Theater, which again would be lent for the purpose. The budget established for the season was $2,500. When members of the organization set out to ensure this (Miss Hogg again taking the lead), they had small trouble in finding 138 guarantors who pledged an average of $25 each.[5] The season would thus start with a cushion of $3,450 in underwriting. It had been settled that Mr. Blitz was to be the conductor; for the time being he would work at the

---

[5] See appendix for a list of guarantors.

same pay rate as the players. The orchestra would be the one he had formed for the trial concert, or substantially that body, with any changes he saw fit to provide. Expenses being assured, the first concert was announced for the afternoon of December 19.

This time there was less reason to worry about public response. The experimental performance had made musical friends; the talk it aroused, plus the campaign to finance the first season, had captured the attention of others. Now it was seen that membership in the new organization would carry with it a certain social advantage. As a result, when tickets were offered for the season, there appeared to have been a sudden and rather spectacular upsurge of the town's passion for serious music. All at once everyone wanted to join, and little time was required to make certain the house would be full.

And so there was a capacity audience when the Houston Symphony Orchestra began its career, six days before Christmas in 1913. The program Mr. Blitz offered was unpretentious enough; it opened with Haydn's *London* Symphony, and in its other matter reflected the preoccupation of that American day with the operatic. There was a baritone soloist, Arturo Lugaro, who sang the "Toreador Song" from *Carmen*; the other instrumental selections were Mascagni's fantasia on themes from *Cavalleria Rusticana*, Gandolfo's "Marche Héroique," from his version of *Don Quixote*, Bolognesi's *Apres la Valse*, and Saint-Saëns's *Coronation March*. Mr. Blitz had probably made a pretty shrewd guess as to the elements he would find in his audience that afternoon.

The press recorded another victory in the form of enthusiasm and hat styles displayed, but not all the reports were unqualified. Though Mrs. Hutcheson wrote warmly enough in the *Post*, she avoided rash musical claims. Her remarks were discreetly keyed to the note of promise, concerning the orchestra, and to the wonders of Haydn's inventiveness. The rest of the program, she made sufficiently clear, was intrinsically rather a stew.

Her disapproval was apparently taken to heart, for the second concert, given in March, brought certain improvements in repertory; it also, according to Mrs. Hutcheson's estimate, showed gains in executional workmanship. The playing had become more unified and expressively varied. Other reports of this occasion were encouraging, too, and audience enthusiasm continued. By the time of the concert closing the series, on May 12, matters were looking up smartly. The program for this affair was the best of the three, combining Mozart's *Jupiter* Symphony with compositions of Donizetti, Grieg, Godard, and Tchaikovsky. Arthur Barbour supplied meticulous program notes, but the program book was excessively formal. The Donizetti number was the sextette from *Lucia*, its vocalists being "Mesdames Kyle, Lillard, and Messrs. Doescher, Juenger, Spurway and Lugaro"—all singing without their first names.

What mattered, however, was that the season had been a success. That was the count from any viewpoint. The public had turned out well; the players themselves were enthusiastic and now began feeling a sense of connection. Will Kendall, the volunteer business manager, could show the movement to be in good condition financially, and the guarantor plan had been accepted, however modestly, as a requisite of the symphony idea. There was another hopeful development, too—the interest displayed in this venture by the city's business community. One of Houston's largest department stores, Foley Brothers, had been a contributor to the guaranty fund; another smart store of the kind, Levy Brothers, had lent help by including the symphony cause in its own advertising. These gestures had done something to give color and weight to the season and established a precedent that has meant much to the progress of musical culture in Houston.

It was a little prophetic, however, that the Grieg pieces performed in the closing concert were the *Two Elegiac Melodies*. The second of these is a tender and shadowed little poem, *Letzter Frühling*—the Last Spring; it is music of a curious longing. Spring's softness was much in the air as Mrs. Parker, Miss Hogg, and the other organizers, happy over the season and the promising outlook, separated to go their ways for the summer. What they could not know, with the Grieg elegy fresh in their memories, was that the partings this year were to have an extraordinary significance. Spring would not come again in the same way, nor would music ever again be made, or listened to, from the same background of emotion. There were two months left in an epoch.

The world's peace was destroyed by shots fired in the Balkan village of Sarajevo on June 28. Before summer was over, most of Europe was swept by war. Nobody had believed it could happen, but it had happened, and it was war of a new terror and magnitude. At first the catastrophe was too vast to be fully understood at a distance. Americans who had grown up in a world of apparent stability were shocked, stunned, and bewildered; neutrality was the cry, however, and affairs went ahead in some manner. Momentum operated where attention was distracted or absent.

The American theater season of 1914–1915, planned well in advance, would be another very generous outlay, with frivolous matter galore. The rate of touring again was spectacular. But the season began in a garish, unreal light, and enthusiasm was hectic or forced. By early September the German armies were sweeping on Paris, and news of the battle of the Marne, with its hideous desperation and carnage, was strange preparation for attending a farce or the latest musical extravaganza from Broadway. With hopes for an early end of the war fast disappearing, the drift of matters was all too evident: Armageddon and world war were terms increasingly and oppressively used.

At this time, however, there was another aspect to the crisis. America, it was said, now had its obligation to grow up and set a model of sanity and responsibility. Civilization was threatened; if the major nations of Europe, which had long been its conservators in the West, were entangled in a savage and terrible folly, it behooved America to take over that guardianship during the nightmare by preserving the civilized customs and amenities. America had sheltered the poor and rejected of various European countries; now it stood in position, because of remoteness, to shelter their cultural arts. There was that much reason for the nation's artistic establishments to continue with normal objectives in an atmosphere greatly disturbed. The Houston Symphony Association, though still so new, was anxious to preserve what it had gained, and in September its board met, reelected Mrs. Parker and the other officials, and voted to go on with the operation.

The second season repeated the plan of the first. There was a preliminary solicitation that enrolled substantially the same body of underwriters, and three more "twilight" concerts were announced for the Majestic Theater. The ticket response was again splendid, and the season began, appropriately enough, on Thanksgiving afternoon, November 26. The program opened with German's "Three Dances" from *Henry VIII*; the other orchestral selections were Grieg's *Four Northern Dances*, the ballet music from Gounod's *Faust*, and the *Spanish Dances* of Moszkowsky, which closed the performance. Midway came a vocal insertion, the waltz from Gounod's *Romeo and Juliet*, with Mrs. McElroy Johnston the soprano soloist.

By midseason of 1914–1915 the mounting emotional tensions of the war were being felt in American concert halls. Programs had to be chosen with care. The playing of intensely German music was becoming a problem; German conductors had begun to feel the audience chill. That this irrationality was not operating too strongly in Houston, however, is indicated by the second program of this season. In the concert of March 12, 1915, the orchestra had its first instrumental soloist. She was the violinist Rosetta Hirsch (sister of Maurice Hirsch), who had played in the ensemble from the time it began and who played for this occasion the G Minor Concerto of Max Bruch, with all its rich German romanticism. The program had opened with Haydn's Symphony in G Major (No. 13), and otherwise included Delibes's intermezzo for *Naïla* and Luigini's *Ballet Egyptian*.

When the season ended in May, another success could be claimed, though the gratification was subdued by the turn of events. All hope for an early end of the war seemed lost. The summer was grim and alarming, but as yet the disturbance of American life, of American habits, was not too great—if one could look away from the headlines. People went to the mountains or seashore for very pleasant vacations, and there was a wide prosperity. Although the cloud above Europe assumed ever more menacing darkness and the Washington news became ever more cause for concern, life in American cities and towns could be very attractive for all that. Prosperity added to the audience for good theater fare. The "twilight" concerts of the Houston society had become an agreeable habit, and its seasons of 1915–1916 and 1916–1917 went better than the two seasons before.

There was one change in the plan. After the 1915–1916 series, Julien Paul Blitz asked to be relieved of his duties as conductor. He was replaced by Paul Bergé, a violinist who had also made his reputation in Houston as a player in its better theater and cafe orchestras. His tenure began with a concert on Thanksgiving afternoon, November 30, 1916, when he led a program of Haydn, a suite by Percy Grainger, Mendelssohn's *Ruy Blas* Overture, and airs from *Manon* and *Cavalleria Rusticana* sung by James Dow, a Houston tenor of more than competent craft. "After yesterday's hearing I do not think that any real musician could fail to appreciate that our new Symphony director is in his attitude toward the art tremendously in earnest," Mrs. Hutcheson wrote in the *Post*. "Most emphatically we are in for congratulations all round, according to my way of thinking."

But congratulations were somewhat absent-mindedly given that day and became more casual as the season progressed. Woodrow Wilson was no longer insisting that America was "too proud to fight." Too many American ships had gone down; the handwriting was plain to be seen on the wall, even theater walls. On April 6, 1917, a month after the close of Mr. Bergé's first season, the United States entered the maelstrom by a declaration of war against Germany. Public reaction was half one of relief; it was better to know the worst, if it had to come, than to go on with an agonizing suspense. The call to action was stimulating, at least, and for a while was accompanied by an instinct to grasp eagerly at any good thing—any momentary pleasure or comfort or beauty—because the chance might not again come.

The Houston Symphony Association went through with a 1917–1918 season, which opened on the afternoon of November 22 with a program consisting of Goldmark's *Rustic Wedding* Symphony, Massenet's *Scenes Pittoresques*, Sibelius's *Valse Triste*, and Nicolai's *Merry Wives of Windsor* Overture. The solo number, "Che gelida manina" from *La Bohème*, was a reminder of how things stood: it was sung by Sgt. Ridgely Hudson. There were the usual three concerts, and the season closed on April 3. Mrs. John F. Grant was the soloist for that occasion, in Liszt's E-flat Piano Concerto; but the fitting title came last on the program. It was Saint-Saëns's prelude to *The Deluge*. At last the grimness had come too close. Men were leaving the orchestra to be trained for war, and with this performance the sponsors accepted the color of the day. They voted not to attempt a sixth season.

Had the organization remained active as a concert-giving society for another seven months, it would have found the road open again. But in April of 1918 nobody could foresee what was to happen in November. By that time the association had taken itself out of the picture, and, in the general confusion that followed the restoration of what was called peace, the promoters of this movement were slow to recover their enthusiasm. The society drifted, and a curious situation resulted.

Chapter 3

The war left Houston a more complex, restless city. In material ways it had benefited from the great industrial effort brought on by the conflict; socially it had acquired a variety of new characteristics, due to heavy gains in population that had not as yet been fully assimilated. The public temper was impatient, erratic, and fickle. Such indeed was the atmosphere over the nation as a whole. And as the second decade of the century gave way to the one later to be known as the Roaring Twenties, the meaning of this reaction to the war's frenzy was not to be guessed. It was a strange lingering fever. The resumption of old habits had not occurred as most people had expected; the past seemed very much past. It was a time of new pressures, dissatisfactions, and doubts.

The Houston orchestra had been disbanded without disbanding its supporting organization. Officially, there was still a society. This continuance was chiefly the work of Miss Hogg, who had become president of the association in 1917 and had seen to it that occasional meetings were held. She had hoped to reestablish the orchestra as soon as conditions were normal, but now, though the crisis was over, she found little to encourage her idea. The immediate postwar air did not invite art projects whose goals were necessarily distant. A year after the conflict Miss Hogg suffered the illness that caused her to remain long in a hospital, and when it ended she was not at once able to resume her accustomed activities.

In 1921 she was succeeded as president of the association by Mrs. H. M. Garwood, and there were other official rearrangements. But this led to no immediate action. The association adopted a waiting policy, and it easily turned into a habit. The mad Twenties were very bemusing. Time passed, and there was no move to reassemble the orchestra. But after a while, in order to hold some public position, the society began to present occasional programs of chamber music, with members of the original orchestra, and to act as joint sponsor of certain visiting musical attractions. For the latter purpose it made an arrangement with Mrs. Edna W. Saunders, who had recently come into prominence as a booker of cultural entertainment for Houston; this connection resulted in appearances of the St. Louis, Minneapolis, and other symphony organizations of note. Altogether, however, thirteen years were to pass, from the time of the orchestra's disappearance, before Houston's own symphony movement would be fully revived. When this did happen, the time was entirely unlikely and the circumstances not lacking a note of the comic.

In the summer of 1929 the nation was at the peak of a wild economic boom, and this giddy prosperity, which had been mounting for more than a decade, manifested itself in an orgy of freak fads and extravagant projects. No other time could have made flagpole-sitting an interest. Among the period's more grandiose ventures that found ready financing was Chicago's Century of Progress Exposition, the plant for which was then under construction. The aims of the exposition included a representative showing of the nation's regional culture, and thus it occasioned a certain venture in Houston.

The Houston musical colony had for many years been enlivened by a personality of rare color, temerity, and impulse, Mrs. John Wesley

Graham, whose impatient rushes to conquer the heights of Olympus left many a legend. She was a teacher of voice, choir director of the First Methodist Church, and organizer extraordinary of sundry ventures intended, as she individually reckoned, to hasten the coming of the city's full cultural glory. The announcement of Chicago's plan to survey regional theater art was to this excellent lady a direct and imperative challenge. "Ma" Graham—for so she was fondly known to her considerable flock—reacted in typical manner. It became her conviction that Houston should be represented in Chicago by an opera company of full mettle and weight, in the form of a spectacular production of Verdi's *Aïda*, elephants included, which she would personally undertake to finance, organize, and direct.

Nobody in Houston said nay to the ideas of "Ma" Graham; the prudent had learned to take cover and give her full freedom of movement. Though the exposition would not open for more than a year, she felt there was no time to be lost; the opera company would need seasoning at home. She accordingly started with a propaganda barrage of her own brand; Mrs. Graham was a pioneer in the saturation technique of publicity. Her campaign had proceeded for some weeks and was just getting the city well blanketed, when the Wall Street market collapsed on October 28. The inflationary bubble had burst. Within a very few weeks, drastic retrenchments of every kind had become the order of American life.

It might have been supposed that such a scheme as the Houston opera enterprise would rank high among locally dispensable items. But that was to reckon without "Ma" Graham. She was not the sort of woman to be turned in her purpose by a mere national calamity. Houston did not at once feel the depression too keenly and was never to suffer its worst blight. Mrs. Graham simply redoubled her efforts. In the summer of 1930, with certain backing secured in her own ways, she left for Europe to scout some of its operatic ideas and available talent. Her trip was to have dramatic results, for things happened that way with Mrs. Graham.

She first visited Italy, and while in Milan met an opera coach and conductor whose talents impressed her. This was Uriel Nespoli. He was still youngish, well regarded, and apparently on his way up. Mrs.

Graham thought so well of his qualities that she made him an offer to become the conductor of her enterprise. Though he probably never understood her completely, Nespoli gladly accepted. He had never been in America and the offer had a flattering sound. Mrs. Graham then left to continue her travels in England, France, and Germany. She was not to be home until September; Nespoli was to meet her in Houston at that time.

But there was a hitch in the plan. Complications developed, and as a result Mrs. Graham arrived in the city in high dudgeon. She had sent back news of the conductor's appointment, and now there was no conductor to meet her. She explained things in a statement given the press. It appeared that when Nespoli, acting on her instructions, had attempted to leave for his new post, he had been told by the Italian authorities in Milan that the quota of immigration to the United States was exhausted for the year, and summarily ordered to forget his plan. Mrs. Graham was indignant and furious. In view of the reason for Nespoli's hiring, she considered this interference an outrage. She suspected a plot against American art, and held Mussolini responsible. The conductor was no less than a prisoner in Italy, she protested, and she would demand state action if necessary.

As a preliminary, however, in order to strengthen her position, to make clear the rare qualities of this musical artist, and to show the absurdity of the law, she would place Nespoli under a new, ten-year contract of spectacular gravity and conditional specifications. She proceeded to do so with all speed. (Her counsel, and the author of this remarkable document, was a handsome and indulgent young Houston attorney, Maurice Hirsch.) She sent a copy of the contract to the American consul in Milan, with a letter demanding redress. When he chose to ignore it, the situation became fully operatic. Mrs. Graham moved on Congress, where she was not altogether without friends. Washington smoked for three days and capitulated.[1] The case wound up in the office of the secretary of state, where it was conveniently found

---

[1] Mrs. Graham had a notable working vocabulary. Sample: She once said of another vocal teacher in Houston, her chief rival: "The difference between Mrs. X and me is that her pupils sing like hell and she doesn't know it, and mine sing like hell and I do know it."

that a small error had been made and that after all one more entry was possible under the immigration quota. As a result the conductor set sail on the first available craft—a cattle boat. It will never be known what he expected to find.

But all this had consumed time, and the season was moving along. It was mid-January before Nespoli finally arrived—tagged and delivered to Mrs. Graham much in the way of a piece of baggage, for he was utterly innocent of English. Nespoli was a stocky, nervous, eruptive little man of forty-seven, myopic and beginning to bald, who peered at the world through round, thick-lensed glasses with the aspect of an unusually emotional salmon. A Neapolitan by birth, he was in fact a simple Italian provincial. He had been a pupil of the celebrated Leopoldo Mugnone, Verdi's favorite conductor. Mugnone could not have had a more diligent or worshipful protégé; to Nespoli, he was a god. But whatever his training in Italy, it had little prepared Uriel Nespoli for the circumstances in which he found himself now. Houston overwhelmed him completely; he could never get used to its ways. It was an alien world of incredible habits, and, although he had been taken into the household of Mrs. Graham, he was bitterly homesick and when not at work wandered about in a daze. He knew much about music and loved it passionately; he was emotional to the point of embarrassment. To watch him rehearsing the opera chorus in Houston was to watch a man suffering acute pain in his effort to communicate. It was pitiful because he lacked the advantage of a ready verbal exchange with his singers. All the same, his direction was clear, and nobody could doubt his sincerity. It was like that of a child. For a time he drudged faithfully at training the volunteer choral performers. But his expression grew increasingly melancholy.

Musical politics are in any case apt to be confusing, and a visitor less alien than Nespoli could have found himself sorely befuddled by the picture in Houston that winter. For "Miz Graham," as he called her, was not alone running the show, and the whole of it was a curious mixture. While businesses flickered and failed over town in the depression's gathering gloom, other musical ventures had sprung up. They now began coming to light.

Before leaving for Europe Mrs. Graham had announced her intention to form a full orchestra for the opera company. She had pointed out that the orchestra's usefulness need not end there; it could also be presented in concerts. Her statement had undoubtedly been noted with interest by members of the quiescent symphony board, though they probably thought the idea would remain strictly an idea in the head of this lady. But once Mrs. Graham had gone as far as to provide herself with a European conductor, the matter began looking a little different. Now there was not much time for the symphony faction to think it over, for with Nespoli's coming the other developments thrust forward.

The most surprising was another orchestra that suddenly sprang out of nowhere—complete with conductor, repertory, sponsoring body, and a plan to do immediate business. There was an odd story behind it. This venture had begun in the winter of 1929 when a group of the city's musicians, mostly professional but including some talented amateurs, anxious to make serious music and weary of waiting for the chance, had decided to act for themselves. The result was an informal association or club consisting of some fifty performers, who paid membership dues of five dollars to be used for the rental of scores. As a conductor they had selected Victor Alessandro,[2] then director of band and orchestra music in the Houston public schools. As a meeting place they had borrowed the basement of the First Christian Church, and for more than a year they had gathered on two evenings a week to rehearse. Having by then worked up a considerable repertory, they became interested in giving public performances.

For that purpose they needed a sponsor, and they found one in N. D. Naman, a quiet cotton and real estate broker, who had long been a lover of music. Invited to one of the orchestra's meetings, he liked what he heard and agreed to furnish a modest underwriting (about $350 a concert) for a series of public appearances. He thereupon, with four associates, chartered the organization as a non-profit enterprise; the name was the Houston Philharmonic Orchestra, which suddenly made itself known by advertising a course of concerts to be given on Sunday afternoons in the auditorium of Scottish Rite Cathedral. The

[2] Father of the present conductor of the San Antonio Symphony Orchestra.

first was scheduled for March 15, 1931, Mr. Alessandro to conduct.

The public was a little surprised by the news; it was not a time to expect such ventures. But hardly had it finished digesting this morsel when it got a companion *bonne bouche*. Still another orchestra and still another series of concerts was announced. This time it was the Ellison Van Hoose Little Symphony. The organizer-conductor, whose name it assumed, was a popular voice coach and director of Houston choral societies, and a very close friend of Mrs. Edna W. Saunders, the city's chief entrepreneur. The Van Hoose ensemble of twenty-two players would give concerts in the Palace Theater (this was the former Majestic, the Houston Symphony's old stand), beginning April 28, with a policy favoring vocal performers as soloists. But what gave this item a particular tang among knowing observers was that the orchestra would be presented under the individual management of Mrs. Saunders. That apparently meant she had ended her partnership with the Symphony Association as a sponsor of orchestral music. It was so. She made it pointedly clear in her advertising, specifying that the operation of the Von Hoose enterprise would be "strictly commercial."

Meanwhile in its own corner the *Aïda* chorus was lustily hymning the Pharaoh. But Mrs. Graham had picked up a competitor. Mary Carson, a Houston soprano with red hair and a European reputation in opera, had returned home to pursue aims as an impresario and was stormily rehearsing a production of *Carmen*—also with civic opera intent. Otherwise Houston was quiet as spring settled in 1931.

The humor of the situation was not lost upon those who could follow the game. At this juncture the *Houston Gargoyle*, a sprightly news magazine that recorded the follies of the day, appeared with an article entitled "Unfinished Symphonies," whose subheading inquired: "Organized Your Orchestra Yet?" It was certainly the seasonal fad. The town's musical factions were clearly divided, and the gossip was lively and apt to be slightly malicious.[3] At smart gatherings the guests winked at each other when the subject was mentioned, thereby implying the

[3] In the fall Ima Hogg had arranged a meeting of fourteen musical spirits to discuss a possible reorganization of the symphony movement. One of them was Edna W. Saunders, who resented the idea and surprisingly told the group she would "fight to the death" any scheme for reviving the orchestra.

obvious question: where was the Symphony Association in all this cultural fury?

That was a little hard to make out. With orchestra movements apparently forming on all sides, the association was pushed into the background. It had nothing to say in all this and appeared to be content with the activity by which it had been chiefly identified for more than a decade—the supporting of chamber music performances. In the season of 1930–1931, these performances were being given by a string quartette, with Josephine Boudreaux, an excellent violinist, as leader; the concerts were presented in homes or in a hall of the public library. They were rather private and discreet little affairs, and by the turn of events they were made to seem tamer than ever. The title of the Symphony Association began to seem rather incongruous, for the organization appeared to have yielded the larger musical field to the more adventurous.

But it was not to be counted out of the game. True, the association had taken a very generous pause; it had done nothing to retake the ground it had claimed for itself prior to the war. Years had gone by when it might have picked up its original aims without having had to face exceptional handicaps. It nevertheless had a case. The organization had existed for seventeen years, thanks to the spirit and determination of Ima Hogg; and although it had been passive for nearly two-thirds of that time, it still had certain advantages. The most important of these advantages was the matter of membership; the association included most of the city's really selective and prominent art lovers—a much greater number than either one of the new ventures could claim. And if the Symphony Association had been in no hurry to resume the orchestra movement, it had worked well to keep Houston reminded of the values of great music when the times were not particularly inviting of cultural efforts. Perhaps the organization was a little intimidated by the size and demands of its own orchestra project; all luxuries were becoming very expensive.

Whatever the case, the association was now sharply aroused. It was given the spur, and the spur hurt. The new movements ignored its existence. Finding itself treated in that rather unceremonious way, the association was in no humor to bow meekly and surrender the franchise.

Its first moves were not immediately evident to the public. As soon as it became apparent, in February, that the Philharmonic's intentions were serious, Mr. Naman and one of the other incorporators of that enterprise, W. H. Hogue, were invited to a meeting in the quarters of the Chamber of Commerce. There they found waiting a committee from the Symphony Association, Miss Hogg being one of its spokesmen. The committee had a proposal to offer. It was pointed out to the Philharmonic visitors that the older society had first cultivated the symphony idea in Houston, that it had spent much time in preparations and planning for an orchestra, and that now the air was being clouded in a way that could prove hurtful to the best interests of fine music in town. The suggestion, in brief, was that a united effort would be necessary to gain the desired goal, that the Philharmonic should accordingly merge with the Symphony Association and under its banner work toward the establishment of a truly representative orchestra. Messrs. Naman and Hogue listened politely. When they quietly declined the proposal (Mr. Hogue going further to mention that in his opinion the Philharmonic *was* a representative orchestra; at least it existed and was ready to play), the meeting adjourned in a chill atmosphere. On that front it would be war, though the tidings were largely suppressed.

At the same time, the presence of Nespoli in town was embarrassing from the standpoint of the association. Because of the flamboyance of his sponsor, Mrs. Graham, the circumstances of his arrival, and his own idiosyncrasies, he had caused a considerable curiosity. His mannerisms were good "copy" and the press had been having its inevitable holiday with the doings of a strange visiting maestro. It was discovered that for some curious reason he could shave only one side of his face. His favorite amusement in Houston was streetcar riding. Because of his podium furies he was nicknamed "Little Caesar," after the fulminous hero of an Edward G. Robinson movie, and when this was picked up by the Italian press and came back over the Atlantic as *Piccolo Cesare*, the local historians were delighted. In one way and another, he had created more interest than the Philharmonic announcement. It was also apparent that he was training a chorus quite ably and that Mrs. Graham's opera endeavor, if it was to be further developed, would very soon have need of its own orchestra. To much of the public, Nespoli had become the symbol of new musical stirrings in town.

One result of all this was that Ima Hogg made a trip to New York. She went as a representative of the Symphony Association to interview conductors who might be suitable to head a revival of the Houston venture. Before she had got far with that effort, however, there was another local development. Nespoli let it be known that he was very discouraged with prospects for the operatic endeavor. His lament was heard where he meant it to be. In late February, the Italian conductor was quietly consulted by a friend of the Symphony Association as to how he would look upon a chance to organize and direct an orchestra for this sponsoring body, an activity which, it was pointedly mentioned, could very well be carried on without affecting his duties to the opera company. Nespoli by now had his Italian advisers in town (Mrs. Marie Vescova, in particular) and through one of these submitted his contract with Mrs. Graham to a legal authority for examination. When told that it seemed to leave room for the orchestral job, he accepted at once with enthusiasm. But he was bidden to say nothing about this to anyone for the moment.

Meanwhile, on March 15 the Philharmonic presented its debut concert to a large and warm-spirited audience. The program performed by the forty-piece ensemble was not one of exacting demands; the critical commentaries struck an encouraging tone and were gentle in citing the all but inevitable flaws of precision in the orchestra's work. Then on April 28 the Van Hoose Little Symphony presented its debut concert in the Palace Theater, with its own goodly attendance and with much the same type of reaction.

Between these events, and without nearly as much notice, the Symphony Association had been busy. Quietly it had executed a reorganization, and as April began it installed Dr. Joseph Aloysius Mullen as president, the first man to occupy the position. Mrs. Garwood became first vice-president, Miss Hogg second vice-president. The other new name added to the roster was that of Bernard Epstein as treasurer. Dr. Mullen was a prominent physician, a devoted lover of music, and a believer in getting to the point. There was a prompt decision and no delay about making it public. A firm announcement appeared that the Symphony Association was back in its original role: it was forming an orchestra. This time the ensemble would be one of full scale, a company of at least seventy-five. The notice concluded by stating that the organization would be presented in two introductory concerts at the Palace Theater on May 7 and 8, which Uriel Nespoli would conduct.

Again the musical public was surprised and the gossips were titillated. Just what was the meaning of all this? Nespoli was supposed to belong to Mrs. Graham, exclusively, and those familiar with the methods of that lady expected a storm. But there was no immediate outburst, which puzzled them more, and the town's musical news was now read with a closer attention than perhaps it had ever had in the past. The truth was that Mrs. Graham, a little ill from her own worry and work, was not wholly opposed to this idea. As she understood it, Nespoli was engaged only for the two introductory performances; she felt that by letting him serve she was doing the Symphony Association a favor, and that this could prove handy a little later when she needed an orchestra herself. Mrs. Graham knew how to be silent when silence was useful.

So the symphony plan went ahead. By mid-April Nespoli was rehearsing for the association an orchestra whose personnel he had selected. They were a mixture of professional and amateur players, including some who had participated in both the Philharmonic and Little Symphony ventures. As might have been supposed, Josephine Boudreaux was installed as the concertmistress. The first rehearsals took place in a cotton warehouse of the new Merchants' and Manufacturers' Building, a great desolate room that, with its low ceiling and baled cotton stacked high against three of its walls, could not have been better designed by a genius from hell to resist and defeat musical sound. The use of it was free, however, and economy was the governing idea. To a man of Nespoli's temper and sensitive hearing, this cavern was a torture chamber fit only for Dante's description. He bore it as he did the other bewilderments of a mad and impossible land, but his nightly distress, as he stood on a deal table before his players and wept, was such as to make that of Canio in the first act of *Pagliacci* seem a relatively undemonstrative form of chagrin. Eventually these sessions were moved from the cotton loft to the salesroom of a dairy concern.

On the whole the results were rather better than anyone might have expected. Nespoli's choice of players spoke well for his judgment and probity; he had made the most of his chances. Also, his preparation of the orchestra again showed him to be a tireless and indeed fanatical worker, which at least meant there was no wastage of time. And this challenge was good for his spirit. His new patrons were understanding and sympathetic with his musical aims, and if the working conditions were somewhat odd, he had the comforting knowledge that this experiment, if it came off well, could offer more solid and lasting benefits than those promised by the rather nebulous opera scheme. The incentive was there to put forth his best, and this he attempted to do by presenting the new band with an order of work that was a flattering estimate of its ready resources—not to mention, perhaps, his own.

Selling tickets for the concerts was no problem, at any rate. The real attraction was not the program, but the town's musical war, obviously made hotter by the Symphony Association's return to the field. Everyone wanted to be present to see what happened. When the night for the first concert finally arrived, the Palace Theater was full and the air somewhat more than expectant. That gathering of May 7, 1931, was discreetly referred to by the press as "a representative audience," which meant that all factions in this struggle were represented in force. There was a tension in the auditorium, hardly diminished when ceremonies began with certain formal remarks from the stage, all carefully emphasizing the fact that the Symphony Association had founded and fostered the orchestra movement in Houston and was here resuming an effort that had only been stopped by a world war. The inference was that it was now time to revive this excellent civic aim—but of course in the orthodox way.

The lights then failed for a moment. When they came up brightly again the spectators beheld, in all proper detail, a stage crowded by an orchestra of seventy-four, and out of the wings strode Nespoli, red, damp, and heroic, to address himself to the gods present and past. Drama had been duly observed. The program itself likewise aimed for the limit in that respect; it was nothing if not dramatic, and was drawn from the canon of the art. It opened with Wagner, the Prelude and Liebestod from *Tristan und Isolde* (for some reason given under their French titles), and included that master's Good Friday Spell music from *Parsifal*. Between these came the Beethoven Fifth Symphony. The *Parsifal* episode was followed by two shorter selections, Saint-Saëns's *Le Cygne* and Schumann's *Traumerei*, and these in turn by the closing scene of Mascagni's opera *Iris*, the Hymn to the Sun, with a chorus drawn partly from the singers Nespoli had been training for the *Aïda* production and partly from other organizations in town.

Doubtless this program was intended to discourage the competitive ventures by indicating the limits of their reach. But it likewise showed the limits of its own. The program asked too much of an orchestra put together as this company had been; the band clearly was ill fitted to deal with the problems, tonal and stylistic, of such a list—even under a leader who bore the name of an archangel and was more than ordinarily willing to wrestle with the other celestials on any terms.

But the effort was not a total disaster. Nespoli's passion, though that of a furnace, did not sweep him away; his work showed enough sign of respectable judgment and method; and the orchestra, catching this intensity well, often met his demands with some grace. The *Tristan* music, with its expressive conundrums, went better than anyone had a right to expect, and the playing of the Beethoven symphony, though rough, had a generous impulse and no solecisms of interpretative procedure. Had it stopped with the intermission, the concert would have been a rather notable effort of its kind. But the rest was over-stretching the odds. Conductor and orchestra were not up to sustaining reasonable interest in the *Parsifal* music, which pulled badly to pieces; and the excerpt from Mascagni's forgotten opera, despite a fresh chorus, displayed an exhaustion that made clear why *Iris* was dead in the storehouse.

The evening had invited attention to certain incidental delights, one of which was that the shoes of the little Italian conductor squeaked loudly. They always did, inside the theater or out. His other mannerisms, worthy of Salvini in Hamlet, had likewise amused those who had come looking for sport.[4] All the same, he had probably brought off the most impressive orchestral performance yet heard from the city's own talents. When this popular verdict was underwritten by all published reports of the concert, the quibblers were left with very little to chew on. The association had made a definite point.

It lost no time about taking advantage of the fact. As early as March 27 the symphony board had voted authority to its president, Mrs. Garwood, "to sign contracts with Mr. Nespoli and the Musicians' Union"; but at that time the board also had certain communications from Mrs. Graham to consider, and these apparently had stayed its hand for the moment. The concert, however, having come out as it did, reheated the controversy, and Nespoli was the chief pawn in the game.

His affairs were in a curious tangle. It is doubtful that he ever quite understood what he was doing in Houston—just why he had been brought, who were the pivotal figures in the city's musical politics, how the various schemes were connected or crossed, or the implications of any arrangement he might make. He was an *enfant perdu* in a strange land, and everything around him was baffling. Cut off by his lack of English from the gossip and shop talk, he remained a confused wanderer, who spun like a weathercock with his own shifting emotions and suppositions.

Whatever the case, after the concert there were swift moves back of the scenes. The first recorded result is a letter to the Symphony Association, over Nespoli's signature on May 12, 1931: "I do hereby agree and offer my services as Director to you for a period of six months from October 1, 1931, to and including May 30, 1932, for the assembling of musicians and their adequate training in rehearsals and in concerts for the presentation of six concerts and to direct the same. . . . I will accept for my services $3,000, or five hundred dollars for each concert, and five hundred dollars for any and all other concerts than the six mentioned." There is no indication that an answer was made. On June

---

[4] He had a way of clapping a hand to his forehead, at a moment of stress, in a manner rendered more widely familiar by the movie performances of Ben Turpin.

4 another version of this letter was sent. Certain small changes appear, but the proposition remains what it was in the first place and the terms are the same. It is unlikely that either communication originated entirely with Nespoli. The careful wording and stress on the fact of an "offer" were rather clearly inspired; this tactic suggests that the possibility of a charge of conductor-snatching was present in somebody's mind.

It should be noted that when Bernard Epstein was elected treasurer of the Symphony Association it meant more than the title strictly implies. Mr. Epstein was a young business executive and psychologist of unusual gift; and when he volunteered to act also as business manager for the society during the reorganization, his offer had been gladly accepted. It was the gain of a clever talent. On various matters of policy and administration his advice was both canny and valuable. Nespoli's letter wound up in the hands of Mr. Epstein, whose action was prompt. On June 10 he received from his brother, Maurice Epstein, an attorney, the following note:

Dear Ben:
Maestro Uriel Nespoli came to see me along with the Italian Consul to act as interpreter, and I examined the various instruments purporting to be contracts between Nespoli and Mrs. Graham. These instruments are dated August 13, 1930, October 10, 1930, and November 12, 1930, all respectively executed in Italy. It is not necessary to interpret the execution of these various contracts, because I am convinced that in any event Mrs. Graham has no claim on Nespoli after August 1, 1931.

Under the circumstances, the Houston Symphony Association is free to engage Mr. Nespoli after that date, unless the latter has some other agreement with Mrs. Graham outside of those referred to above.

Meanwhile, without waiting for this legal opinion to be rendered, the society had opened negotiations with Local 65 of the American Federation of Musicians. The result was a contract with the union, also drawn by Maurice Epstein, which was signed under date of June 4. It bound the labor organization to furnish "sixty first class and competent musicians, and all instruments, necessary and appropriate to form a complete symphony orchestra, for the purpose of performing six concerts during the season beginning November 1, 1931, and ending

August 31, 1932." The union would receive $1,200 per concert guaranteed, and, if attendance receipts for any concert exceeded the association's true cost, 75 percent of the profit up to the sum of $1,750. The union agreed to pay its performing members at the rate of $1.50 an hour for nine two-hour rehearsals and $7.50 for the concert proper, a total of $34.50 per man. The contract made it certain that the orchestra would consist chiefly of professional musicians, but a special condition was that avocational players could also be used, if the sponsors desired, along with the sixty union performers.

Having this agreement in hand when it received Maurice Epstein's opinion concerning the legal status of Nespoli, the society waited no longer. The conductor was informed, in the briefest of notes, that his "offer" of June 4 was accepted. On June 18 Dr. Mullen, the new president, addressed a letter to the public of Houston, declaring that in view of the very successful May concerts, the Symphony Association was fully active again, and announcing a series of six concerts for the 1931–1932 season, with Nespoli as conductor, for which ticket subscriptions were invited. This confident horn call seemed to indicate a resolution of the town's musical strife. But the comedy was not ready to end.

Houston now had three symphony orchestras and supporting organizations, and the other two, though presented with what appeared an embarrassing coup, were in no humor to give up and dematerialize. There was more to them than that. The Philharmonic had given its second concert on May 3 (four days before the symphony's appearance); the Van Hoose Little Symphony had followed on May 12 with its own second event. Both had received certain encouragements in the form of audience interest, as well as in actual playing results. Their sponsors were intelligent, earnest, and not lacking in material means; and with this challenge their pride was affected. They accepted Dr. Mullen's announcement with poker-faced calm and shook off the news of the symphony's contract with the union. But the private talk was resentful and biting.

Nobody quite understood everything that had happened. A question that flew about in the gossip was where Mrs. Graham was now left. Oddly, she had been silent for some weeks, though in view of the involvement of Nespoli with the symphony venture, it was from her quarter that lightning had been fairly expected. But Mrs. Graham remained quiet and let the mystery develop as it would.

Meanwhile, having opened headquarters in the Chamber of Commerce, the Symphony Association was losing no time in pressing its advantage. Committees were organized and affairs given to stress the civic nature of this original movement. These included a large and glamorous luncheon, at which the society let it be known that its concerts of the coming season would be moved from the Palace Theater to the City Auditorium, with its seating capacity of 3,400. Among the reactions to that news was a prompt reply from the Philharmonic Society, which announced it had also contracted for the use of the City Auditorium and would offer a series of *twelve* concerts in the 1931–1932 season. Moreover, it instituted a price war by setting its minimum ticket for the series at five dollars; the symphony was asking ten dollars for its series of six. And further, in behalf of its own civic image, the Philharmonic announced plans for a scholarship fund to assist the city's deserving musical young.

The Van Hoose Little Symphony could think of no immediate premium offer to make, but its professional sponsor (Edna Saunders was a greatly practical and imperturbable woman) declared that the orchestra needed no recommendation beyond the making of good music, and that its plan to present six concerts in the coming season was unaffected by anything that had happened. Thus no fewer than twenty-four concerts were scheduled for the next winter by three orchestra organizations, which inevitably would have to draw in some measure from the same pool of performers. The situation was doubtless a shade sanguine in a week when a Wall Street market report spoke of "a world fast turning to defeatism and passive despair."

In late June Mrs. Graham recovered her health and full vigor. Familiars of Nespoli whispered that he had been "thrown" from her house. The description was perhaps slightly exaggerated. Nonetheless, the storm had at last burst and the maestro's ejection was summary. It left him at night on a curbstone, his startled baggage around him, where he stood forlorn in a wet wind until rescued by a friend with Italian sympathies and an automobile. Nespoli moved to the Warwick

Hotel, and Mrs. Graham spoke of a contract suit—among other things. A day or two later she announced to the papers that preparations for the *Aïda* production had been temporarily halted, "owing to the very hot weather."

It was indeed hot, and the summer seemed to last longer than usual. But everyone was thus given, if not a chance to cool off, at least adequate time to consider the hard facts of the town's musical tangle. They were now more readily seen. It was apparent that the Symphony Association, by its contract with the union, had secured an important advantage in the competition for players (its degree of substantiality, as against that of the newer movements, would not be overlooked by musicians with an eye to the future); and along with this stroke it had neatly sacked up the conductorial lionet of the moment. The influential public of Houston, both social and musical, took notice of these facts and directed its favor accordingly. Also, the times were getting no better, and the future looked very forbidding. Quietly the other two movements declined under the heat. By autumn they were gone, and the Symphony Association again had the field to itself.

Chapter 4

There are today some twelve hundred orchestras in the United States, thirty belonging to the so-called major classification, with budgets above $500,000 a year. The oldest orchestra has a record of 128 years; many of the others have existed for considerable spans. It is then rather a curious thing that of all this number, not more than ten or twelve are conceded to be organizations of a really superior character. In a nation so rich, the percentage is not greatly impressive. Though luck may have played its own part in the situation, it would look as though the sponsors of many of these ventures had been either unable to conceive, or unwilling to accept, the full task necessary for the creation of a first-class musical body. Obviously time is not as important a factor in that task as it is often represented to be. Neither is the mere question of money. If time gives chances for an orchestra to ripen its style, it also gives chances for indifferent standards to become established as matters of habit.

The Houston orchestra's beginning was modest indeed; so was the reorganization of 1931. But in neither case were any flighty or easy illusions entertained as to the range and demands of the undertaking. And as one follows the history of the thirty-nine years of unbroken endeavor since the revival, the orchestra's chief blessing becomes clear: the consistency shown by its sponsors in preserving toward the endeavor a fully realistic and balanced perspective. Chance figures to some extent in the evolution of any such musical organization, but the Houston venture is proof that good luck is more apt to drop in when the door is held invitingly open.

The name of Miss Ima Hogg ever recurs in this story. She has been called the heart and soul of the orchestra. The poetic description is justified, though it hardly suggests the variety of her practical service. Miss Hogg's part in the creation of this musical enterprise cannot be summed up in a phrase; but it is fairly to be said that the greatest of her contributions has been a rigorous concept of first quality standards, to which she has held with an iron probity. Refusing to accept less as a goal for the orchestra, she has influenced its character strongly. She has been its exigent Juno, never easy to please, and at the same time its most devoted evangel; and to have had that service throughout its career, along with the invaluable social gift of Miss Hogg, has indeed been an advantage of great measure.

The immediate steps taken in the reorganization represented her judgment of the best to be done in the circumstances. They were in no way drastic. The economy standing as it did, it took some courage to ask donations for the start of a new cultural venture in the summer of 1931. Accordingly, a budget of some twenty thousand dollars was declared for the first season, and the campaigners who set about making it sure, in the form of either ticket subscriptions or underwriting, were much indebted to Miss Hogg for the resolution they took into the field. Another who fed that spirit in ways that are well remembered was Mrs. Edgar Odell Lovett, wife of the president of Rice Institute, whose comprehensive support, like that of her husband, helped forge the first link between the orchestra and the new university.

The association's decision to move to the City Auditorium (the Palace Theater would not be available for evening performances during its

own season) was not made without due thought. There were two risks
to consider. The first was the size of this hall, which meant that a serious overestimate of the orchestra's drawing potential could have an embarrassing revelation. The second was that the building had a certain
grimness about it, bestowed partly by man's genius for error and partly
by the hard usage of time. Designed as an all-purpose auditorium in
accordance with the notions of 1910, this structure on Texas Avenue,
a few steps from the Palace, had accumulated some curious history.
The auditorium stage was of classic proportions, with a beautiful arch,
and was a splendid setting for certain operas and other large spectacles.
But the building's main floor was level, and here there were no permanent seats. Collapsible wooden chairs had to be placed on the flat
surface when the hall was in theatrical use. They were hard, noisy, and
cramped; besides, as one's distance from the stage increased, so did
one's chance of seeing anything much without risking a spinal separation. The side and loge boxes afforded a better view, as well as com-
forts approved by their own day. They had large upholstered chairs,
though due to the building's miscellaneous uses (it was discovered
shortly after the orchestra's move) the velvet cushions and other ac-
cessories had acquired their own life—small, animated, and startling
—and a war of extermination was necessary in order to give patrons
of music the unchallenged possession of these quarters. The dress
circle and gallery had adequate pitch and offered certain acoustical advantages not to be had in the main floor seats, which of course were
supposed to be premium positions. This was awkward for theatrical
promoters using the building, since naturally the cheaper seats were
preferred. All in all, the City Auditorium, which had harbored everything from poultry shows to athletics and had often served as a public
hurricane shelter, was not a greatly inviting place for the practice of
the cultural arts at this date. It had nevertheless held some of the city's
most memorable theater occasions (in 1930 a full staging of Wagner's
Ring des Nibelungen, with Johanna Gadski as Brünnhilde, in four
consecutive evenings!), and for some time it would continue to do so.

By late summer, at least one of the hazards the symphony sponsors
had accepted was out of the way. Notwithstanding the uncertainty
and increasing gloom of the times, the ticket subscription campaign

had been very successful. The field efforts were called off well in advance of the season—which meant that immediate worries concerning the budget were much eased.

And so in the old temple, with its worn fittings and strangely mingled tradition, the orchestra's resurrection began with a concert on the evening of November 16, 1931. There was a capacity audience representing the city's taste, status, and social elegance, all turned out at their own brightest and best. Uriel Nespoli's orchestra was the one that had been heard in the May concerts; the program consisted of Wagner's *Meistersinger* Overture, Beethoven's Sixth Symphony, Grieg's Piano Concerto, with Drusilla Huffmaster as soloist, Verdi's overture to *I Vespri Siciliani*, and the "Dance of the Hours" from Ponchielli's *La Gioconda*.

In presenting Miss Huffmaster the sponsors had assured the dramatic success of the evening, besides reinstating an admirable policy of recognizing true musical brilliance at home. Drusilla Huffmaster was a Houston prodigy of fourteen, beautiful into the bargain, the daughter of Hu T. Huffmaster, a fine organist and pedagogue of the art. Her combination of astonishing poise, technical means, musical intelligence, and high personal charm made certain the place of Grieg's vehicle as the audience hit of the evening. Miss Huffmaster was voted a triumph, and thus began an association between this artist and the orchestra that has come down to the present day, with results ever more fruitful and gratifying.

The rest of the program was ably performed, considering the orchestra's newness. It naturally called for some tolerance. Representing the *Gargoyle*, this writer reported that Beethoven's *Pastoral* Symphony, heard in this way, was less like taking a pleasant trip to the country than like having to live there for a year; but that is a hazard of the Sixth from which older and quite eloquent orchestras are not entirely exempt. Nespoli and his company had done quite well.[1] Their work

---

[1] Miss Hogg was again to be thanked. She had shrewdly perceived that while Nespoli was a good opera conductor, he was not as sure of himself in the symphonic literature. Her suggestions had caused him to accept coaching in this program (as he apparently did in others) from a splendid German musician, Walter Welschoff, one of the city's best teachers and organists.

showed any musical listener that talent was there in the ensemble, awaiting polish and full sensitization. The audience had been more than agreeable in receiving the effort, and the general opinion of the press was that the new movement had made a rather victorious start.

The next concert, however, given on December 14, was a somewhat unsettling affair. It defeated the traditional jinx of the Christmas season by fetching an audience about equal in size to the first, and it offered the orchestra's concertmistress, Josephine Boudreaux, in a performance of Beethoven's Violin Concerto. But the other music was a raffish layout for an orchestra evening at this time of the year or any other—Weber's *Freischütz* Overture, a drizzle by one Bettinelli entitled *Caravane Notturna*; Bizet's second *L'Arlésienne* suite, and Tchaikovsky's *1812* Overture. Apart from the work of Miss Boudreaux, which was that of a skillful and heady musician, the performing level was decidedly below that of the opening concert, and at times there were sounds that must have startled the Christmas angels severely.

But other opinions were entertained. After remarking that the trouble of performing the Bettinelli item could well have been spared, Ina Gillespie, critic of the *Chronicle*, went on to report that "the orchestra was in unusually fine fettle from beginning to end," and of Nespoli that "with every performance this fiery Italian who so amply justifies that overworked word, dynamic, gains prestige with his listeners; for his personality, as well as his musicianship, is of such sweeping quality that he commands from his audience the same respect that is shown by his players." Some of the reviewing of that season was at least as impetuous as the music making itself.

The third concert, which came on January 18, had Schumann's *Spring* Symphony (No. 1 in B-flat) as the principal work for the orchestra. The soloist presented was Card Elliott, a popular Houston baritone, who sang the Prologue to *Pagliacci*; the other pieces were Wagner's *Flying Dutchman* Overture and Weber's *Invitation to the Dance*. This time Nespoli was in better control of himself and the situation in general; the result was that the orchestra showed its cleanest and most effective performing. It cast a spell in the slow movement of the Schumann symphony. It was beginning to express, to have a little glow, a little more intonational unity, a litttle more freedom and confidence.

And at this point there were other conditions to encourage the society's confidence. The box-office continued to thrive and there were many good signs from the audience. By the year's end Dr. Mullen was able to declare the assurance of the movement's continuance and to announce that the auditorium had already been booked for a 1932–1933 series of concerts. This was a small marvel, considering how the depression had dealt with the city's other theater life.

With that cheerful prelude, the fourth concert took place on February 18, featuring another young pianist, Rhodes Dunlap, a student of Rice Institute, who played Chopin's E Minor Concerto. The list opened with Bach's Orchestral Suite in D Major (No. 3); its other items were the symphonic interlude from César Franck's *Redemption*, a *Carmen* fantasia, and Wagner's overture to *Tannhäuser*. The audience was thus offered a chance to be redeemed twice in an evening, which is properly recognized as a bargain, and the Franck-Wagner solemnities, added to the rest, made certain another pious and heated approval from the house.

Much of this audience tribute was directed to Nespoli. His acceptance, from the start of the series, had been quite warm, trustful, and generous, and now perhaps there was a touch of affection in the public approval of his work. Whatever the case, the audience attitude brought about a dramatic change in his own feelings concerning the city. He had found that a large number of its people stood ready to receive serious musical effort with understanding and gratitude, and it seemed that his sponsors had assured him sufficiently that his own qualities were respected and valued. The sun came out, the city made sense to him at last. He was ecstatically happy—with or without enough reason.

The programs here listed reveal something of the man who had charge of the orchestra. He was intensely loyal to Italian music, especially that of his own colleagues of the Rome-Milan schools of composition, an allegiance that, if perfectly natural, could render him somewhat blind. He was apt to perform their works for rather trivial reasons. He had a strong predilection for the music of Wagner, which was also natural enough for the day. But the frequency with which the

Wagnerian literature was used in the orchestra's first season, considering the limitations of Nespoli's band, could hardly be reckoned a prime instance of conductorial judgment. Grandeur of sound was too much to be asked of the instrument. On the other hand, he was not solely responsible for his programs; a program committee had authority to work over his choices. Wagnerianism was the reigning musical cult in America, and it may be that the ambitious committee was responsible for giving Wagner the share that he had of these 1931–1932 evenings.

Whatever the case, Nespoli planned to wind up with another gesture to modern Italy. It was announced that the final concert of the season would be a production of Lorenzo Perosi's oratorio, *The Passion of Christ*, a contemporary creation of which the composer (who held by Papal *regolamento* the awesome title of Perpetual Master of the Pontifical Chapel) had brought out a revised version in 1923, after his recovery from an extended illness. The plan was to gather into this venture a number of choirs from the city's principal churches, to which organizations the maestro now issued a call. But that was not to be the way of the matter. The gods who had cast Nespoli in his role were still watching the show and were not ready to end good sport.

If strictly musical gifts and capacity for hard work were the only requirements for success in orchestral conducting, the world's musical problems would be simpler and so would the writing of orchestra histories. It is extremely naïve to suppose anything of the kind and in the United States it is laughable. But nowhere on earth do conductors long thrive by acute musical talent alone. It is clear that the organized practice of musical culture is bound up with certain rites of a purely social variety. These are intended as manifestations of the cultural spirit, and in such games the conductor, as god of the temple, is expected to present a model of *delicatesse*. It is part of his job.

Nespoli's merits did not include this particular brand of urbanity. He was neither handsome nor otherwise physically striking. Sometimes, when at work, he had the dignity that simple honesty gives, but he was a plain little man. Though he put his thoughts well in Italian or French, nature had not formed him to play the role of the gallant in the presence of cocktail crackers. He was too restless for that. Tension caused him to speak with abruptness and extravagant gestures, and often to say more than enough. His shoes continued to squeak; it was apparently an incurable case. And he drank soup in a rather resonant way. Although he was not lacking in letters or wit, the impression he gave on social occasions was of a somewhat *goffo* quality.

These characteristics had hardly escaped notice at dinner parties, receptions, and other functions related to the musical season. Perhaps they were a little painful to some patrons of art who regarded the finer punctilio as important. In any event, as fate managed to show, the season ended in April without the production of Perosi's devotional composition. And the end of the season was the end of the man who had hoped to perform this document.

There is some mystery in the processes by which every great symphony orchestra has evolved, and there is some in connection with this early decision of the Houston orchestra's board. Official records of the reorganization were rather sketchily kept, and a veil of discretion hangs over the precise reasons invoked for the dropping of Nespoli. If an investigator were very ingenuous, he would have to conclude that the trouble began with the fifth concert of the season, in which the conductor, misunderstanding or disregarding the will of his sponsors, allowed the evening's soprano, Daisy Elgin, to add a rather luxurious encore to her listed selections. There appears to have been official reaction to this; in any event, the oratorio project was suddenly cancelled and an all-request program was ordered for the orchestra's final appearance on April 25. This one also had a couple of singers, however (Nancy Swinford and Walter Jenkins), and it seems the conductor was again warned about encore policy. Whereupon, one is further invited to believe, Nespoli compounded his original sin by indulging *this* pair in a repeat of the lovers' duet from *Pagliacci*, the program being already overloaded, and thereby committed insufferable *lèse majesté* against "a very prominent member of the Association." The member, not named, had apparently found her chair hard.

If all this seems ludicrous as the cause of a crisis that lay beyond hope of adjustment, the fact remains that Nespoli was summarily fired. The conductor believed that he knew the actual reasons; they were set forth in a letter he wrote to a Houston lady in August. She had anonymously risen to his defense, and his answer was published in the *Gargoyle*:

Dear Unknown Lady:

The letter you sent to The Gargoyle has echoed in my soul with a deep and stirring sense of emotion, because it has given me splendid proof that in this magnificient city there are people capable of feeling admiration and hospitality for an artist who devoted all of himself, heart and soul, to the task of helping to give Houston a Symphony Orchestra.

I can't yet, for personal reasons, enter into the deep of the question . . . but I owe you, Dear Lady, and the public of this city an explanation with regard to that famous "encore" which seems to have so greatly disturbed the equilibrium of some members of the Symphony Association. No instructions were ever given me not to grant an encore, for I can safely assure you that even though I may drink broth with some noise, I would have been polite enough to follow the Association's desires, regardless of my personal opinion.

As soon as word reached me that a very prominent member of the Association was very displeased with the encore, I hastened to write a letter of explanation, of which I will quote only the last sentence: "I would have preferred to lose the check of this last concert rather than a word of praise from you."

I have never received a reply. Now, I may give you my word of honor that among artists, even if one drinks his broth with more or less noise, we consider it a strict rule to always answer a letter when it comes from a sensitive soul . . .

After considering all things, I believe the Board of the Houston Symphony may be informed that in view of the strict relationship that it seems to be developing between the imbibing of broth of chicken and the interpretation of Wagner and Beethoven, I will urgently make a suggestion to the principal Music Conservatories that, with the same severity they impose on the study of the musical classics and of composition and contrappunto, it shall be required of pupils to penetrate into the deep mysteries of the different broths and of the manner of drinking them.

I shall do this in the hope that also the conservatories will institute special classes teaching pupils how to reply to letters sent them by well-meaning people who are not accustomed to forget their contractual obligations.

Yours faithfully,
Uriel Nespoli.

With that dramatic apology, the comedy ended. The implications of Nespoli's letter were never answered. He stayed on in the city a while to deliver an opera production of his own—*Madame Butterfly* with Nancy Swinford as Cio-Cio San. In November he sued the Symphony Association, claiming breach of a contract he had held for the 1932–1933 season and asking damages amounting to eighteen thousand dollars. By that time, however, attention had turned elsewhere, and so had the maestro himself, who wound up in New York.

Chapter 5

The Houston orchestra association began a campaign for support of its second auditorium season with no conductor announced. It would hardly venture to try such an arrangement today, notwithstanding great changes in the orchestra's status and prestige. But the confidence shown by this 1932 gesture was rather characteristic of the period. Though the times were not good, perhaps partly because of that fact, there was a new interest in great music and a new audience ready to receive it.

The movement that so dramatically altered the musical habits of America, beginning about 1925 and attaining its peak in the years just after the Second World War, supplies one of the most significant chapters in the cultural history of this restless and discovering nation. It was the movement that spread the symphony cult to all parts of the country; it sprang largely from the influence of radio, which, with its broadcasting of many fine orchestras, had introduced millions to a world of enjoyment they had never suspected before. It was the movement that gave the idea of the symphony orchestra a new personal and civic connotation.

The reorganizational season of the Houston Symphony had illustrated the working of this trend. From the standpoint of public interest and eager reception, the first season had been a heady success. The association had enrolled more than 600 ticket subscribers for the series, but another figure was much more striking. The average attendance had been 3,500 per concert. As a result, the total income for the season was $12,002, which fell only $884 short of exact balance, costs having mounted to $12,886. Subscribers had paid a maximum of 83 cents and a minimum of 67 cents per ticket. With such tempering of the wind to the shorn lambs of a bitter depression, the symphony had an excellent case. It appeared to be doing, if not the Lord's work, at least business of a sort with which the banks could not find any serious fault.

Now in the early summer of 1932, the association set out to ensure an income, by subscription, of fourteen thousand dollars for the second season. It was a thoroughly organized campaign. The arguments taken into the field by its workers, the ideas used in its printed matter and given to the press of the city, were largely the ideas of Miss Hogg. Again they attest to her very clear vision of this enterprise, her keen practical sense, and her understanding of the community mind. The aims she defined then were the ones from which she would never depart. But there were many excellent leaders. As chairman of the society's ways and means committee, Card Elliott recruited the soliciting forces; Ethel Brosius was the tireless publicity chief; Dr. Mullen was a powerful spokesman and influential among business and professional elements; Dr. and Mrs. Lovett, Mrs. H. M. Garwood, Mrs. Underwood Nazro, Leopold Meyer, Miss Mary Elizabeth Rouse, Randolph Bryan, Mrs. J. G. Flynn, Miss Helen Saft, Mrs. W. H. Hogue, Tom Flaxman, Mrs. Ray L. Dudley, Mrs. Walter Walne, Mrs. W. A. Paddock, Dr. Henry Barnston, Dr. R. A. Tsanoff—all these, prominent in one field or another, gave invaluable aid and advice. And as they labored in the heat waves of a much distressed summer, they implanted the idea of the Houston Symphony in a way that was destined to last. Their spirit is in the orchestra's voice today.

But while the fund-raising proceeded the conductorial question was open, and the town wondered about what had occurred. Nespoli's letter had been eagerly pounced upon and enjoyed by the gossips. Was it really his social *gaucherie* that had brought about his precipitate downfall? And if so, who had ordered the stroke? It would be perhaps history's first case of a conductor's losing his job because he was out of tune with his soup. But that question would never be answered. Whatever the reason for dispensing with Nespoli, the association's officials had been looking in other directions well before he was notified. And when they made a decision, the choice might easily have been seen as a confirmation of Nespoli's published suspicions.

Frank St. Leger, the conductor they called upon to replace him, was a man of very different characteristics. It would have been hard to discover a person of his calling, within reach of such an organization, who contrasted more sharply with Nespoli. The search had led to Chicago, where St. Leger had been on the staff of that city's prestigious Civic Opera since 1929. Here again Bernard Epstein was the instrument of symphony policy. Before himself moving to Houston from the midwest, he had been a close friend of St. Leger's, and it was he who directed the society's interest and eventually brought about the connection.

Born of English parents in India, Frank St. Leger was a product of British education and a graduate of London's Royal Academy of Music, where he was a medal winner and the object of blessings by such Olympians as Hans Richter and Nikisch. He had reached the United States in 1917 under the amplitudinous wing of Nellie Melba, as conductor of Dame Nellie's own opera company, and after that tour and a short time as conductor for the ill-fated American Opera Company, had joined the Chicago enterprise. His professional background was thus not too much different from Nespoli's, but there all similarity ended. St. Leger had the qualities that go with British precocity, when that precocity includes the flair for theatricalism that is also part of the heritage of British blood. The combination has produced some of the world's best actors. In his early forties he was tall, erect, handsome, suave, and sophisticated. He radiated vitality but held it always in a certain reserve; his speech was clipped, precise, and elegant, touched up with a ready wit when it suited the moment; he wore his clothes with the air that is bred only in London, and they were models of Bond Street fashion. He was at home in all the tongues of international society—the polite ones, at any rate; he was a golfer, a bridge player, a connoisseur of fine foods and rare wines to go with them; and few people could mention an exotic or romantic spot of the globe, if it was in any way fashionable, of which he did not have an experience. In short, he was a polished man of the world.

Though every podium lion must have a drawing-room presence that matches in some measure the interest of his theater image, all are not naturally gifted with this quality. Sometimes the party act is no more than an act, which the conductor has taught himself to perform with an air of relish as a necessary part of his job. This was not so of St. Leger. His social instinct was a real one. He loved company and it brought him out at his best. A beautiful drawing room, filled with bright spirits, was his perfect theater. There was a streak of the entertainer in his nature, and he was ready with tricks to throw any such gathering into convulsions of mirth. He could sit at the piano and with a sober face play part of the overture to *Tannhäuser* by brushing in with a whisk-broom the descending figuration that runs over the melody of the Pilgrim's Chorus. It came out perfectly. He could render another florid and mellifluous salon piece by rolling a grapefruit over the piano's black keys. He could killingly imitate operatic divas being choked by emotion and bust straps. But he knew when enough was enough. His parodies never got into burlesque; they stopped short of scandalizing the art. They were deft, clever, and beguiling.

With these manners he devastated the ladies. They buzzed about him with giddy delight and, if they were beautiful, stimulated him to the best of his repartee. Everything he did seemed to arouse their curiosity. There was the fact that he and his wife Kay, as smart in her own right, were installed for the season in the guest house of Miss Hogg's queenly estate, Bayou Bend—which indicated a great deal. They seemed very much to belong there. But it was not only the women who found St. Leger engaging; he had also the British talent for playing the man among men. The contract had been signed on July 6; he arrived with his lady in good time, and after a grand dinner at the Houston Club on October 21, which formally introduced him to the musical elite of the city, he had things going in much his own way without sounding a note. Businessmen liked his remarks, which were diplomatic and avoided the arty, and they took to him as they were shrewdly invited to do.

"I cannot predict anything about the Houston Symphony Orchestra," he had said at the dinner. "I do not know the possibilities of the musicians; in fact I have met only a few of them. I do not come with a promise, but with a plea of cooperation and hard work from the orchestra." This indicated, for the time being at least, no drastic demands of other kinds. You could not get into trouble in 1932 by taking that line before a gathering of businessmen who uneasily felt that perhaps they were going to be asked for substantial donations to sweet culture. They esteemed this sensible fellow. Very soon St. Leger was appearing before all the more prominent luncheon clubs, where his clever talks were applauded and got him invited to poker games. So much had he done without music.

Three weeks after his arrival he met the musical public in general. The society's 1932–1933 season began with a concert on the evening of November 7. With a new conductor to offer, the opening had a double attraction. Anticipation had been much whetted by the stories of St. Leger as a personality, which the press had played up with its usual enthusiasm for almost any change in the arts, and the public was eager to know more. The society felt challenged to produce an event, and for this special occasion the grimness of the City Auditorium was relieved in some measure by pretty floral displays, arranged by tense feminine hands. At concert time there was a fine gathering that filled every part of the hall.

St. Leger had promised no immediate miracles with the orchestra, and in this he was shown to be a prophet of incontestable truth. There were certainly none to record. The program was a rather drastically modest beginning; it consisted of three works, opening with Glinka's overture to *Russlan and Ludmilla* and closing with Dvořák's *New World* Symphony. Between these came a pretty little amenity: Julien

Paul Blitz, the orchestra's original conductor, was presented as soloist in a cello display piece, Boëllmann's *Symphonic Variations*.

The audience that came with expectations of a more elegant stage picture was not disappointed. St. Leger was indeed a handsomer figure before the orchestra than Uriel Nespoli had ever been. He came nearer the aspect of a podium noble. But other conditions were unchanged. Essentially the orchestra was the one that Nespoli had assembled, and essentially it worked in the same ways. It was a somewhat curious mixture. About sixty of its members were union musicians; ten or fifteen were avocational players (the number varied from one concert to another), admitted under the union agreement. Some of the amateurs, whose attendance was not certain, were of excellent skill and vital to the best work of the orchestra. As this season began they included three Houston physicians, Drs. H. L. D. Kirkham and H. L. Bartlett, violinists, and Dr. Raymond Selders, who was the principal flutist. There was apprehension about emergency calls on concert nights.

But St. Leger enjoyed the full company for his opening affair, and the organization was a better one than he appeared to have realized. For his handling of it in this program was such an extreme model of caution as to extinguish much of the interest of which the ensemble was capable. The playing was too careful to have vigor. St. Leger seemed chiefly intent upon fixing the image of a rare and fastidious leadership, to be admired for its immaculate scruple, and perhaps that was the idea for the hour. If so, it was not an exciting one. After the hot passions and charges of Nespoli, this performance seemed lacking in color and unsporting in point of hazards accepted. It was nevertheless voted a major success by most of the audience, which was not to be cheated of the privilege of crowning a hero, and it made no difference that one or two critics did not thoroughly join in this accolade.

When November at last delivers Houston from long summer, the transition is dramatically sudden and overexhilarating. Everything then appears a little more exciting than it actually is. In a month or so the stimulation abates and the air is more thoughtful again. St. Leger had started with cool weather; by the time of his second appearance with the organization, on December 12, conditions were a little better adjusted for calm judgment. This time he gave a program with Beethoven's Eighth Symphony as the principal item; the other orchestra pieces were indeed a scratchy collection—Wolf-Ferrari's overture to *The Secret of Suzanne*, the intermezzi from that composer's *Jewels of the Madonna*, and Tchaikovsky's *Capriccio Italien*. The soloist was Evelyn Duerler, a San Antonio soprano, who sang a couple of Mozart airs. St. Leger had recovered a little from the rigors of the opening concert and the music was less stuffy and prim. There was a certain neatening up of the ensemble and a little more life in the sound. But, while there was some reason for gratification, reviewers were still left with quite limited praises to grant, and Ina Gillespie of the *Chronicle* caught more than the momentary truth when she wrote of St. Leger the next day: "On the whole, they [the audience] find him highly satisfactory, with a sure sense of the fitness of things. Mr. St. Leger is often too restrained to get the fullest interest from the music he essays, but he is at all times an excellent taskmaster and one feels that were he quite sure of the response of his players he could let himself go. . . . As yet he is still first of all a drillmaster and second an interpretative instrument which only whets the appetite of his listeners."

This was an accurate diagnosis. It was curious that the man who was so lively and winning a social entertainer should lack the same ease and often give the impression of chilly and excessive reserve in the concert hall. But that was the paradox to consider as the season developed. The January occasion was a Mendelssohn evening, the orchestra giving the *Midsummer Night's Dream* music, which followed the same master's Violin Concerto. The fourteen-year-old soloist, Raphael Fliegel, signalled the day, still more than a decade in the future, when he would take over the concertmaster's position with this organization.

The repertory notes show what St. Leger conceived his mission in Houston to be. He apparently envisioned a sort of "music appreciation" course with a double action. He would attempt to work out his designs for the orchestra with material equally suited to lead a newly interested audience into the art by steps that were simple and painless. This approach was hardly an accurate judgment of the city's musical character. Whatever may have been best for the orchestra's training at this stage, the Houston musical public was in no need of being pampered to such an extent. It was bored and impatient with some of the trifles St. Leger presented. His attitude tended to produce effects that were academic and dry; it was patronizing and thus a little repugnant.

All this time, however, he continued as a busy and popular propagandist. He spoke to the luncheon clubs, he appeared before innumerable ladies' societies dedicated to improving their own taste or that of others; he became the intimate comrade, at card sessions or on hunting or fishing excursions, of wealthy gentlemen of the practical world who might otherwise never have found reason to notice the orchestra cause. St. Leger could phrase the symphony doctrine in many clever and interesting ways, and in this gift he appeared to delight and thus often delighted his audience. He was a natural promoter of music, and the service he rendered in linking the orchestra movement with the business community of Houston was of much value indeed.

But what had the orchestra otherwise gained in the period? When the season closed it was harder to take that measurement. Some pleasant programs had been given, but it was too much to say that the real drama of orchestral performance had occurred in any of these. They had lacked even the thrill that brave failure can sometimes give. Prudence in the choice of repertory had produced a monotony of effects. The orchestra had begun as a company of hopeful but rather oddly assorted musicians; it was difficult to mark any advance toward a stronger, more unified character. But there was no clear case to be lodged against the conductor, and nobody attempted to make one. From the standpoint of attendance the season had duplicated or bettered the record of its forerunner, and the orchestra movement had gained footing in town. The curtain descended on a note of success, and nothing was more taken for granted than the prospect of St. Leger's retention.

Matters were not so idyllic, however, that this was to happen altogether smoothly. No doubt feeling his grandeur a bit, the conductor retired for the summer to Norwich, New York, to play golf and another popular game of the podium brotherhood. At a distance he became coy and elusive. He had received $3,000 for his first season in Houston; the society offered him $3,600 for the second. St. Leger demurred, holding out for a minimum of $4,000 by contract. His argument was that a promise made by the society to assist him in augmenting his first-year income by teaching had not materialized (because of resentment of other vocal teachers in town), and that in consequence he had lived in Houston at a personal loss. This seemed strange in view of the fact that he had lived as a guest. But as letters mounted between the golfer, Dr. Mullen, and Epstein, the conductor's replies modulated to an injured and rather querulous tone. It seemed he had so many other offers to consider, and so on, and so on. Finally, after two months of this solemn and delicate shuttlecock, the association's executive committee agreed to make up the extra $400; the contract was concluded on June 4 and the tidings announced to the city. Coincidentally the contract with the musicians' union was renewed, no change being made in its terms.

Thus the orchestra was placed in position to continue "the mixture as before," and this it did for the 1933–1934 season. The St. Legers returned on cue and in character, the social formalities of the previous season were repeated, and there were more stories and *bons mots* to be relished, even if some of these began to seem rather familiar. The same could be said of St. Leger's program designs for that 1933–1934 season. And the orchestra's typical forms of discrepancy lingered.

These discrepancies were not painfully evident; they seldom thrust out at the uncritical listener. Everything went with some style. They were nevertheless there in the organization, to be noted with irritation by any discriminating ear. There was a great deal of enthusiastic and trustful applause, but the critical listener was entitled to wonder how long this interest would last unless the orchestra did more from the stage to induce honest excitement. How much blandness and humdrum in the making of music should be excused because an orchestra's budget was modest?

The difficulties of St. Leger's position were obvious. Strict professionalism in music, as in other fields, is not conclusive of anything, but in an orchestra it makes possible a sort of discipline that is not to be had with a mixed group. St. Leger worked with the band he had inherited. The qualitative unevenness of its membership was apparent; another unevenness lay in the instruments being used, some of which were of very low grade. The soul, even if it is stirred, cannot well be expressed through cigar box fiddles and gas pipe. There was scant budget allowance for replacement of players by better talent; there was none for replacement of instruments. Absenteeism interfered with rehearsals—the result of a low pay scale no less than of amateur participation. At least one concert had been given in which saxophones played the bassoon parts because there was not a bassoonist in town that week, the fishing having become unexpectedly good. And whenever the woodwind demands of a program were a little extraordinary, it was common to find players imported from Chicago, St. Louis, or other points for the single performance. It was a willing but very uncertain assembly that St. Leger commanded. This had to be allowed in estimating the outcome of his second season.

When the season was nearly over, a change of administration occurred. Dr. Mullen resigned the presidency of the association for reasons of health. He was succeeded by Joseph S. Smith, a prominent insurance executive, whose agreement to serve was another sign of increasing civic concern for the orchestra. Mr. Smith brought wisdom, dispatch, and a winning geniality to the office. There were no immediate changes of policy, and St. Leger's contract was again renewed to extend through the 1934–1935 season. Under Mr. Smith a very clear, realistic, and businesslike plan was worked out for the summer's subscription campaign and for other moves to secure the orchestra's underwriting. He stressed the point that the organization should not rely chiefly on ticket sales; it would increasingly have need of donated support, and he urged every possible effort to make the city familiar with this fact. It had been Miss Hogg's theme from the outset, and her own endeavors were now greatly encouraged by this sturdy and far-sighted endorsement. The society's constitution was revised under the supervision of Mrs. Oveta Culp Hobby as parliamentarian, and its business affairs systematized. It was preparing for bigger things. By September the campaigners reported $10,935 in ticket subscriptions for the coming season, a gain of more than $2,000 over the advance sale of the previous season.

But the musical course itself hardly sustained the bright hopes. A third season for any conductor, whatever the quality of his orchestra, brings up the hazard of familiarity. The conductor's personality is no longer a novelty to the audience; he has given his "act" and, very likely, has exhausted his little package of specialty items that show him off at his best. He is now challenged to hold interest in the ways that are more strictly essential. He must get down to the making of new terms with his listeners.

The Houston orchestra's 1934–1935 season ran into this hazard full on. Again the music seemed all of a kind. St. Leger perhaps did as well as he had done in the earlier seasons; it was just that he did as well in the same ways, and he did no better. He may have realized that there was no more he could do, conditions being as they stubbornly were. It was a disenchanting discovery on both sides of the footlights. There was little real heart in the music making of that winter. Too many programs provided as soloists young wonders who were not quite wonders, and the routine of slick prettiness palled. When the orchestra was not spending its time on trifles, it did little of interest with music of a more substantial variety. The sixth and last program, on April 15, was a particular hodge-podge—Saint-Saëns's B-Minor Violin Concerto with yet another boy wonder (Arnold Caplan) in combination with the ballet music from Grétry's *Céphale et Procris*, some musical caricatures by Leo Sowerby, Wagner's *Rienzi* Overture, and Sibelius's *Finlandia*. My review of that concert, for the *Houston Press*, contained the following comment:

Your correspondent has been one of the firmest supporters of the educational efforts of the Houston Symphony Orchestra, and yet even a good idea can be carried a little too far. The closing program of the season by Conductor Frank St. Leger and the organization, a sort of effort to be all things to all men, women, and children, was the least worthy and interesting performance we have had from the orchestra in a year. I do not think the production of mere prettiness in the concert hall is an educational work of much value, and there has lately been a persistent disposition to bend the programs of the Symphony at that angle. Whatever the case, the results of this winter should have shown clearly enough that the orchestra fares best when it has something more than a program of glorified charm music to offer its public. The average musical listener is above the average indicated by such a seasonal layout, and the orchestra society needs clearly to recognize that.

A few days later the conductor departed for Central City, Colorado, where his friend Robert Edmond Jones, as director of a summer festival project, was getting ready to stage a period drama for which St. Leger was to direct musical interludes. There was no announcement by the society of its conductorial plan for the next season—a *tacet* that struck some as significant. Weeks passed and the silence continued. Then the question was settled from the other end. In late summer St. Leger, still in the mountains and perhaps sensitive to the silence himself, wrote his Houston employers that he would not be available for the season to come. It was a graceful solution. St. Leger was headed for a place on the staff of the Metropolitan Opera Company, a position that well suited his talents and other characteristics.

Although the society had not been taken entirely by surprise, it was not as ready to meet this news as it might have been. It had perhaps dallied a little, in summer's languorous heat, about choosing the move to be made should the situation occur. Now there was small time to decide; the new season was at hand. The movement had been going along very well; all the same, it was still on trial. It was easy to see how a mistake at this time, if it disappointed the audience, could prove fatal. No great salary could be offered a conductor as yet—so what then was the turn? Committee meetings were called, and much earnest discussion ensued. The decision was against taking a plunge. In the end the board voted to place the orchestra entirely in charge of guest conductors for the season of 1935–1936; it would thus have time to look over some prospects more closely before awarding the position again. Meanwhile, the audience could be expected to welcome the novelty.

Accordingly, three men were selected, each to direct two concerts. Two of the trio, Vittorio Verse and Modeste Alloo, were of the younger division, ambitious and of modest repute; they could be considered postulants. The third was a man of distinction. He was Alfred Hertz, then conductor of the San Francisco Symphony Orchestra, a post he had held since 1915. The background of Alfred Hertz was broad and impressive. Born in Frankfort-am-Main in 1872, he enjoyed talents of a measure that eventually made him one of the high priests of Wagnerianism in Germany, comparable to Richter and Muck in that field. He thus belonged to the order of podium aristocracy that dominated the last quarter of the nineteenth century and the first thirty or forty years of the present one. In 1902 Hertz had been brought to New York to become head of the German wing of the Metropolitan Opera, where he remained until taking the California position. Those years were the glory of the Wagnerian cult at the Met; it has never since been as strong in that literature. The reputation of Hertz was equally solid in England and other quarters of Europe, and at this time of his life there was no higher authority, in his special domain, to be found anywhere in the world.

But the orchestra's season began under Vittorio Verse, who had also worked for the Metropolitan. He set it off in October, introducing a new method of displaying the orchestra, which was seated on elevated platforms for the first time. His program included a contemporary note, Luigi Mancinelli's overture to *Cleopatra*, as well as Beethoven's Fifth Symphony, Bach's Third Suite, the *Andante cantabile* movement of Tchaikovsky's Fifth Symphony, and Berlioz's *Rakoczy* March. It is not necessary to trace further the work of Mr. Verse with the organization (his concerts were consecutive), or to discuss that of Modeste Alloo, whose pair came at the close of the season. These gentlemen did as they were able, giving performances whose most notable characteristic was the ease with which they were forgotten. But no one who attended that season would ever forget the visit of its midwinter conductor, or the things that he did with the orchestra.

Alfred Hertz in his sixty-third year was a model of the Teutonic conductorial majesty such as only his epoch produced. He was a short, broad, thick-set man, who at this time walked heavily, slowly, and rather uncertainly with a cane, for he had suffered a stroke and was slightly paralyzed. This evil he resisted with a Bismarckian will, reinforced by that of his wife Lillie, a Christian Scientist as well as a German (and as a singer, a magnificent artist in her own right), who refused to acknowledge the impediment. He had steely blue eyes behind round, silver-rimmed spectacles; their expression could be mild, but when he stood to conduct they were piercing. He was quite bald but had the bristling mustache of a field marshall and a beard fit for the chin of a prophet. He spoke in a deep voice and his English was heavily accented. In short, he was the picture of the imperious musical *Kommandant*. Brought up in a tradition of absolute discipline and expecting it everywhere, he represented a kind of authority that was bred only in the German music theater prior to World War I.

The decisions of Alfred Hertz were autocratic and final. He had known nothing of Houston before he arrived, and what he found in the auditorium gave him rather a shock. After one taste of the orchestra, he laid down the baton with a snort. *Lieber Gott!* he could not be expected to give concerts with such an organization! Why had they called him for this? His bald head became pink with emotion. There would have to be replacements in certain positions at once; otherwise he would go on his way.[1]

The sponsors were intimidated and thrown into a state. What were they to say? There was indeed nothing to say, for the conductor had already been proudly announced. Clearly he knew what he was asking —and why. The only possible thing was to give in to his ultimatum and ask mercy. The *Herr Doktor* was reasonable too; he would settle for the importation of five more experienced and competent players— an oboist, an English hornist, two bassoonists, and a French hornist to take over the principal chair. They could be had from points no more distant than St. Louis or maybe Chicago. The plan would add about $785 to the cost of each concert, including two extra rehearsals. This gave the society worry, but it had to agree. Notified to that effect, the old martinet consented to resume his command.[2]

Under his care, the orchestra received in a week the most strict and intensive music lessons it had ever sustained. They were greatly illuminating and a little frightening. For these sessions the conductor, who was an honorary member of the San Francisco Police Department, appeared with a silver police whistle suspended on a cord from his neck. He used it shrilly and often for the purpose of halting the orchestra. Though this was amusing, nobody dared laugh at the idea. His comments to the players could be withering.

---

[1] It was Joseph S. Smith who had booked him, and he delivered himself to the president.

[2] What probably did as much to placate him were the dinners he was offered in Miss Hogg's beautiful home, Bayou Bend. Hertz was a famous gourmet, as were Sir Thomas Beecham and Georges Enesco, who later celebrated the cuisine of this mansion.

"Gendlemen," he would say, after a graveyard silence of half a minute, "I tage dis chance to remind you, *vonce* more, dad de sign BB in music does *nod* mean 'bowerful as bossible.' Iss clear yet? . . . Ve repead." The players shrank under his gaze.

But with all this he was teaching some of the secrets of orchestral refinement. His first program, given on January 13, consisted of Saint-Saëns's prelude to *Le Déluge*, Schubert's *Unfinished* Symphony, the Prelude and Liebestod from Wagner's *Tristan und Isolde*, and Respighi's *Pines of Rome*. In his second performance, on February 17, he conducted Tchaikovsky's *Romeo and Juliet*, an expansion of the *Andante cantabile* movement of that composer's D Major String Quartette, also his B-flat Minor Piano Concerto, with Leslie Hodge, a protégé of Dr. Hertz's as soloist, and two more Wagnerian numbers, the prelude to *Lohengrin* and overture to *Tannhäuser*.

These were evenings of revelation for most of the orchestra's listeners. The voice of the instrument seemed to have changed; it was richer and more expressive than ever before, and there was often a singing in it that delighted the senses and echoed in the memory. The climaxes were noble and broad, without feeling of strain; the shadings were exquisitely managed. Every piece became a different experience because the whole of its character emerged. With such handling the poetry of great music was there with the sound, and the audience was completely enthralled. The spell of the first evening was repeated in the second of Dr. Hertz's performances, and those who had been interested in the symphony movement before were left with a new kind of excitement. They asked themselves what had occurred.

The answer was both simple and mystic. Plainly the first moment of truth had arrived for this organization. The extra and well-seasoned performers in key spots had made a measure of difference in the orchestra, giving it more expressive variety. That was a lesson to absorb. But the other reasons for this lovely experience lay in the personality and style of the man in command. The mystery of the conductorial office itself, when it is significantly occupied, had been everywhere felt in these programs. But where it was felt most—and where it shivered the soul prepared to receive—was in the music of Wagner, the *Tristan* and *Lohengrin* episodes in particular. These were for the first time properly heard from this organization, through the presence of a masterful leader who communicated the transcendentalism of Wagner as well as any conductor has ever done.

In that sense, Alfred Hertz was a bearer of light, and the concerts he gave Houston, not long before the end of his earthly career, were certainly among his most noble bequests as an artist. They form a cardinal page in the musical history of the city, for they showed it for the first time what its orchestra could be like, given certain improvements and with the full authority present before it. The vision had been caught, and its haunting effects would remain. The goal urged by Miss Hogg had received a dramatic clarification.

Chapter 6

When officials of the orchestra paused to take stock, after five seasons of the new operation, they had reason enough to be pleased. From the popular standpoint the orchestra was in a solid position. It had been a success since the reorganization. Its business affairs were in good order; deficits had been small. Finding of enthusiastic and able volunteer workers was no longer a problem. As to artistic conditions, there was certainly a gain to be noted, modest but entirely respectable; and now the peculiar beauties of the Hertz performances, which continued to be talked of, had shown the possibilities latent in the orchestra and supplied excellent arguments for its fuller support. There remained problems enough, to be sure, but as 1936 entered its second quarter the association was sanguine. In that spring mood it amended its charter, changed its name, and became officially the Houston Symphony Society.

Better still, there were signs that the depression was at last beginning to lift. They were scattered and evanescent, but more apparent in Houston than in most cities; and this sense that the monster was losing its hold gave the air an exhilarating tang. Emergency measures remained much in effect over the nation, however; and with a little more luck the society would have benefited from that condition to the point of finding one of its difficulties removed.

In 1935 the Works Progress Administration had been set up by the federal government to create employment. Under this plan a great many unlikely and rather wonderful things had been built, including municipal bath houses, dams across waterless creeks in anticipation of their possible changes of habit, animal quarantine stations, and brave monuments to forgotten glories of history. Houston had been awarded a share of these grants, and among the needs locally declared to be pressing was replacing the old wooden hall of assembly, a few paces from Buffalo Bayou, which had been built for the National Democratic Convention in 1928. It was quickly decided to substitute a permanent municipal coliseum of 15,000 capacity (the indoor circus idea was beginning to take hold at the time), with a music hall of 2,500 capacity joined to its east side.

So rapidly had this project developed and been put into work (the buildings were now nearing completion) that few people had been fully consulted about it—nobody of much judgment from the musical and theater factions, at any rate. As a consequence, this hasty construction received a stage that perhaps was unique in theater history. Intended to serve both buildings, it had identical openings into the Music Hall and Coliseum and was thus a tunnel whose sole merit was the clarity with which it transmitted disturbing sounds between the one and the other. Two remodeling operations were necessary to cure this fault. But even then, the hall was unsatisfactory from the symphony's standpoint. The main trouble, which might have been quite easily avoided, was that it would not accommodate the orchestra's average attendance at one sitting. The hall's auditorium, a rectangular box with drab walls, was a fit reminder of the state of depression, and altogether the building displayed less theatrical charm than the better grade hospitals were achieving at that date. So the orchestra's chance to get into a new home was lost. Because of the bungles in planning this building, the society would continue to operate in the City Auditorium, one season excepted, for another eighteen years to come.

But in April of 1936 the immediate problem was that of finding another conductor. This was a delicate matter to settle, and as the guest season concluded the handling of it was complicated by another administrative change. Having served the society in valuable ways for two years, Joseph S. Smith retired from the presidency. It was an unexpected development, and Miss Hogg was named chairman of a committee to find a replacement. She proceeded in typical manner.

One afternoon in late April, eight business and professional leaders of the city were invited to have tea in Miss Hogg's beautiful home. No reason for the meeting was mentioned. As they arrived, each was covertly handed a small slip of paper, on which were the words: "You have been nominated to be president of the Houston Symphony Society." The results were amusing. With each man thinking himself the lone nominee, a wily competition ensued. The idea was to gain privately the ear of the hostess, into which the "nominee" murmured the reasons why, though terribly honored by the selection, he would be unable to serve. Then he felt smug and secure. All that done, Miss Hogg revealed the little joke of the eight uniform slips. In the laughter that followed, the guests found themselves made a committee to single out one of their number for the office. The one upon whom it was more or less thrust, and who accepted with good humor and a slight modification (by Kentucky bourbon) of his tea, was Walter H. Walne. It had been a very fortunate meeting.

Symphony orchestras in the United States have been nurtured by two forms of support. The first has come naturally from persons with a direct interest in music and some experience of the symphony mode. Thus the movements originate. But they cannot proceed far without support of another kind, which has to be given as an act of faith or civic responsibility. There must be those who see fit to contribute, in personal service or fiscal assistance, although they do not have, at least to begin with, any real interest in music. If they are converted, the conversions must be by logic. The test of any orchestra movement in this country is the degree to which it has been able to gain this type of support. No American orchestra has ever become better than ordinary without having it in considerable measure.

Walter H. Walne was such a man from the "outside," and the model he left was a rare and exemplary case of this spirit. A highly successful and very busy attorney, he had never had more than a casual interest in serious music. He claimed no knowledge of the art.[1] His recreations were apt to be hunting and fishing, and he was persuaded to accept the presidency only by strenuous pleading and the fact of his wife's musical leanings and work as a member of the orchestra board. His acceptance, however, was in earnest. And because he was a person of logic and probity, Walter Walne set out to learn the job he had taken—and the art it supported—as few men could have done more faithfully. The result was that he found himself captured. Fine music became his dominant passion and remained so to the end of his life.

He began with the study of Henry Lee Higginson, founder of the Boston Symphony Orchestra, whose writings he accepted as gospel. The glory of the Boston Symphony was there to prove Higginson's wisdom. This direction of Walne's interest was to be of great meaning to Houston. Toward the middle of summer he visited New England on business, and it was no matter of chance that he spent most of that visit in Boston. Serge Koussevitzky, who had conducted the Boston ensemble since 1924, was at the peak of his remarkable reign. The magic of it all was imparted to Walter Walne as he sat evening after evening in Symphony Hall. He also heard the faith put into words by the master. Miss Hogg had written letters to Boston that produced an introduction to Koussevitzky. The Russian conductor received the Houstonian in a mood of benignity. He listened with patience to the lawyer's description of the musical situation in Houston (it must have been only a name to Koussevitzky, but at least the name sounded a little like Boston) and proved to be gracious and helpful. He thought he understood the requirement. There was in Boston a young conductor whom Koussevitzky, after the immemorial way of his kind, chose to

[1] At one of his early board meetings he was said to have told the directors: "Our conductor tells me that what we need most, to improve the orchestra's woodwind section, is a couple of good bassinets."

look upon as a protégé of his own. That was hardly the case, but he recommended this musician to Mr. Walne's attention, and himself arranged a meeting between them. The man was Ernst Hoffmann, conductor of the Commonwealth Symphony Orchestra, another emergency enterprise of the Works Progress Administration.

Whatever Walter Walne had expected of this meeting, he probably received a certain surprise. He found himself with a brisk, slender, very articulate young man of thirty-seven, handsome in a quiet way, with strikingly fine brown eyes and a thoroughly businesslike air. Everything about Ernst Hoffmann's appearance was as neat as a pin—a German pin—and this characteristic appeared also in his exact ways of expressing himself. But there was little Germanic tinge in his accent. And there was nothing at all arty about him. He was a man you could talk to. The Houston attorney, accustomed to judge character quickly, liked Hoffmann's directness and logic. There was one small point that disturbed him. When he thought of a cocktail before lunch and inquired what his companion would have, the conductor asked for a cup of hot water. Walter Walne was not certain he heard right. But then he considered the moral extremities of Boston—or perhaps his guest had a touch of malaise. He did not allow it to influence his judgement.

Ernst Heinrich Hoffmann was a native of Boston. His father, a violinist, had emigrated from Germany and had for many years played in the Boston orchestra. Ernst was a prodigy who graduated from Harvard, *cum laude*, at seventeen and was promptly offered a place on the university's faculty as an anthropologist. He had done brilliant research in that field. But he had likewise distinguished himself in a musical way (his piano teacher was the great Harold Bauer), and it was to this art that he had decided to devote the rest of his life. The war intervened, but after serving through part of it in the United States field artillery, he went to Germany in 1920 to complete his artistic education in the Berliner Konservatorium für Musik, and by work in the city's theaters. There he met a pretty, slender blonde girl, a native, whose faith in his talent was infinite. By an odd bit of coincidence she was already the bearer of his name: she was Annemarie Clara Hoffmann, a teacher of mathematics and languages. They fell in love, were married in 1922, and five years later had a son, Clifford, their only child.

After completing his studies Hoffmann had gone into conducting in the land where the testing is hardest. He was successful. In 1924 he was appointed conductor-in-chief of the Breslau Opera and Philharmonic Orchestra, a post in which he remained till the creeping poison of Hitlerism set in. Then, despite an excellent record of achievement and because of his American citizenship and outspoken opinions, Hoffmann lost his position. It meant he would find no other employment in the state theater of a nation whose political climate he had come to detest. He returned to Boston in 1934 and was shortly given the responsibility of organizing the Commonwealth Orchestra. As this was apt to be only a temporary affair, he was interested in any opportunity that seemed to offer more solid and challenging prospects. He spoke with the charm of a natural and intelligent candor.

There was to be a performance by the Commonwealth Symphony on the following evening, and Walter Walne went to the concert. In the hall he was again strongly impressed. As he listened to the music that Hoffmann delivered and thought over what Koussevitzky had said of the younger conductor, he decided that Koussevitzky was right. When he returned home a few days later, he presented Hoffmann's name to the symphony board, along with his own recommendation.

Although the orchestra's stewards were uneasily conscious of another season approaching without a conductor in hand, they were disposed to be as careful as possible this time. They were chary of a hasty decision. For that matter, Ernst Hoffmann had indicated some caution himself. He had left Mr. Walne to understand that should an offer develop he would want to know more about the orchestra in Houston, and about the city itself, before giving his answer. The attorney could only approve that attitude. And now the board members, having heard his report, decided to bring Hoffmann to Houston for an interview, his expenses to be paid. The conductor would thus have an opportunity to look over the city, the officials could look over the conductor, and everybody would be in position to make up his mind with full evidence.

The invitation was accepted and in due course the time came for the visitor's arrival. It was a Sunday morning, dark, sodden, and oppressive. The welcoming delegation consisted of Mr. Walne and one member of the press; I had joined him for breakfast and a slippery drive to the station. We awaited the train, which finally pulled in with its windows heavily misted. Ernst Hoffmann stepped from his Pullman and put his feet on Texas soil for the first time. He saw Mr. Walne and came toward him. Possibly fifteen seconds had elapsed, during which the conductor had obtained his sole impression of Houston—the grimy train shed of the old Grand Central Station.

He put out his hand with a smile. "Mr. Walne, I've decided to come!" he said. "I can see I would like it here."

The president was somewhat taken aback, but he managed to hold a straight face. He was a man of the world. After all, four-thousand-dollar-a-year musical jobs were not growing on bushes in 1936, and Hoffmann was too intelligent a man to play coy. Doubtless the greatly practical Annemarie had spoken to him since the meeting with the president in Boston. Whatever the case, simple candor was always a large part of his natural appeal.

The board too was a little stumped when it learned what had happened. It looked as though it had been left with not much to decide, which amused some of its members. But there were no further whimsical tid-bits. The formal interview was full of sobriety and hard sense, and everything went to the credit of the man under examination. He impressed all the officials, as he had impressed Walne, by his earnestness, logic, and realistic appraisal of the problems of creating an orchestra. His credentials were sound, his personality pleased, and after deliberating the board voted to ratify his "acceptance" and give him a contract for the season to come. It was a fortunate decision. Ernst Hoffmann was to be the symphony's leader for eleven years—the longest tenure yet achieved in the office—and during those years the foundations of the orchestra's artistic character were much strengthened.

The new conductor drove his family from Boston to Houston in a car that had made two Atlantic crossings and between these logged a hundred thousand or so miles on the *bahns* of Germany and Middle Europe. Hoffmann had bought it in Boston and taken it abroad; it had come back with the family. It was well over ten years old, but that was evident only because of its styling; there was no other sign of this usage. The motor continued to run with a salesroom murmur, and the upholstery and fittings were immaculate. The exact measures of gasoline and oil used for the trip had been neatly inscribed in a register kept in the glove box. The tally was precise, from the day the union between owner and car had been consummated. It was a proud automobile, in the way that a beautiful woman is sometimes proud who has been cherished and lovingly used with full regard for the perishable nature of beauty.

Hoffmann's hat suitably complemented this vehicle. It was small, round, and in style seemed of a date with the car. It rested high and precisely on his head, as though it had never been taken off after leaving the store; changes might since have occurred in the man, but none had occurred in the hat. The family sat up quite straight in the vehicle, all very composed, and thus they arrived at a new home. The picture suggested that it might have been twenty minutes from East Prussia.

As all the world knows, German methodicalness has its two sides, the drear and the dear. With the Hoffmanns it seldom appeared in the ways that exasperate others, but in the second form it was richly displayed. Ernst and "Mini" Hoffmann had many a quaint habit and characteristic; they also had a rare kind of devotion. The finest thing to be said of this pair is that the qualities of one could not well be considered apart from the qualities of the other. They were truly inseparable, and must always be remembered together.

But Houston, engrossed with other interesting changes, did not at once give them much notice of any kind. The new excitement was that of release. After more than five crippling and dull years, the boom condition that had so long been characteristic of Houston was again taking effect. The city had continued to grow; its population had risen to more than half a million; its business was reviving well ahead of the progress shown nationally. Streetcars were about to disappear from its scene in this autumn of 1936, amid a rush of new projects and innovations. Social life quickened, and the pace was the liveliest since the "good old days" of the late twenties. Ernst and Annemarie Hoffmann were a little bit lost in it all.

But to those who took time to observe the orchestra's early rehearsals, it was evident that the wheel of fortune had again turned in its favor. At this point nothing could have better suited its needs than a resident commander who brought German method, German thoroughness, German order and drill and sobriety, in combination with German frugality, patience, and expediency. All these things Hoffmann conferred, though he did so with no imperious airs. His manner was mild to the point of abnegation at times; he was seldom excited and never caustic. But under his mildness was a sharply analytical mind, a perfectionist spirit, and great firmness of will. The orchestra found that out quickly enough. He asked of no man what he himself was not willing to give, and he was a fanatical worker. His musical god was Richard Strauss, Germany's most celebrated conductor of the day and most widely renowned living composer. As a violinist in the theaters of Berlin and other cities, Hoffmann had often worked under the illustrious Richard, famous for stuffing the pages of his scores with superfluous notes and tough riddles for orchestral performers, and for his scathing sarcasms with any who faltered over the difficulties.

It was now the more typical music of Strauss, the masterful tone poems with their tricky involvements of rhythm and texture, with which Hoffmann tested his performers. It was a new language to some. He determined quickly the orchestra's faults and shortcomings and methodically made his report to the trustees. There were two principal troubles. The first was a matter of technical incapacity—too many players whose ability was substandard or hopeless. The second condition was instrumental. The orchestra was pocked with instruments of inferior quality, which in measure defeated the efforts of players equipped to do acceptable work with the right tools. This of course hampered the balance of the choirs.

Hoffmann asked the board for remedial steps; the board listened and did what it could. The money granted was small in proportion to the needs, but Hoffmann took what he was offered and promptly replaced some of the players where better material was at hand. The purchase of new instruments—by the society, at any rate—was quite out of the question. So informed, the conductor set out to do what he could in his own ways. A certain sound haunted his mind; it was hard to explain, but maybe with patience it could be shown in degree.

The season's first concert had to be given, however, with very limited renovation of the orchestra. It remained much the same organization that St. Leger had left. Hoffmann made the best of the bargain by not asking too much of his company. The society still had a program committee, which had decreed a plan of imported soloists for the season and engaged for this concert Richard Bonnelli, the Metropolitan Opera baritone, and Hoffmann was content to let the vocalist go as he would. Bonnelli helped himself to four numbers. As these included Wolfram's air from *Tannhäuser*, the Barber's *Largo al factotum*, and (as seemed inevitable for the day) the "Toreador Song" of Bizet, the time left for the orchestra's strict service was not too great. Hoffmann used it for the *Freischutz* Overture and Tchaikovsky's F Minor Symphony.

An audience of 3,700 attended this opening and found reasons for greeting the new conductor with more than merely courteous interest. As a figure on the orchestra stage, Hoffman made a pleasant rather than a striking appearance. He was no model of physical grace; he had no theatricalism. But he was clean-cut and assured. His beat was precise, he was thoroughly watchful, and a certain authority made itself felt in his work. It was clear, intelligent music making; the shape and sense of the pieces were there. He had seated the orchestra in a way not used before, the woodwinds outside to his right. There were improvements in that section, as well as in the work of the strings, where strict unity of bowing prevailed. All in all, the concert gave signs of imagination and a warm heart at the helm, and everybody responded to that appeal.

The schedule again called for a season of six concerts, and the next of these, given on December 14, being entirely for the orchestra, was a better index to the taste and characteristics of the man. Pre-Christmas occasions are dangerous temptations to orchestra leaders, who are apt to borrow the motif unduly. Hoffmann's choice of a little Mozart piece, *The Sleighbells*, as the only seasonal reference, showed gratifying restraint. Along with it the gathering received Schubert's great C Major Symphony, also his first *Rosamunde* ballet suite; Beethoven's

Leonore Overture No. 3, and two Johann Strauss items, the *Fledermaus* Overture and *The Blue Danube* in its original concert version. A truly Viennese evening, and all in order as to spirit and style of rendition. The orchestra sang well where the singing is best in this music, and the critical listener learned something about the imagination that animated the talents of Ernst Hoffmann.

It was a Christmas bright with the candles of hope. The American public, relieved of some of the anxieties under which it had lived for half a decade, had reason to show its best side. The nation was recovering full vigor. If the distant horizon continued to present a very troubling appearance, that could be put out of mind for the moment. There was much gratitude in the air, and this Christmas the benevolent spirit was manifested in unusual ways.

The orchestra felt some of the warmth, for it was certainly now tended with an extraordinary degree of affection. The making of good music is always a labor of love, and with the Hoffmanns it was a sort of religion. During their first years they bestowed on the organization a devotion that was simple, open-hearted, and sentimental—a compound of the feelings with which they had left Europe, a natural and somewhat childlike goodness, and a real appreciation of the opportunity given them in Houston. The players could not fail to be touched by this ardor, and it helped discover the orchestra to itself.

Hoffmann yearned for complete professional capacity in the orchestra; it was hard not to have funds to do quickly the things that he knew to be needed. He worried, fretted, and schemed. Though the orchestra had a manager in that opening season, Harry Bourne (one of its double-bass players), it was Hoffmann who handled most of the office affairs with a scrupulous eye on costs.[2] He would himself set out the chairs for a concert; it saved a few dollars that could then be spent for improvements. Pride certainly was not one of his faults, and his energy seemed unlimited. But along with great practical sense he had a curi-

---

[2] The office staff otherwise consisted of two ladies—Mrs. Anita Rall and Mrs. McClelland Wallace—who performed a prodigious variety of duties, from the sale of tickets to the sweeping of the stage. Mrs. Rall remains (1970) the society's auditor; Mrs. Wallace has long been on the board of directors and is now a vice-president.

ous touch of superstition. He would not think of conducting a concert except in the same pair of shoes in which he had made his professional debut in Germany. They were put on his feet by his wife in the dressing-room, at the last moment, and never used for a step more than was necessary to get him to the podium and back. They were of patent leather, perfectly preserved, and were kept in a special case with a felt lining.

It would be tedious to list many of the things that were done by Ernst and Annemarie Hoffmann, beyond the strict call of conductorial duty, for the sake of the orchestra's nourishment. Little was known of these acts by the public, which only felt some of their benefits. To overlook them entirely in this story, however, would be to ignore the reason for some of the virtues that are found today in the orchestra's character. The Hoffmanns had charity equal to their carefully planned ambitions. There were few lengths to which they would not go, if the promise was that of aid to the band. They had a talent for finding, in faraway places, violinists or woodwind players, of better than ordinary grade, who were victims of the times and in conditions of extra-ordinary distress. They knew of other musicians in Germany, suffering bitterly, who would do anything to escape. By means greatly involved and demanding of patience, they brought some of these cases to Houston—and then found they must rehabilitate them in order to make use of their skills. It was privately said in the orchestra that Mini Hoffmann would do the laundry of any fiddler who could play Brahms well enough, in order to get him into the orchestra, and moreover would find him a shirt if he needed one. She had indeed done that service at times; she had fed, sheltered, and tenderly nursed indigent players from abroad, or their wives or children, while they struggled to get on their own feet. Was it love for the orchestra, or ambition for the man she adored? It did not matter; in the heart of Mini Hoffmann the two emotions were one.

Other oddities of recruitment occurred. One morning the telephone rang in the conductor's office. It was an official of the police department.

"Got any use for a bass drummer down there?" he inquired.

Hoffmann was puzzled. "Why?"

"We've got one here."

"Where's that?" asked the conductor.

"In jail. He says he's a bass drummer."

"Where did you get him?"

"Out of a boxcar. Last night in the freight yards."

"Is it a serious charge?"

"No; vagrancy. Just riding the rods."

Hoffmann calculated a moment. "Bring him over," he said.

It was true. The candidate proved to be an experienced percussion player of European extraction, temporarily down on his luck. He was obtained at the cost of a five-dollar fine and for years served well in the orchestra. The second flute in that opening season (later the first), Paul Rubinstein Kepner, was a veteran just out of a United States cavalry band; he had seldom made music before save in the saddle or under the sky. Frances Albertin, the second bassoon, could only play at her best with her shoes off and was happy at last in an orchestra that understood this need of her temperament. She had felt stifled in Boston where conventions were tighter. Herman Weiss, the veteran chief timpanist, who liked his cigar, had a habit of vanishing through a slit in the back curtain when he had a long rest in his part. It terrified Hoffmann, but this seasoned performer could count musical measures in his sleep and never failed to reappear, without attracting an audience eye, at the last possible moment.

Walter Walne's interest had helped bring more of the city's prominent business and professional leaders into the orchestra's administration. The roster for 1936–1937 included John E. Green, Jr., Harry C. Wiess, and Mrs. J. G. Flynn as vice-presidents; Milton R. Underwood as treasurer; Mrs. C. J. Robertson, recording secretary; Mrs. Ray Dudley, corresponding secretary; and Mrs. W. P. Hobby, parliamentarian. Among those named to the board of directors at the annual meeting in January was another outstanding attorney, Maurice Hirsch, the second generation of his family to serve. He was elected together with Mrs. Harry C. Hanszen and Mrs. J. A. Tennant. It meant something for the movement to have that order of representation. The tradition of trusteeship was developing along with the orchestra.

Hoffmann's work had assured a renewal of his contract. The board voted him a salary increase to six thousand dollars and gave him other signs of its confidence. He was authorized to put on in the coming season a course of six "pop" concerts, which he wished to model after the Boston Pops plan, and, although the society still had a program committee, the selection of the regular programs was left much in his hands. He had made a very happy beginning in Houston. He was grateful, and spent most of the summer in town, busy with schemes for improving his opportunity.

Certain results of this labor were felt with the start of the 1937–1938 season. The opening was another remarkable evidence of the symphony's popularity; every seat in the City Auditorium had again been sold. Hoffmann offered this gathering a program whose chief works were Richard Strauss's *Don Juan* and Rachmaninoff's E Minor Symphony. The orchestra, numbering seventy-four, showed various changes, including a new concertmaster, the fourth it had had in a year. This time it was Joseph Gallo who headed the violins. The playing in general was better balanced than that of the previous season, and its spirit was very engaging. One interested listener, Moses Smith, music critic of the *Boston Transcript* and a friend of Hoffmann's, who had come down for the evening, reported back to his paper that the former Boston conductor had put together in Houston the makings of a very good orchestra.

As might have been expected in a man of his background, Hoffmann hoped to see the orchestra turned to the uses of opera, and the third program of this season was a showing of his credentials in that wise— a concert production of Puccini's *Madama Butterfly*. Cio-Cio San was an excellent Houston soprano, Nancy Yeager Swinford, who had sung the role in a standard production put on in this hall by Uriel Nespoli shortly after his release by the symphony. Mrs. Swinford repeated the beauties of her earlier work, and Hoffmann gave a winning account of his own instinct for the operatic form.

The fifth program was an evening of Shakespeare in music, with performances of John K. Paine's *The Tempest*, Tchaikovsky's *Romeo and Juliet*, and Mendelssohn's *Midsummer Night's Dream* music, among other material. When the series concluded on April 12 with the

Brahms Second Symphony, Grieg's *Peer Gynt* Suite, and two Wagner selections, the prelude to Act 3 of *Lohengrin* and the *Tannhäuser* Overture, the society had been given a season of unusual pattern and taste. Everyone recognized progress achieved; a certain character was coming into the orchestra's work. Most strikingly, perhaps, a richer, darker, more dramatic quality had been heard in the brass tone of the final concert. It was hauntingly felt in the Wagner creations and lent a lovely solemnity to the music of *Tannhäuser*.

The explanation was that Hoffmann had bought with his own money, from the Schmidt factory in Germany, a set of large-bore, rotary-valve trumpets and matching trombones, such as are favored in the German orchestras. The Houston players complained of them at first but soon found that their efforts to use them were richly repaid. Hoffmann was poorer but happy. These instruments gave part of the tonal character he had dreamed of for the orchestra; and such was the typical sound of its brass choir for the rest of his time as conductor.

Only one scheme of the season had not been a success. The "pop" concerts had failed to attract the young public for which they were intended—or any other in suitable numbers—and that project was dropped.

As indicated earlier, the Music Hall, which had been under construction for about two years, was a product of rather curious planning. Whatever the case, in the summer of 1938 this edifice was declared by its builders to be finished and ready for use. The announcement was happily read by the city's theater public. It had been a long time since Houston had received a new theater facility of this type, and in the climate of optimism produced by the growing economic recovery, people were very much in a humor for change and a more elegant note in their entertainment. The newness of the hall was appealing, and they were eager to see it put into use.

The society's officials were not quite so enthusiastic about it. Some of them had been watching the work. They were painfully conscious of the hall's unimaginative design; they were put to great wonder by its strange, two-way stage. The other problem it offered, from the orchestra's standpoint, was disconcerting. With its seating capacity of

2,500, the hall would not accommodate the symphony's whole public at once; if it were going to be used, concerts would have to be given in pairs. The officials hesitated before that prospect, and their reason was a rather curious one.

At some point in the dim past of the city, and for what reason no record reveals, Monday night had become known as "society night" in the Houston theater. Though the foolish designation itself had long since disappeared, the custom it indicated had not. The city's elite had for generations made Monday the preferred evening for theater attendance. So firmly was this tradition, or superstition, established that it had been the most natural thing in the world for the Symphony Society to pick Monday as the night for its concerts. What would now happen if it had to ask part of its audience to attend on another evening? The officials worried about it.

But if there were misgivings, the society also was tired of the problems presented by the City Auditorium, which were getting no fewer as time ran. And how would it look if all the other art organizations of town went to the Music Hall, and only the orchestra stayed on in the dingy surroundings of the old plant? It would hardly seem very progressive. The expectations of the public were evident and were taken into consideration. In the end, perhaps more for that reason than because of its own confident judgment, the society announced the transfer of its 1938–1939 concerts to the Music Hall.

Although the initial reaction to this news was enthusiastic, the paired concert plan ran into the difficulty expected. When season tickets were placed on sale a little later, nearly all the subscribers preferred Monday. When some of these, the box buyers especially, had to be told that only Tuesday accommodations were available, they tended to be rather indignant. The old voodoo was still working, and Tuesday was somehow looked upon as a lesser value than opening night.

This problem was not a great one, however, and no doubt would have ended quickly enough had the hall itself proved to be an indisputable improvement. It proved to be more of a shock. The builders had prepared an expensive disappointment for the Houston theater public, and the orchestra became one of the agencies unhappily bound to reveal it. The Music Hall utterly lacked glamor and theatrical interest. With its boxlike shape and its dark, roach-colored walls, it amounted to a Quaker house with a stage. It was little more comfortable or acoustically favorable than the City Auditorium, and was less flattering to pretty dresses displayed. The musicians liked it no better than the public, and Hoffmann's programs, though again very tastefully fashioned, seemed to meet in this building a stubborn and chilly resistance. Moreover, the hall's first season was haunted by the constantly more somber news coming from Europe, and everyone was a little distracted. Attendance declined, especially on the orchestra's second nights, which became indeed cheerless and drab.

With so much disenchantment and apprehension around, the season of 1938–1939 left little for the symphony's friends to remember. Such improvements as appeared in the band itself were lost in the prevalent melancholy. It was a warning, and the society took it to heart. Well short of the season's end it announced a decision to return to its old quarters the next fall.

Before that could occur the world changed. Hitler's armies invaded Poland on September 1, 1939. The grim horsemen appeared in the skies above Europe again, and the last hopes of the pacifists were destroyed by events of the next few days. Every heart felt the weight of a deadly depression, for each sensed in its way that the story of 1914 was repeating itself, with even more terrible prospects.

Yet if the stage had been set for another world war, whose course could be all too easily imagined, it remained for the moment, as in the earlier case, altogether a European war and for that reason a trifle unreal. Outwardly life changed little as America oriented itself to the tragedy. In Houston, as elsewhere, the main effect of the war for two years was to heighten the economic boom. The inevitability of the nation's involvement in the holocaust, sooner or later, was accepted by some as the months passed, but the subject was nowhere welcome. To avoid it, however, was futile. More and more, as the war moved westward, there was a feeling of time running out. It created another hateful suspense. In such a condition it is natural for people, frustrated, resentful, and restless, to seize upon any distraction that offers a momentary pleasure.

Faced with the same situation that had caused its abandonment twenty-one years before, the orchestra society was of no mind to be scuttled again. It was in far stronger position (the annual budget had now risen to some seventy thousand dollars), it had a popular conductor and a definite image, and it had the authority of the public itself, very clearly expressed, to keep going. There was no thought of doing otherwise. Back in the City Auditorium, the organization gave sign of its confidence with a 1939–1940 season that in every way represented expansion.

This time there was a ten-concert schedule, compared with the former series of six, and most of the soloists were of national or international repute. They included two pianists, Jacques Abram (a brilliant credit to his Houston teacher) and Robert Casadesus, the violinist Albert Spalding, and the Brazilian soprano Bidu Sayao, at that time a particular darling of the Met. But the more significant study of that season is to turn the pages of its programs and consider the repertory that Hoffmann presented. One is offered the picture of a conscientious and gifted orchestra builder at work. There can have been few cases in this country in which a young orchestra was brought along with better judgment or more canny regard for the opportunities offered, both in the orchestra itself and in the audience. Hoffmann's programs were designed to lead interest, and to lead it in ways that yield increasingly rich musical substance. Improvements continued to appear in the orchestra, notably in the work of the strings. When the season ended in April with a program headed by Schubert's great C Major Symphony and including the *Tristan* Liebestod, with Nancy Swinford as the beautiful singer, there were many damp eyes in the hall. They were testimony to an orchestra's character and sensitivity, no less than to emotions resulting from the tragic conditions of the hour.

The audience was reluctant to part with the spell of this music. Outside there was an ever grimmer and lonelier air; the world seemed to plunge deeper and deeper into madness. On the night of this concert the agony of Dunkirk was beginning. The desperation of France and England, earlier sensed, had now become starkly apparent. Under the impact of that realization all beautiful music, whatever its spirit, seemed to mourn for the civilization out of which it had emerged.

Chapter 7

Franklin D. Roosevelt had made a phrase to define the nation's quasineutral position. It was to be "the arsenal of democracy." This was clever political psychology. For while the slogan gave comfort by suggesting that America was fully aroused to a great danger, it further implied that the war's democratic combatants, given enough help in the form of American goods, might reasonably be expected to take care of the fighting itself. That idea much suited the public attitude of the moment. The president was also long on individual fitness, physical and mental, as an obligation of the critical times, and this too was approved as fine logic by most of his listeners. It accordingly seemed that everyone was entitled to continue his pleasures, without serious problems of conscience, because it is well known that recreation is healthy and contributes to fitness of both body and mind. People found themselves able to indulge in a wide range of delights with the feeling that thereby they were serving the cause of preparedness.

These principles laid down, the American theater proceeded much as it had in the 1914–1918 conflict. It got rich. There was nothing unusual about the theater's case; it merely followed the business curve shown by the nation as a whole. Prosperity spread to most fields. Employment and wages were high, and the instinct was for good living while the living was good. There was a new theater rush, and play touring resumed on a scale unknown since the boom days before 1929.

The musical medium caught its own share of the traffic. Opera houses and concert halls overflowed with a fresh, discovering audience, and found they could hardly provide enough offerings to satisfy this eager demand. A supplementary scheme, which caught on with new force, was that of the summer symphony concert played in the open air. Various eastern orchestras took to this plan, more or less imitating the *al fresco* seasons the Boston orchestra had been giving since 1937 in a woodland setting at Tanglewood, Massachusetts. Outdoor music was a fad of the hour, and this resulted in a Houston development that requires the momentary injection of a personal note into this history.

One day in the late summer of 1940, as music and theater critic of the *Houston Post,* I received a letter from a reader (he was the operator of a grocery store) who asked why summer symphony music—the outdoor kind—should not be provided in Houston. The letter was quoted in a column the next day, which went on to discuss the new vogue. The general idea of the piece was that, although getting into the open air on a summer evening may be a very nice thing for the audience, it is not the best working arrangement for a symphony orchestra. The peculiar values of the orchestral form, which involve the acoustical advantages of a hall, were taken into consideration, and the article closed by suggesting that the best way to enjoy symphony music is to seek it under its natural conditions.

But what is reason against the pull of a fad? Instead of closing the matter, the column resulted in a surprising number of letters from people in every part of the city and in neighboring towns, all supporting the grocer's idea. Some of the writers gave reasons enough why they could not attend regular concerts of the Houston society; the rest argued for the novelty simply because of its novelty and romantic attraction. This mail evidently represented a lot of enthusiasm and raised the question of whether the orchestra was not missing a good chance to deliver its educational message.

There was one reason at least to consider a possible test of the idea. Among the facilities of Hermann Park, the city's chief demesne of the kind, was a structure called Miller Memorial Theater. Designed in somebody's conception of the neo-Greek style, with stone colonnades flanking a stage too narrow for its height, the building had stood for twenty years without having any regular use. Now and again it had served for choral performances, political rallies, or the showing of outdoor movies. It was not an unhandsome construction and was quite beautifully framed by a wide green mall bordered by sentinel pines. By moonlight Miller Theater was highly romantic and more inviting of fine music than of most of the other things it had held. I wondered how it would do as an orchestra setting.

The result of my ruminations was that I showed the collection of letters to Ernst Hoffmann. He was astonished by the number and spirit of the writers. He felt strongly that something ought to be done to acknowledge such a demonstration of interest, and the upshot of our meeting was that together we paid a visit to the office of Walter Walne, taking with us a sampling of the mail. That day, however, the society's president was busy with other things; he was very depressed by the war news, which continued to worsen, and for once he was not sympathetic to Hoffmann's enthusiasm. He listened politely to everything; he was glad to be told of such a public desire for the orchestra. But he added that any notion that the Symphony Society should engage in a summer experiment was entirely out of the question. As things were going, he said, the organization would need luck to supply its regular seasons. That apparently settled the matter.

But outside in the street Hoffmann was thoughtful. He shrugged as we were ready to part.

"I wish we could have tried it just once," he said. "Maybe it's the kind of 'pop' they're waiting for here."

"How much do you think it would have cost to find out?" I asked.

"One concert? Not very much. That stage would hold only about forty performers. Say six hundred dollars for players."

"What about you?"

"Nothing," he said. "That would have been a donation."

The word suggested an idea. "I wonder whether the people who want these things would be willing to share part of the cost."

"How could they?" he asked. "There's no way to charge admission at Miller Theater."

"What about passing the hat?"

"And what if nobody responded?"

"We'd be out six hundred dollars."

Hoffmann smiled. "*Who* would?"

"Well," I said, "don't leave town till you hear from me again."

We parted and I went back to my office. Feeling that some answer was owed to the letter writers, I wrote a column for the paper explaining what had occurred and why the Symphony Society could not act. The column went on to suggest that those who wanted quality music should be willing to help support music. The possibility of contributions at Miller Theater was mentioned, and as a postscript I added that if some benefactor in Houston would put up a thousand dollars in underwriting, I felt certain a concert could be arranged as a test of the idea.

Next morning I received a mysterious telephone call. The caller, who declined to identify himself, said he had read the column and was interested in supplying the guaranty. He would say no more, but gave the number of an office in the Union National Bank Building and a time at which I could drop by if I cared to. My curiosity was sufficiently primed. A few hours later I drove to the downtown building, located the office, which bore no sign, and pushed open the door. I found myself in the presence of a bright-eyed gentleman of middle-age—mysterious, maybe, but no stranger. He was N. D. Naman, the quiet man of finance who had fostered the Houston Philharmonic venture ten years before. He looked up from his desk with a smile, thoroughly pleased by his little joke.

"I hope I didn't take you out of your way," he apologized.

"Not a bit," I replied, joining the fun. "But what does all *this* mean?"

"I hope it means you're going to have a very interesting concert. Do you think a thousand will cover the cost?"

"I imagine it will, if the thing can be managed at all. There may be questions to settle."

"Well," he said, "you can see about that." And he thereupon wrote a check which he handed over with one specification—that he should not be identified as the sponsor.

I was uncertain. My proposition in the paper had been met, but I hadn't counted on having it met in exactly this way—by an old rival of the symphony organization. I could think of reasons to hesitate, but in the end I accepted the check.

At first I could not even let Hoffmann into the secret. He had to proceed on faith. But Hoffmann could understand a deposit slip—and so could the boys at Union Hall. And it was a case of do something at once or do nothing; summer was waning, August was nearly half gone. The Symphony Society would not be involved in the venture, but its conductor and some of its players would be. How then would it take to the idea? It was characteristic of Hoffmann that he never seemed to consider the question. He saw only a chance to build interest in music.

The anonymous gift was announced in the paper, forty-five union musicians were hired by the conductor, and the evening of Wednesday, August 21, was picked for the concert. Hoffmann's program consisted of the March and Procession from Gounod's *Queen of Sheba*, Jacob Gade's *Jealousy* tango (a popular hit), Johann Strauss's *Wine, Woman and Song*, Wagner's *Tannhäuser* Overture, the "Dance of the Hours" from *La Gioconda*, the first movement of Schubert's *Unfinished* Symphony, and Sibelius's *Finlandia*. There was one rehearsal at Miller Theater on the morning of concert day—temperature 100 degrees.

Night came with a full moon rising over the theater, and there was a revelation indeed: by seven o'clock all roads leading into the park were choked. At eight-fifteen, when the concert began, police estimated the crowd spread before Miller Theater at fifteen thousand. Nothing like it had ever before been seen at a concert of orchestral music in Houston.

Those of us who had put together the venture were stunned, and so was at least one visitor, Walter Walne, who had come out to observe. He could hardly believe what he saw. And then he witnessed another phenomenon. At the program's intermission the audience was invited by a speaker, Dr. Reginald Platt, to contribute whatever it saw fit, if it wished a continuation of this plan. Donations were collected in tin buckets by a company of youngsters who had volunteered. The amount they brought back to the stage, in sums ranging from pennies to ten-dollar bills, was well over eight hundred dollars. The concert had earned more than it cost.

More dramatically, however, it had discovered a new, unsuspected and greatly impressive interest in the orchestra. It was this that fascinated and charged the imagination of Walter Walne. Without leaving the scene, he proposed that the Symphony Society take over the enterprise. But that was a bit awkward. He was reminded of the way in which the concert was ensured; the anonymous sponsor would have to be consulted about what was to be done with the idea. I felt pretty certain that gentleman would not leap at the first chance of a transfer.

The supposition proved to be right. Mr. Naman was glad to receive news of the offer, but he gently suggested that the plan in effect be carried along until it was seen whether the interest would hold. Meanwhile his thousand dollars remained on deposit with the proceeds from the concert. What happened, therefore, was that another performance was arranged for the following week. It repeated the scenes of the first and brought another collection that more than covered expenses. There was not time for a third concert. Summer was ending and Hoffman had duties preparatory to the opening of the regular season. The park audience, however, was left with the promise that a longer series would be given at Miller Theater the next summer, and that was to be the way of the matter.

With the same plan in effect, the 1941 outdoor season consisted of six concerts. It began with another grant from Mr. Naman (this time it was $1,500), and the chartering of a small organization, the Public Music Association, to present these evenings. Mrs. Oveta Culp Hobby, vice-president of the *Post*, became president of this body; Mr. Naman was represented by his son, Bernard; Roy Demme acted as treasurer, and his beautiful wife, Genevieve, was an indefatigable arranger of many operating details.

This series went off with delightful results, the concerts again meeting the costs of production and leaving the guaranty untouched. The plan was extended again, and two more seasons were given in this manner before the park venture, completely successful, was turned over to the Symphony Society on condition that the series be fully sustained.[1] Meanwhile Mr. Naman's part in providing the series had become known, and he was elected to the Symphony Society's board. But that office he politely declined. The founder of the Philharmonic had had his little riposte and was satisfied. He had taught the society a lesson.

With this change in operational method, the custom of taking collections at the park was dropped. Since 1943 the outdoor concerts have been financed by the society, aided by annual grants from the municipal government. Eighteen concerts per season are now given. The original Miller Theater is no more, having been demolished to make way for a much more commodious structure. In this beautiful modern facility, opened in 1968, the park audience hears the full orchestra instead of a provisional unit. So much did it win by its first showing of interest and the nickels and dimes it invested.

National prosperity at the cost of a great war was not a gratification, but it was an American fact. By the middle of 1940 the stimulation was felt in every phase of the country's activities, including the recreational arts. In May of that year, Walter Walne asked the Houston orchestra's stewards to create a new office, the position of chairman of the board. The orchestra's uses were expanding. He foresaw that its costs would become steadily larger, and, with income from ticket sales already at its reasonable limit, there would have to be more and more funding by substantial and outright gifts. The times now offered a chance to vigor-

---

[1] Perhaps the most remarkable of these concerts was given in 1942, when Tchaikovsky's *1812* Overture was among the selections. In place of the cannon shot called for in the score, it was decided to use rockets that could be tossed by a mechanical sling and would explode 150 feet in the air. Nobody thought to announce this. As a result, the audience took it to be an air raid, and there was a spectacular rush that nearly ended the concert.

ously press that idea, and Walter Walne felt that he needed administrative assistance.

His recommendation was accepted, and T. E. Swigart became the first chairman of the board. It was a very fortunate choice. Mr. Swigart was not only a prominent oil company executive, but a true musical spirit who understood fully the symphony's problems and aims. He gave the society a carefully planned method of soliciting aid by contribution, and it was much due to his labors that the orchestra's civic position was solidified in spite of the competing pressures of wartime.

Meanwhile Hoffmann's work as a builder was fruitful. The 1940–1941 season marked changes of note in the orchestra; a better finish came into the playing in general, and with it a wider range of expressive effects. Of these the conductor took canny advantage. He had a machine that did its work with increasing dependability; his aim as a good teacher was now to give it full ease and a certain style of its own. For that purpose, the more work the better, and Hoffmann's efforts to promote the use of the orchestra were extraordinary. He especially sought to enlarge its regional service. This season the orchestra gave fourteen concerts on the road, visiting Texas towns as far distant as San Antonio, Abilene, and San Angelo, as well as Lake Charles, Louisiana. Added to the regular City Auditorium series were two productions of Handel's *Messiah*, on December 3 and 15, an extra concert as a bonus for season subscribers, and four student performances.

The final spring program, in the spirit of Easter, included two German examples of the beatific—the Prelude and Good Friday Spell music from *Parsifal*. They were beautifully played and produced their inevitable feelings of religious exaltation—a slightly ironical circumstance in view of the fact that German bombs were then raining on the people of England.

The next orchestra season would be strange, and the strangeness began with the first concert. On that evening the orchestra's patrons, gathered in full number, found that something disturbing had happened to a very familiar piece of music, or happened to themselves. The composition was *The Star Spangled Banner*. When it was played to open the program and the audience tried to sing along (as every audience did at that time), most of those in the hall were unable to do so. The song's musical difficulties seemed to have mounted, and the singers were left baffled or panting. They looked at each other in wonder.

An odd thing had occurred. One of the most distinguished of America's adopted composers, the celebrated Igor Stravinsky, had expressed his own patriotism by making what he called an arrangement of the national anthem, and this had been widely distributed by his publishers. It was one of Stravinsky's more curious ideas. For in fact his arrangement amounted to little more than a simple transposition of the song, which was taken out of its customary key of B-flat major and put into the key of C major, a full tone higher. This was contrary to musical logic, since an anthem is a piece of music intended to be sung and the effect of transferring this model to the key of C is to shut it off to most amateur singers, who are thus asked for a G over the staff. More than patriotic emotion is needed to reach that level. Hoffmann's use of the transcription at this concert was a mark of respect to Stravinksy. He promptly put it way—which was a mark of respect to the audience.

Fall had come on with a gray face. Before the era of smog, Houston was not apt to receive an unfriendly November, but this one had been dark and depressing. Ragged low clouds, drifting in from the gulf, hung over the city like dirty vagrants asleep in the streets; and day after day had a curious, trancelike stillness. The spell continued into December, and Sunday the seventh was such a day, with the air dead and a ghostly mist caught in the treetops. At four in the afternoon it became quite dark; and this was the setting in which the people of Houston, halfheartedly preparing for the celebration of Christmas, were told that the Japanese had attacked Pearl Harbor. The greater strangeness began with that broadcast.

Nobody now knew what to expect, but among the things that Houstonians did on the first day this country was at war with Japan was to attend a performance of the Houston Symphony Orchestra. The third concert of the 1941–1942 season took place on the evening of December 8. It was a weird, unreal ceremony, not only because of the feelings that were taken into the hall (attendance was very little below normal) but in some of the music making itself.

The formal program began with a recognition of the one-hundredth anniversary of Dvořák's birth, but the principal work was not his. It was Tchaikovsky's Sixth Symphony, the *Pathétique*, the "Symphony of Death"—as though it might have been chosen with the turn of events twenty-odd hours before. The curiosity, however, lay not in this stroke of coincidence, but in the manner in which the symphony was performed as the closing work of the concert.

If people had been much in a humor for program reading that evening, a good many would have noticed an oddity in the listing of the *Pathétique*. Only three of its movements were indicated, in the usual way, by their tempo marks under the heading; the final section, the *Adagio lamentoso*, was missing. The musically knowing would doubtless have attributed this to a printer's omission; but they would have been more thoroughly puzzled by what took place on the stage. For when the moment arrived, the program proved strictly correct: the symphony ended with its third movement. On the final chord of that wild and rather terrible march, Hoffmann put down the stick, abruptly walked from the stage, and the evening was over. He did not even answer the bewildered applause that began after a moment or two. At another time this would have been an offense; but the audience that night was in no humor to trouble itself over the reason, and once it became certain that the symphony was not to continue, was probably glad to be gone.

Some thought the conductor had become suddenly ill. They were wrong. The truth was that Hoffmann had acted on one of his superstitions. He believed the *Pathétique*—or at any rate its last movement— to be evil. Shortly after arriving in Houston he had conducted the work, and it was while he was so engaged that news came of the death of his father, which had followed an accident in Boston. The message had arrived toward the close of the symphony and was kept from him until he had finished. When he was told, the shock became linked in his mind with the somber conclusion of the *Pathétique*, and he swore never to conduct it again. The program committee had ordered the Sixth for this concert, believing that Hoffmann would not dare to carry out his intent. Having learned better, it never again asked him to violate his conviction that the symphony's last movement was deadly. He continued to end it with the march.

By January the dislocations of war could be felt in the hall; they were evident on both sides of the footlights. Dr. H. L. Bartlett, the society's excellent program annotator, had left to join a medical unit in training, familiar faces were missing in the orchestra, and some of the box-holders were gone. The rest of the season would be a time of leave-takings and a time of discovery of this organization by strangers in Houston, themselves uprooted and sent to the city as part of a feverish preparation for war.

As it worked out, this emergency shifting of population was somewhat to the orchestra's gain. For while Houston sent thousands of men and very often their families to distant parts of the land or overseas, it received a greater number of migrants, military and civilian, because of its own vital position as a training and industrial center. The orchestra accordingly suffered no loss of attendance; in fact, it recorded an increase. Though the City Auditorium at this time was being made to accommodate four thousand, there was often an overflow crowd.

But this appearance of prosperity was rather deceptive. The boom economy brought its own problems. Operational costs mounted along with attendance, and wartime was not a time when increases in ticket prices could be gracefully managed. The orchestra was expected to go ahead doing its job because that was the spirit of the day. But in making this effort to encourage morale, amid scenes of apparent wellbeing, it was playing itself into financial difficulties.

Walter Walne had been doubtful, from the start of the war, that the normal cultivation of music should be attempted while the struggle continued. He had never supposed otherwise than that American involvement was certain; now that this had occurred, he found himself heavily burdened. His legal firm was a large one and his professional duties were multiplied. He was no longer a young man. For five years he had made a hobby of looking after the orchestra, and he had enjoyed the experience. But early in 1942 he notified the society that he must retire from the presidency. It was a blow to the board, which depended so greatly upon him, and to Hoffmann, who had always been able to count on the attorney for understanding of a special degree. But there was a more serious overtone. A few days after the president made known his decision, an extraordinary meeting of the society's officials was held with Mr. Swigart presiding. He placed before the assembly a full statement of the orchestra's financial position and outlook; and the question the directors were asked to decide was an echo of 1917—whether the orchestra should be disbanded for the second time as a victim of war.

The reasons offered for that possible course were the obvious ones. Clearly the organization would face serious personnel problems; many of its players would be subject to military call. But the main considerations were administrative and fiscal. There was a serious deficit to be dealt with; in order to continue, the orchestra would need more and more help in the form of direct gifts. Such aid had been hard enough to obtain under the best of conditions, and nothing was certain any more. As things now stood, where were the leaders to be found who could go out and produce this help? Every prominent citizen of Houston appeared to be engaged in some way with the war effort. If entertainment was to be continued—which nearly everyone agreed was a good idea—it was certainly a minor concern among those of the moment. It looked as though every person of influence in Houston would have the same reasons that Walter Walne gave for subordinating the symphony's claims at this juncture. There was no real shortage of entertainment anywhere in the country; there were critical shortages of other things. The disaster of Pearl Harbor had shown that "preparedness" was a hollow fiction indeed; air raid drills were being ordered for American cities, including Houston. The war was now a shocking reality beside which everything else seemed suddenly trifling or frivolous.

Such was the mood of the meeting. The orchestra might easily have died that afternoon; for it is not likely that public enthusiasm could have been found for a second revival of the enterprise. But when no decision had been reached at the end of two hours, Mr. Swigart held open an escape hatch. He proposed that a special committee be formed —first, to study further the orchestra's prospects, and second, to see whether a suitable replacement for Walter Walne could be found under the existing conditions. The committee would represent the city's most responsible leadership; its recommendations would be final. And as chairman of this body Mr. Swigart appointed H. R. Cullen, who was not an official of the Symphony Society but whose wife, Lillie, had long been one of its most active directors.

By thus naming a gentleman who was not at the meeting, Ted Swigart accomplished his most notable stroke in behalf of the orchestra. As he very well knew, H. R. Cullen was much too busy to be interested in any further committee work, however worthy the cause might be. But Mr. Swigart was further aware that Lillie Cullen's concern for the orchestra movement was a real one. He knew that she was fully alert to its danger, and he counted on her gentle persuasions.

His calculations proved strictly correct. Mr. Cullen was not agreeable to becoming the chairman of a symphony committee of any kind. But, after hearing from his wife what had occurred at the rather desperate meeting, and seeing her real apprehension, he decided that perhaps the matter could be more expeditiously handled. Rather than bother himself or any others with committee affairs and formalities, he would agree, if it suited the rest, to act as president of the society for the duration of the emergency or, as he put it, "as long as this country is at war with Germany, and no longer." For H. R. Cullen it was a typical gesture; for the orchestra society, which delightedly accepted, it was the best possible assurance at this critical hour.

Hugh Roy Cullen was a unique figure and force. Although he was not musical in the ordinary sense, he was a dreamer on the widest of scales, and at the time of this act, in his sixtieth year, the controller of a spectacular fortune. He was indeed often described as "the richest man in the world"—which may have been true for the time, though the phrase generally was applied in the wrong spirit and without knowledge of his characteristics. Roy Cullen was rich in the sense of achievement and because he had lived with a rare fullness. The four years in which he served as administrative head of the symphony movement form only part of a fabulous story, too extensive to be told here.

Hugh Roy Cullen represented a type of American character that is now disappearing because the conditions necessary to its development no longer exist. He belonged to the frontier strain. He was a strapping man, physically massive and big in the way that he saw things, a product of so-called rugged individualism in a form peculiar to the Southwest and to one brief period of Southwest history, the first forty years of the twentieth century. That was the time of the oil giants, and Hugh Roy Cullen was a titan among them, "the king of the wildcatters."

Born on a farm in Denton County near Dallas and early taken to San Antonio, where he went to work as a boy to help care for his mother, Roy Cullen was self-made in the classic tradition. His schooling was meager, but he took to the books of his own choice with an omnivorous appetite. They gave him enough for his needs. He had the characteristics, the natural intelligence, that made the pioneer strength of the West, and he applied these to the search for oil.

Roy and Lillie Cullen enjoyed the simple blessings of life—good health, a loving family, and the beauty of the world. They early began expressing their gratitude by placing their means at the service of others. The list of their gifts, ever larger in sum, is a noble chapter in the history of Houston. Finally, in 1947, Roy and Lillie Cullen afforded themselves what they described as their greatest happiness. They created a philanthropic foundation that added to their other benefactions the income from properties with an estimated value of 160 million dollars—a gift said to have been the largest ever made by a single family within the lifetime of the donors.[2] It completed their charities, which in whole amounted to 93 percent of the fortune Roy Cullen had made. The benefits of the foundation go chiefly to educational and medical ends. The University of Houston, with its magnificent plant and enrollment of more than twenty thousand, and the great Texas Medical Center in Houston are among the manifestations of the wisdom that Roy Cullen acquired in becoming "the richest man in the world."

[2] *Hugh Roy Cullen*, a biography by Ed Kilman and Theon Wright; New York, 1954.

Chapter 8

Roy Cullen adopted the orchestra as simply as though it had been another acreage lease. Once he took charge, its business detail was reduced to the absolute minimum. The war was the big and enveloping fact, and his interest in the organization was chiefly what it could do for the war effort. He had his own notions of how a musical body could best serve, and his decisions and whims, often on the spur of the moment, could make policy changes that in other times would have caused lengthy and cautious debate. Perhaps his ways were a little autocratic, but nobody minded at this time; and when any plan he suggested meant an orchestra service would have to be given without charge or could only result in a money loss, it was understood he would personally take care of the bill. The amount of his help in that way was never fully recorded; it often consisted of simply writing a check and handing it over to Ernst Hoffmann, no record being kept of the matter.

On the other hand, he did not pamper the organization with gifts. The society's regular policy of solicitation remained in effect and was expected to produce its own part of the operating revenue. Thus the orchestra's habitual donors were not lost, and indeed new help of this order was found during the war years. Much of it came by reason of Roy Cullen's example, and it is fair to say that the movement survived this crisis because of his spirit and generosity. He asserted its right to exist in a Jovian voice.

Here, too, much was owed to the personal attraction of the Hoffmanns. Annemarie Hoffmann and Lillie Cullen had developed a close, sympathetic friendship, which certainly had counted in winning over the interest of Roy Cullen himself. And now he developed a real fondness for the energetic and clear-headed conductor. It took a bit of understanding—especially on the day when Roy Cullen discovered that Hoffmann drank nothing but hot water on social occasions. The tough old wildcatter's amazement was equalled only by his roaring delight. He was bound to admit that this world is a place of great wonders.

Roy Cullen's habit in business had been to think of the region as a whole, and he continued to do so in his musical office. What could be regionally done with the orchestra? Much was already being done. The symphony had started its 1942–1943 season with a schedule of thirteen out-of-town concerts booked, in addition to a list of ten subscription performances in the City Auditorium and other extras including four student events. On March 25, 1942, the orchestra had given its first production of Beethoven's Ninth Symphony. This was a regional venture; the singing body for the work consisted of two choirs from North Texas State Teachers' College in Denton, directed by Wilfred C. Bain. During the rehearsals a warm friendship developed between this gentleman and the Houston conductor, later to be of much value to Hoffmann.

Uniforms were now thick in the auditorium gatherings, and the national anthem (in its singable version) began every concert of the orchestra. But as the first war season arrived at its end on April 13, selections from *Die Meistersinger* and the quiet spirit of Mendelssohn's *Reformation* Symphony gave the evening a touch of tranquility, and the unhurried monotonies of Ravel's *Bolero*, which closed the program, were even farther from suggesting the state of things in the world of reality.

It was to be different thereafter. The crowds at the park concerts in the summer of 1942 were the largest of all, but the audience picture was changed; its colors became principally those of the military. Travel restrictions began to be felt and small conveniences disappeared in the course of everyday living. In the newspapers there were casualty lists. The war was beginning to press home.

While the orchestra went through the outdoor series it bore its own share of the mobilization. More of its younger members were gone by the start of the 1942–1943 Auditorium season. Their talents were missed and, although their replacements were able, these evenings were heavy with reminders of separation and of savage passions inflaming the human heart. The season began, almost inevitably, with a performance of Beethoven's Fifth Symphony—symbol of Allied victory—and there were the messages in the program books. The one for December contained, where Christmas sentiments might have been expected, two advertisements facing the musical listings. Their headings were "Hounds of Hell" and "We Will Win!" They were pleas for the purchase of war bonds.

The programs given for subscribers this season were not, on the whole, ambitious, but they were adequate, considering the circumstances. The music of Sibelius was much favored, mostly in the form of his first two symphonies, and Bruckner's Fourth Symphony made its appearance in the repertory. But there was a very full roster of soloists, varied and charming, including the singers Helen Jepson, Lucille Manners, Milla Dominguez (in an all-Latin evening), and the trio of Elva Kalb Dumas, Edward Bing, and Myron Taylor, who combined to deliver the third act of *Aïda* in concert form. The memorable violinist was Fredell Lack (in the Brahms concerto); the visiting pianists, José Iturbi and Monte Hill Davis, a Texas prodigy.

Little has been said in this story of Hoffmann's own gifts as a pianist. They were large. He had started his musical life with the idea of making a solo career at the piano; he might well have gone farther in that role than he did in conducting, for his qualities of imagination and expressive control were extraordinary. In the February 15 concert of this series he joined Miriam Follader Lurie and Virginia Jean in Bach's C Major Concerto for three pianos, which could not have been more gracefully handled. It was one of the few times that the symphony audience had a glimpse of this side of Hoffmann's musical personality.

The appearance of Lucille Manners, however, stirred the winter's greatest excitement. Representing Roy Cullen's particular interest, his idea of a musical war service, the event provided the first national broadcast of the orchestra. To recall it is to mark the great change that has taken place in the nation's typical home entertainment since 1942. At that time radio had the air to itself, and radio fed concert music to the public on a scale that television has never approached. The dominant stars of the radio epoch were conductors and concert artists. One of the most popular broadcast programs—of the "semi-classic" variety —was the weekly Cities Service Concert over NBC from New York, with Lucille Manners as its glamorous prima donna. She had thus reached the attention and become a favorite of Hugh Roy Cullen. It now occurred to him that if the beautiful blonde singer could be presented in Houston it would be a good thing for everybody; it further occurred to him that if the Cities Service program were broadcast with the Houston Symphony Orchestra, it would be a good thing for the orchestra. Nor did his reflections stop there. What then if Miss Manners and the organization should give a concert especially for servicemen stationed in Houston? Roy Cullen decided it would be a fine thing for morale—and that settled the matter. It was a characteristic decision. He put in a telephone call to the New York sponsors of the program and told them what he would like to arrange. They were stunned and, not knowing how else to reply, referred him to the office of NBC. The radio people were even more stunned; they tried to explain that the program involved a very elaborate studio setup and could not be moved on the spur of the moment. Mr. Cullen replied that he hadn't asked that; he could give them a week—which ought to be enough for anybody.

There was no more haggling about it. He enlisted two members of the orchestra board, Ted Swigart and Leopold Meyer, to put through any necessary details, and NBC found itself left with very little to do but keep out of the way. The entire engineering and production staffs of the New York program were summarily moved down, Miss Manners herself was duly delivered with her glamor intact, and the Cities Service broadcast of January 15, 1943, originated from the Music Hall in Houston, the orchestra having half the air time for a "pop" concert of its own.

Two days later, on Sunday, Miss Manners again appeared with the organization in a concert given free for the officers and men of Ellington Field, and the next evening was soloist for the fourth subscription concert of the season, singing "Voi lo sapete" from *Cavalleria* and "Il est doux" from Massenet's *Hérodiade*. With all this and the entertainment she had further sustained between concerts, the lady had demonstrated at least her own physical fitness and high state of morale. But her smile had become a little wan.

In discharging Roy Cullen's concept of its wartime role, the orchestra likewise met tests of its own physical hardihood.[1] His policy aimed at the maximum service to the military—and great military establishments had sprung up in every quarter of Texas. The territorial U.S.O. was arranging entertainment for these bases, and the Houston orchestra was available at any time its home duties allowed. What this meant was indicated by the program for the last subscription concert of the 1942–1943 season; a note mentioned that in addition to seventeen regular out-of-town concerts the orchestra had given nineteen full-length programs and one hospital performance at seventeen army and navy cantonments. "The services of Conductor Ernst Hoffmann and all the players were donated for this project," the note added. "In carrying it out, the orchestra traveled more than six thousand miles, slept when, and where possible, or slept not at all in traveling at night." No other large musical organization of the region was half as active in that way.

These added exertions, though sometimes painful and producing

---

[1] On one famous occasion, at the urging of local sports writers and his own patriotic emotions, he allowed the orchestra to be used in conjunction with a professional wrestling match, as part of a war bond show. It was a grotesque spectacle, with the orchestra sounding a dirge while the gory gladiators beat each other about in the ring. Unluckily, the scene was recorded by a newsreel camera and the pictures created a scandal. What was not told was that this atrocity sold hundreds of thousands of dollars in war bonds.

their own casualty lists, had come at a good time for the orchestra. Finding itself able to meet the demands, the group gained a new sense of position and worth. The extra work, too, was good for its musical muscles; an orchestra plays better for having the chance to play much.

On November 8, 1943, the Houston Symphony opened its thirtieth season with fifty-five concerts booked, thirty-six to be played out of town. The winter's program included another national broadcast that had grown out of the Cities Service occasion. This one was to be on the "Voice of Firestone" on January 25, with Richard Crooks, tenor, and William Primrose, violist, performing as soloists. Altogether the 1943–1944 season consisted of eleven subscription performances, four "pops," four student concerts, eleven visits to army and navy installations, and twenty-two other appearances in cities of Texas and Louisiana.

Meanwhile the orchestra continued to lose men. The program for the opening concert of this season named seventeen players who were absent on duty in the armed forces. Among those missing was Joseph Gallo, the concertmaster of the season before; the orchestra again had a concertmistress, Olga Henkel, blonde, pretty, and efficient, who had moved up from the second stand of the violins. Hoffmann had continued his program of player recruitment, and there were no musical cripples among his replacements. The orchestra came to attention that fall in fine spirit and played with an evident pride, but it was in no way brash.

Soloists for the 1943–1944 regular series included Albert Spalding, who played Beethoven's Violin Concerto in the opening concert, the pianists Claudio Arrau, Virginia Jean, Drusilla Huffmaster, and Oscar Levant, and sopranos Helen Traubel and Risë Stevens. There were likewise many additions to the repertory; the programs were spattered with asterisks indicating first Houston performances. These included contemporary styles in the form of Walter Piston's Concertino for Piano and Chamber Orchestra, which Miss Jean performed, Morton Gould's *Guaracha*, and Franco Hernandez's *Serenata Regionale*, which the composer (a violinist in the orchestra) conducted with very pretty results. Among other firsts for the series were Falla's *Nights in the Gardens of Spain*, Rachmaninoff's *The Bells* (for voices and orchestra), his *Isle of the Dead*, and the Immolation Scene from *Götterdämmerung*, Miss Traubel ending her evening with that celebrated *tour de force*.

There was another novelty from the policy standpoint. Hoffmann had all along argued that opera should be added to the orchestra's service, and some of the officials agreed with him. Now, at last, he won consent for a trial of this idea. In consequence an opera production took the place of the final subscription concert on the evening of April 10, 1944. The work was Puccini's *Tosca*. Elva Kalb Dumas, an excellent Houston soprano, sang the role of the Roman diva with memorable beauty and fire, Myron Taylor sang Cavaradossi, and Edward Bing was a notable Scarpia. Staged by Lawrence Carra in borrowed settings (which had been through earlier wars), the production was undistinguished as spectacle, but it was greatly alive as a drama in music and thrilled the audience fully. When it ended the demonstration was one of the most excited of the orchestra's history. That evening the society appeared definitely to have entered the business of opera.

Things were not to come out in that way, however. The orchestra, although it had another success to record, became the victim of its restless ambitions. Stimulated by the fevers of war-time and the open-handed encouragement of Roy Cullen, it had lately been rushing ahead. The recent diversification of its work was exciting, but it was a strain, and the effort began taking its toll. Though the spirit was willing, the orchestra did not yet have the reserves, physical or artistic, that such a program of expansion demanded.

The pace was illustrated by the layout for the 1944–1945 season. The orchestra found itself with a total of seventy-two engagements to be filled. They were in the following forms: ten subscription concerts and one extra for its seasonal patrons; a series of six "pop" programs, to be given mostly on Sunday afternoons in the City Auditorium; four opera productions; eight student performances; twenty-eight regular out-of-town concerts, requiring travel as far distant as Monterrey, Mexico; and twenty-three dates at military establishments scattered across Texas and Louisiana. The operas were *La Traviata*, to be presented December 27; *Il Trovatore* on the following evening; *La Bohème* on April 16, with a repetition for students; and a version of

Hansel and Gretel. The "pop" list also added to the unusual demands, for this series, arranged under the energetic chairmanship of Caroline Wiess, had a complement of expensive and glamorous soloists, including Grace Moore, Oscar Levant, and other reigning divinities of radio.

All of it was asking too much. The conductor, though vastly enthusiastic, was mortal; the orchestra was an instrument with human failings and needs; and travel was what it was in the war. The season had a somewhat desperate note, and its offerings at times suffered from an obvious weariness. Too, there had come a change in the war outlook that caused feelings of letdown everywhere. The end of the fighting seemed within sight. When spring came and the soft beauties of *La Bohème* ended the Auditorium series, everyone felt suddenly tired. It was good if everyone could assure himself he had done his bit for the victory. There was a momentary feeling of peace. The world was about to be made as safe as the atomic bomb could make it.

The revelation of that fact, however, would not come for another four months. Meanwhile Germany surrendered on May 7, 1945, and with this turn of events Roy Cullen, who had personally underwritten the orchestra's 1944–1945 season to the amount of $125,000, considered his obligation discharged. He had agreed to serve as head of the movement only as long as the war with Germany lasted, and five days after the Nazi collapse he submitted his resignation from the presidency.

In his letter to the board he pointed out that the orchestra's affairs were in good shape. The Women's Committee had sold virtually all subscriptions available for the 1945–1946 season, a Chamber of Commerce committee was pledged to raise funds for the symphony, and Mr. Cullen now offered to give 20 percent of any sum this committee secured. He further took note of the fact that the city government had appropriated ten thousand dollars toward the cost of the summer's outdoor concerts, and added that, if a deficit should result from the park series, he would be pleased to absorb it. He was proud of what the orchestra had done to make itself useful during the crisis, and he wrote warmly of his admiration for Hoffmann. There was no immediate response to his letter, however, for the summer was too filled with the shocks and excitements of the world cataclysm arriving at its terrible end. Finally, in August, there was Hiroshima, and in the blank, stupe-fying silence that followed, the real meaning of victory began to be realized.

For whatever reasons, the society did not act upon Roy Cullen's request until its annual meeting in January, 1946. His resignation was then accepted, with official regrets, and Joseph S. Smith, who had served as president from 1934 to 1936, was elected to the office again. Mr. Cullen was named chairman of the board. Their terms were to start on May 1.

At the time of this meeting the orchestra's activities proved its considerable wellbeing. It was midway of a season of more than ninety concert performances. Some of the extra events of this list were important, an efficient organization of the schedule had produced results better than those of the previous winter, and attendance continued to run very high, both at home and for concerts on the road.

The next development, then, was surprising. Shortly after the January election it began to be whispered that, although matters were indeed very well with the orchestra movement, they were not altogether well for Hoffmann. The story was that the board of directors was divided on the question of conductorial policy; a faction had arisen that thought it time to replace the conductor of ten years' standing. Reports named Mr. Smith as the head of this faction, opposed by Roy Cullen, who contended that Hoffmann, on the strength of his record, had every right to continue in service. The gossip spread and in due course got into the newspapers, with speculation concerning the division of power in the board, and this guessing game continued when official denials of the schism proved more than a little ambiguous.

During the war years Hoffmann had had no formal contract with the Symphony Society; he had worked under a simple agreement. His official critics used this as an opening. In April they succeeded in having passed by the board a resolution providing that Hoffmann be given a contract for the 1946–1947 season, with the understanding that this was to be his last. There was no immediate implementation of this motion, however, and on April 23 the storm broke. Roy Cullen announced his resignation as chairman of the board. His letter made it explicit that he was acting because of efforts by certain board members to replace the orchestra's leader, and he strongly recommended the retention of Hoffmann. To this he added another pointed suggestion—that henceforth the president of the society "assume full responsibility" for raising donations in support of the orchestra. Roy Cullen's implication was plain. The next turn of the drama was swift. On May 8, Joseph S. Smith resigned from the presidency, having served only a week of his term. The reasons given were somewhat vague; the true reason was pressure from Roy Cullen, whose indignation was as hot as an oil well blaze and who was said to have fired the new president.

Ima Hogg was in Mexico City when this eruption occurred. On receiving the news, she hurried home. Her concern was peace, and she was promptly enlisted by the executive committee as a mediary, delegated to call on Roy Cullen and try to persuade him that the board's decision could not be altered. Then it was hoped to reinstall Mr. Smith in the presidency. But Ima Hogg knew what to expect; she felt it was more than she alone could be expected to handle, and she prevailed upon Gus S. Wortham, one of Houston's most powerful men of finance, to go with her to see Roy Cullen. Her apprehensions were not unwarranted. The old wildcatter sat through the discussion of the board's motion with a certain restraint, but when Mr. Smith's case was presented he blew sky high. He roared his refusal and issued a blunt ultimatum: Miss Hogg herself must become the society's president. Otherwise, said Roy Cullen, he would cut off his support of the orchestra movement entirely.

The two delegates knew that he meant it. So did the board members, when they heard the report of this meeting. So Ima Hogg was elected president of the Symphony Society for the second time. Her agreement to serve was conditioned on the formation of a strong supporting committee representing the business leadership of the city; and this she received, with Gus Wortham appointed to succeed Mr. Cullen as chairman of the board—a greatly important connection.

At the same time a significant operational change was adopted. The directors voted to engage a professional, full-time business manager for the orchestra; the man chosen was Francis R. Deering, an experienced theater executive, just returned to the city from war service. A budget of $192,890 was approved for the 1946–1947 season.

Hoffmann now wondered about his position. Roy Cullen, in his letter of resignation, had recommended an increase of the conductor's
salary from ten to twelve thousand dollars a year. This request had
been met by the new administration, but Hoffmann had had no official
notification of what its ideas were for the future. Francis Deering had
been given to understand that the 1946 season would be Hoffmann's
last, unless he made "an exceptional showing," but that ended the manager's knowledge of board policy, and he kept what he knew to himself. Meanwhile three guest conductors were engaged for the season to
come: Carlos Chavez, of the Mexico City Symphony Orchestra, Efrem
Kurtz, of the Kansas City Philharmonic, and Reginald Stewart, head of
the Baltimore Symphony.

This season of "peace," which began in November, 1946, was a
time of bright social affairs that took advantage of lifted restrictions, of
happy reunions and of special artistic events. Hoffmann opened the
season with a program that included first playings by this organization
of Dvořák's *Carneval* Overture and Richard Strauss's *Rosenkavalier*
Suite. The soloist of the evening was Edward Lear, a Houston tenor
just discharged from the Air Corps; and the Women's Committee took
a page in the program book to embrace the conductor, remarking that
"it is with deep affection and ever increasing pride that we salute our
own Ernst Hoffmann." The conductor was grateful—though probably
somewhat puzzled.

Carlos Chavez, a model of Latin gallantry on elevator heels, took the
orchestra for the next concert on November 18, half the program consisting of his own compositions. Hoffmann's second performance introduced to this audience Gillis's *Short Overture to an Unwritten Opera*
and Albert Roussel's *Rapsodie Flamande*, on a program with the *New
World* Symphony and Brahms's B-flat Piano Concerto, with Jacques
Abram as soloist.

Next came Efrem Kurtz. Although he had earlier been in the city as
a theater conductor, this performance of January 6, 1947, was his first
in Houston as the chief of a full symphony unit. He opened his list
with the *Meistersinger* Prelude, gave two symphonies, Haydn's No. 88
and Shostakovich's Ninth, and closed with Tchaikovsky's *Romeo and
Juliet*.

Efrem Kurtz, then forty, was a personality from the world of ballet
—specifically the Franco-Russian ballet as it was operated in Paris by
the prodigal Sergei Diaghileff. The conductor himself was an elegant
figure in a way that narrowly escaped the grotesque, for he was a musical Ichabod Crane—tall, lank, over-long in the limbs, and sometimes
ungainly in motion. But he was a man of style and fastidious instincts,
with immaculate taste and the means to indulge himself fully; and nobody knew better how to dramatize the suave manner, the air of *no-
blesse*, the stage picture of grandeur, than this son of a Russian fur
merchant. Kurtz had come to America in 1934 as conductor of Wasily
de Basil's Ballet Russe de Monte Carlo (the survivor of Diaghileff's
magnificent troupe), and as he appeared to the Auditorium gathering
on this particular evening he recalled the exotic delights of that wonderful dance ensemble. Many were present who had heard him conduct
its performances, and they welcomed him back in another role with a
sweeping enthusiasm.

The society's officials were also firmly impressed. Thus a few days
after the concert Francis Deering was quietly dispatched to Kansas City.
His instructions from Gus Wortham were to ascertain whether Kurtz
would be interested in the Houston conductorship and, if so, what his
terms would be. Deering came back to report that Kurtz's reaction had
been favorable. His conditions were that the orchestra's player budget
should not be less than $160,000; as for what he would expect for
himself, it would be "about $30,000 per season."[2]

Having delivered this information the manager found himself handling some other interesting duties. The orchestra was about to play for
the national public again, this time in a more important connection. It
had been asked to perform on the NBC program called "Orchestras of
the Nation." Election to that spot was a recognition of an orchestra's
merit and import; it assured a full hearing by radio with a vast potential of listeners. The broadcast took place on the afternoon of Saturday,
February 22, 1947, before a gathering of three thousand in the City

[2] But money was not the chief object. Kurtz wanted the position, and the fact that
his sister was married to one of the wealthiest men in New York, William Rosen-
wald, whose interests were many, was of a certain influence in Houston. "The
intrigue was clear," says Miss Hogg.

Auditorium. Hoffmann's program consisted of the Gillis overture mentioned above, the finale of Handel's *Water Music*, the rondo movement of Mozart's *Haffner* Serenade, and Brahms' Fourth Symphony. It was one of his finest days with the orchestra. He was always at his best in the symphonies of Brahms, and the Fourth, in particular, appealed to the mystic side of his nature. His instinct for the poetry of this great document was never more sensitive than when he unfolded its drama to close this concert.

One listener in the hall was indeed surprised and profoundly affected. He was Burt Whaley, NBC's national program director, who had come down from New York. "I consider this one of the finest orchestras we have ever had on this series," he said after the concert. "It is a wonderful orchestra and you have a conductor who is truly distinguished. It was the most satisfying performance of the Brahms Fourth I have ever heard—bar no orchestra or conductor." Mr. Whaley's obligations as a sponsor and guest did not require him to go that far. His excitement was real. He had experienced a thrill of discovery and it made him a genuine convert, as subsequent recognitions of the orchestra by his powerful company would attest.

But the immediate aftermath was ironical. On February 9 the society's executive committee had held a meeting at which ten of its twelve members were present. The business manager was not bidden to attend, but at the close of the meeting he was told the committee had decided to ask for the resignation of Hoffmann. He never knew more of the matter.

It was not Deering but Ima Hogg who was given the hateful task of transmitting this decision to Hoffmann.[3] She had broken it to him a few days prior to the broadcast, which perhaps accounted for the extraordinary keenness of feeling with which he performed that program. And now in the same state of emotion he was called upon for two other special endeavors. These were part of the season's Azalea Trail Festival: a production of Bach's B-Minor Mass at the City Auditorium on March 8, with the Denton Choir as the singing body and Anna Kaskas, Agnes

---

[3] "He was very sweet about it; he was always so reasonable; and I shall never forget how it hurt me."

Davis, James Jackson, and Robert McDonald as soloists; and a staging of highlights from Gluck's *Orpheus*, with Miss Kaskas in the titular role, the same choral contingent, and the Houston Civic Ballet.

The operatic production was *al fresco*, arranged for presentation amid the shrubbery and other formal delights of Miss Hogg's garden at her Bayou Bend estate. It came at five o'clock in the afternoon of Sunday, March 9, under lowering skies that suggested nature was not strongly in a humor for Gluck. This proved to be so. With the audience seated on collapsible chairs, the opera began in a light drizzle. But half an hour later, when Hades had just been fully evoked and Miss Hogg's bushes were full of Furies and Blessed Spirits in diaphanous costumes, the most vicious spring norther of seasons swept in like a williwaw. Hell had no power to resist it. A great gale blew, as though from the polar ice cap, and centered its fury on these grounds. The Elysian Fields stiffened and everything came loose from its moorings—including the Breslau hat of Ernst Hoffmann, to which he had resorted in the crisis down by the Versailles fountain where the orchestra sat. Pink nymphs in the bushes turned drastically blue as the audience fled. Much of the production was lifted by the boreal sweeper, and for some time afterward residents of southwest Houston, a mile or so distant, were startled by showers of bright tulle and printed musical parts that fell out of the skies. Thus ended the festival and the idea was never repeated.

Several days after this disaster, Miss Hogg, Mr. Wortham, and Frank Deering left quietly for New York City. Their purpose was to make a contract with Efrem Kurtz, who was there as a guest conductor of the New York Philharmonic. They left with the feeling that Roy Cullen was sufficiently agreeable to this idea, for Miss Hogg and the board chairman had taken pains to consult him about it. But the case of Hoffmann would not die in the papers. He had let it be known that his "resignation" was in the hands of the Symphony board;[4] it was sensed that his feelings were bitter; and now it was hinted that he would "have something to say" to the audience at the final concert of the season on March 17. This promptly brought a letter from Mr. Cullen

[4] He had not actually sent it in written form.

to Hoffmann on March 5, which counseled against any such speech to the public. It was a benevolent letter, but the past president's emotions were also disturbed, as he made clear in this message: "There are only two professions that I know of that are not appreciated because of long service, one being the clergy and the other conductors of symphonies. It appears that congregations, churches and audiences at the symphonies become restless—often without cause—and wish a change. To my way of thinking, this is a peculiar psychology and one I do not understand."

Roy Cullen's next act was typical. A few hours after the Houston delegation arrived in New York, and before negotiations with Kurtz could be started, he sent an abrupt wire to Gus Wortham. It said that because of the dismissal of Hoffmann, he had decided to sever his connection with the Symphony Society entirely. Roy Cullen was very angry—no doubt of the fact this time. His telegram was a shock, and it stayed the hands of the New York delegation. They were not ready to disaffect permanently one of the orchestra's most generous patrons, if anything could be done to avoid it. They accordingly decided to temporize, giving feelings a chance to cool off, and they made no overtures to Kurtz. But what was to be done in the meanwhile? The committee, idle in a New York hotel, was caught in a very awkward position. With Hoffmann's "resignation" accepted and another season approaching, the society needed some sort of conductorial plan to sell tickets.

This dilemma was eased by the more or less benevolent efforts of Kurt Weinhold, a shrewd musical agent, who suggested a season of guest conductors for 1947–1948. The idea was accepted, and Weinhold made it possible for a list of ten batonists to be quickly announced from New York by the Houstonians. The implication was that some of these artists, at any rate, would be candidates for the Houston position, and that the committee would thus be afforded an opportunity for close study before choosing a successor to Hoffmann. Efrem Kurtz was among those listed. So was a young fellow named Leonard Bernstein.

Hoffmann followed his patron's advice. For his last regular concert on the City Auditorium stage he gave a program consisting of David Diamond's *Rounds for String Orchestra*, Schumann's *Spring* Symphony, Hindemith's *Metamorphosis of Themes from Weber*, and Men-

The Houston Symphony Orchestra on the stage of the Majestic Theater in 1915. The conductor is Julien Paul Blitz. *(DeMarler Studio)*

Julien Paul Blitz, first conductor of the orchestra, 1913–1916. *(E. Raba)*

Ernst Hoffmann, one of the chief builders of the orchestra, conductor from 1936 to 1947. *(Paul Peters)*

Efrem Kurtz, conductor from 1948 to 1954.

Houston's City Auditorium, where the orchestra played from 1931 to 1954, one season excepted. Constructed in 1910, the auditorium was demolished in 1963 to make way for Jones Hall. *(Harper Leiper Studios)*

The Music Hall *(right)* and Coliseum complex, after the remodeling of 1953–1954. The Music Hall became the orchestra's home until 1966. *(Harper Leiper Studios)*

A typical gathering at Miller Memorial Theater, the orchestra's outdoor home, in the summer of 1941. The audience numbered more than ten thousand.

(Pervin and Assoc.)

F. M. Law, chairman of the board, Houston Symphony Society, 1948–1950.

(Bob Bailey)

Gus S. Wortham, chairman of the board, Houston Symphony Society, 1946–1948.

(Gittings)

Warren S. Bellows, chairman of the board, Houston Symphony Society, 1950–1953. *(Y. Karsh)*

Harmon Whittington, chairman of the board, Houston Symphony Society, 1953–1954. *(Gittings)*

Gluck's *Orpheus,* in the gardens of Miss Ima Hogg's Bayou Bend estate on March 9, 1947. A few minutes after this picture was taken, the production was devastated by a whirlwind. *(Pervin and Assoc.)*

Gen. Maurice Hirsch, president, Houston Symphony Society, 1956–1970, now president emeritus.

Hugh Roy Cullen, president, Houston Symphony Society, 1942–1945. (*Gittings*)

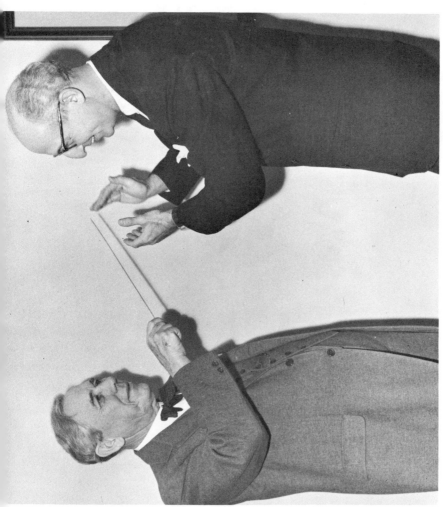

Hugh Roy Cullen takes baton from Efrem Kurtz to give the conductor a few pointers.

(Arrow Arts Studios)

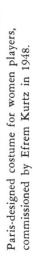

Paris-designed costume for women players, commissioned by Efrem Kurtz in 1948.

Joseph S. Smith, president, Houston Symphony Society, 1934–1936, 1945–1946.
(Gittings)

Dr. Joseph A. Mullen, president, Houston Symphony Society, 1931–1934. *(Gittings)*

Walter H. Walne, president, Houston Symphony Society, 1936–1942. *(Gittings)*

Charles F. Jones, president, Houston Symphony Society, 1970–. *(Gittings)*

Sir Thomas Beecham rehearsing. He conducted the orchestra from 1954 to 1955.

(Andrew Schulhof)

Leopold Stokowski, conductor, 1955–1961.

Leopold Stokowski is inducted as an "honorary Texas cowboy" at a pony track in Hermann Park. The "cowboy" is a deputy sheriff in borrowed costume. *(Richard Pervin)*

Arriving for one of his seasons, Leopold Stokowski is greeted by Gen. Maurice Hirsch, president of the Symphony Society. *(Houston Press)*

Sir John Barbirolli and Miss Ima Hogg.

Tom M. Johnson, Sir John Barbirolli, and Miss Ima Hogg, conferring about plans for the orchestra's fiftieth anniversary season in 1963.

Tom M. Johnson, manager of the Houston
Symphony Orchestra.
(Blackstone Shelburne)

André Previn, conductor, 1967–1969.

Drusilla Huffmaster,
soloist for the orchestra.
(Kaye Marvins)

Sir John Barbirolli, conductor, 1961–1967.

Lawrence Foster conducting. In March, 1971, he became the orchestra's conductor-in-chief at the age of twenty-nine, the youngest man to hold the position.

(James Benfield)

The orchestra and Houston Chorale in Jones Hall, A. Clyde Roller conducting.

(James Benfield)

The foyer of Jones Hall on a symphony evening.

delssohn's Violin Concerto with Erica Morini as soloist. After the symphony, with its tender emotions, he spoke briefly to the players and audience. He acknowledged the help of his fellow performers and officials of the organization, and added only the words: "This audience has been wonderful to me. I feel very close to the people who have come to these concerts, and that is why I wanted to say to you personally that I am resigning at the end of this season." In fact, he stayed on to conduct a postseason concert in the Auditorium on April 14 and to handle the summer series at Miller Theater and the radio series that lasted for most of that time. His duties thus ended in August.

Perhaps Hoffmann had done all that he could. He was by nature a builder. A visiting critic (it was again Moses Smith of the *Boston Transcript*) had written in 1945 that Houston was getting the best symphony music, per dollar invested, of any city in the United States. This could well have been true. Hoffmann had doubtless formed as efficient an orchestra as could then be had in the country on a budget under $200,000 a year, and had given it a spirit of the kind not to be measured in dollar value. It was what he was peculiarly fitted to do, and no man could have done it with a fuller devotion. The orchestra bore deeply the stamp of his character.

In any case, after eleven eventful years in Houston, Ernst and Annemarie Hoffmann departed, leaving Clifford behind to complete his studies for a medical career. They sold their home (it was a pretty white house and they had kept it in spotless condition), and now shipped their belongings to Boston. Unknown to the public, Hoffmann took with him a gift of ten thousand dollars from Roy Cullen, to tide him over while he looked for another "congregation" to serve.

It is an odd fact of the Houston orchestra's history that until 1970 it never invited back one of its early conductors as a guest. This absence of a custom rather common to other symphony orchestras is explainable in one way or another; but Hoffmann, who was sentimental and who had put so much of himself into the venture, perhaps felt it more keenly than the other men. He was to wind up as director of orchestral music at the University of Indiana, an appointment received through the influence of his old friend Wilfred Bain; and in that position he would fully distinguish himself, especially as a conductor of Wagnerian opera. For some time after he left Houston, however, things went badly for Hoffmann. Idleness poisoned his spirit. Unable to find regular work, he fell into a state of melancholy, and in the winter of 1948 he petitioned the Houston society for a chance to conduct one of its concerts as a guest, the idea being that he could thus impress sponsors of another orchestra who were planning to change their conductor, and who were willing to come and hear him in Houston. His request was turned down, without much ceremony, and there would not be another chance of the kind.

After settling in Bloomington, Indiana, the Hoffmanns made occasional visits to Houston to see Clifford. They came for Christmas in 1955. On the night of January 3, after visiting with friends, they set out for the return journey to Bloomington. A few hours later, on a desolate, foggy road in Louisiana, a heavy truck crashed into their automobile and Ernst and Annemarie Hoffmann were killed.

Chapter 9

As a personality show, the second all-guest season of the orchestra measured up to the Ziegfeldian concept of variety. It finally offered not ten, but thirteen visiting conductors. The 1947–1948 schedule consisted of ten subscription performances, three extras, and the customary student events; the gentlemen who had charge, in the order of appearance, were Carlos Chavez, Hans Schwieger, Maurice Abravanel, Frieder Weissmann, Leonard Bernstein, Georges Enesco, Walter Hendl, Tauno Hannikainen, Charles Munch, Efrem Kurtz, Igor Buketoff, and Massimo Freccia. The thirteenth conductor was Frederick Fennell, who came in March to direct two added affairs, a concert of contemporary Texas composers and a production of Verdi's Requiem Mass, as part of a Creative Arts Festival in connection with the annual Azalea Trail.

The orchestra tendered to all these gallants was the one Hoffmann had left, save that Raphael Fliegel, just out of military service, had now taken the concertmaster's position. What the visiting conductors accomplished would prove things about the organization—as well as about themselves—that had either a generous interest or certain comic delights for the critical listener. The number of people who listen critically in any symphony audience is a very debatable factor; but this was a good time in the orchestra's history for its patrons to hear it work under an extraordinary variety of leadership. At points during the series the orchestra showed both how well and how indifferently it could deliver the art, and thus afforded its public a telling index of what conducting itself is about.

Most of the podium visitors were young and theoretically bound somewhere. They could be considered possible candidates, and to these were assigned the soloistic performers of the season—Helen Traubel, the lone singer, two pianists, Claudio Arrau and Eugene List, and a cellist, Edmund Kurtz, brother of Efrem but allocated to the concert of Hannikainen. One conductor, Leonard Bernstein, aged twenty-nine and very full of himself, essayed a double role, acting as his own soloist in a program that included Ravel's G Major Piano Concerto with two symphonies, Mozart's *Linz* and the Second of Schumann.

The two senior conductors had already made distinguished careers. Charles Munch, who, at fifty-six, carried the prestige of long service with the Société des Concerts du Conservatoire in Paris, was now headed for the Boston conductorship; Georges Enesco, ten years senior to Munch, came as one of the world's highly respected composers and one of its great musical educators. Enesco, appearing with the orchestra on January 19, 1948, gave the series its most dramatic event. During the war the Rumanian violinist-composer had been a victim of bitter privations in Europe, and the marks were left heavy upon him. He was cruelly bent with arthritis and his movements were painful; it took little imagination to see that he was otherwise ill, wasted, and driving himself by sheer willpower. Indeed, as it proved, he had only a short time to live. But the flame of his spirit still burned when he came to the stage that evening, and it was kindled to full glow by the music he chose to perform. The spell of it affected both players and audience; and for a while they experienced that deep, greatly rare form of communication which is the mystery and glory of the art.

The program began with the playing of Mozart's overture to *The Marriage of Figaro*, and two symphonies followed—Enesco's own Second and Beethoven's *Eroica*. In this instance they made an ironical contrast, for Enesco's symphony is anything but a work for a solemn occasion; it is essentially jubilant, and there was something immensely touching about watching its crippled author conduct it. The Beethoven Third, if read deeply enough, combines in its slow movement the pathos of all farewells; and thus it was read by the thin, pallid, stonelike figure who commanded the orchestra with gestures so slight as to be scarcely perceptible from the auditorium. The result was overwhelming in emotional force. Music and spectacle were not to be separated and, forming one drama beyond all words, were of infinite sadness and glory. The old artist put all that he knew and felt into this reading; the orchestra played under the spell of a transcendent respect. The colors were like those of a high stained window in a cathedral wall, suffused by the light of the setting sun. There has not been another experience in the musical quarters of Houston such as this *Eroica* rendition produced.

Midway of the season the orchestra received a new manager. Francis Deering had been working under the handicap of an illness and asked to be relieved of his duties. In his letter to Miss Hogg he recommended another young man in the field, Tom M. Johnson, then manager of the Austin Symphony Orchestra. Johnson was invited to meet the Houston directors, and on December 23 Miss Hogg announced his appointment to the managership.

A native of Missouri, Tom Johnson had exceptional qualifications, including the degree of Bachelor of Music along with experience of managerial practice. He had attended Southern Methodist University and the Juilliard School of Music (where he studied under Fritz Mahler and Ferde Grofé), likewise Southwestern University, for which he had acted as publicity director. He had conducted the bands of both Southern Methodist and Southwestern before entering the army in 1942; he was then made leader of the concert band at Camp Hulen. Overseas, as an officer in the Quartermaster Corps, he was assigned to organize and conduct an army symphony orchestra, and after VE day was director of this unit on tours of the American, French, and British occupied zones in Germany and Austria. After leaving the service he had operated a concert management bureau in Fort Worth until his appointment to the Austin Symphony post.

Tom Johnson had natural attraction of personality and great zest for the musical cause. He was a young man with a fine mixture of vision and common sense; he fitted perfectly into the postwar spirit of Houston; and from the time he took office in January of 1948, the orchestra's promotional policies began showing a touch of imagination where imagination is not too often the fortune of such American ventures. During the years of its greater expansion the Houston organization has been lucky to have its business affairs in the hands of a greatly clever and amiable gentleman, with a sense of humor as well as a cool and very logical head. It owes much to the planning of Tom Johnson.

The season proceeded, and the younger conductors did as they were able to do. Sometimes this was exceedingly well; more often their efforts were richer in good will than in promise of Olympian glory. Among the more positive performers was Leonard Bernstein. With his flair for theatricalism and a reputation as a sun-child of the art, he took occasion to spread himself to the limit and worked his audience up to unusual pitch. For a time it looked as though he were the front runner in popularity. But the shrewdest, most polished and elegant showman of this seasonal troupe was Efrem Kurtz, whose concert fell on March 8.

The lateness of Kurtz's appearance may not have been wholly an accident. In the theater it means something to be closing the bill, and the beau-ideal from Kansas City was not one to undervalue the implications and advantage of such a position. He came with intent to give a sense of occasion, and he gave it by playing a Mahler symphony, the First (seven horns among its other heroic effects), together with the Beethoven First and the *Tristan* Prelude and "Liebestod." This was a layout calculated to flatter the connoisseur trade (the big Mahler revival was then on), and it was presented with platform manners to match.

The show produced its intended effect. Though all was not ease in the rendition of the Mahler creation, Kurtz held it together without too much loss of his own image, and the rest of the music was made to seem tidy and firm. The result was that he had another audience triumph. The public had not been blind to late hints in the papers concerning Kurtz, and its welcome was an indication of what it expected when the orchestra's nominating committee took action. For this it did not have to wait long.

There were two more concerts in the series—those of Buketoff and Freccia. Igor Buketoff, the young, handsome, and able conductor of the Fort Wayne, Indiana, Symphony Orchestra, came in to deliver a very pleasing account of himself. The society, however, did not wait for Massimo Freccia to finish his bid—or indeed even begin it. On the day preceding his concert, Sunday, April 4, Miss Hogg announced the appointment of Efrem Kurtz as conductor and musical director of the orchestra, expanding the title and implying a new authority vested in the office.

The appointment received a flattering measure of press notice, both in this country and abroad. One reason was that Efrem Kurtz, suave, charming, and wealthy, was a darling of the new society known as the International Set, which had sprung up since the end of the war. He and his elegant wife, Katherine (whom he had met in Berlin and married in 1933), were often seen in the favorite gathering places of this clan in New York, London, Paris, or on the Mediterranean. In addition, the conductor afforded himself an expensive and ingenious press bureau.

That agency quickly let it be known that his salary in Houston would be thirty thousand dollars a season, which the Houston society neither confirmed nor denied. Meanwhile there was a buzz in its ranks when the maestro returned briefly in April for auditions. He announced plans to enlarge the orchestra's company to ninety (that meant little, as it had used eighty-four members in 1947–1948) and to increase the subscription series from ten to twelve concerts, supplemented by a new course of winter "pops." Rumors flew that he meant to fire 90 percent of the old orchestra's membership, and in general the situation was lively. Nothing of a drastic nature occurred, however, and after a week Kurtz departed to spend the summer in Europe, with a bit of guest conducting to do. As deputy conductor in Houston, he appointed a handsome young fellow, Orlando Barera, who arrived to finish the auditions and handle the summer series at Miller Theater.

In August the annual maintenance fund campaign was begun with Harmon Whittington acting as chairman. Mr. Whittington was executive vice-president of Anderson, Clayton and Company, a cotton firm of great reach and importance, and his leadership significantly increased the symphony's claims on the business community. The orchestra's budget for 1948–1949 was established at $311,000, an increase of $100,000 over that of the previous season.

Tom Johnson, settling into his job, had been busy with ideas for enlarging the orchestra's earned revenue, and some of these began getting results. With assistance from F. M. Law (ever one of the orchestra's best friends), the new manager was able to interest the Henke and Pillot corporation, operator of chain grocery establishments, in sponsoring five extra concerts for the next season, to be offered free to the public on Saturday evenings. And the Texas Gulf Sulphur Company, patron of the orchestra's radio series since 1944, announced another extension of its contract, calling for a season of twenty-six broadcasts over a statewide hookup.

Through the summer Kurtz added his own propaganda from Europe. He sent back plans and more plans. Among other ideas he commissioned from his own pocket a number of new works for the orchestra, including a suite by Aaron Copland to be drawn from his score for the film version of Steinbeck's *The Red Pony*. Altogether the air was full of symphony news with a bright edge and the promise of change. There was a great bustle and stirring of committees, and as summer drew to a close it was evident that the organization had entered a new order of living.

So indeed had the city itself. With the end of the war, Houston had begun to change. There was a feverish rush of development, and nowhere were experiments bolder. The wild beauty of Space Age architecture, with its lean towers of incredible balance, increasingly dominated the midtown scene, obliterating venerable landmarks. New fortunes were made, new leaders arose, and with its population rapidly approaching a million the city swept into a new epoch. The orchestra, though long a respectable enterprise, had been one of comparative plainness. It now took up the note of the times. Efrem Kurtz stood for the glamor of the musical art. He had been professionally bred in a lavish and indulgent theater, Diaghileff's playhouse, and everything about him reflected the nature of a fastidious sybarite. He had a beautiful wife, a beautiful wardrobe, a beautiful collection of paintings, a sophisticated and beautiful dog (French poodle, Dandy by name, who had personally endorsed a popular whisky in a national advertisement), and a taste for beautiful people around him in the orchestra, especially beautiful women. Some of these he brought with him from the Kansas City Philharmonic—most notably Marion Davies, Laila Storch, and Elaine Shaffer, lovely young players who became, respectively, first cellist, oboist, and flutist of the newly designed ensemble. In his other recruiting Kurtz looked with a favorable eye on the applicant who had natural attraction to go along with his musical skill. He was a theater man and he saw no reason why an orchestra concert shouldn't have as much theatrical charm as it could.

When he next returned to the city he brought Katherine along, and his other characteristics began to appear to his new public. It was discovered by the local press, with no little delight, that the orchestra chief was a deft needleman—if there is such a term in the language. At any rate, he admitted to sewing for his lady; it was part of his preoccupation with high fashion. And he was a bustling and meticulous housekeeper. He settled Katherine at the new and extravagant Shamrock Hotel, in a choice apartment that he had furnished all over again; and his passion for the broom, the pretty curtain effect, the right doily, and the apt floral arrangement was carried into his schemes for the orchestra. (At the time he arrived he displayed drawings of a sort of feminine full-dress suit, which he had designed with the help of a Paris *coutourière* and which he hoped to make standard in the organization. When it was tried out, however, all the more bouffant ladies of the ensemble looked strikingly like Edward VII; the idea thus met a certain resistance and failed). Kurtz would gladly have dynamited the City Auditorium, whose invincible drabness offended his instincts as a decorator. But as nothing could be done about that for the moment, he accepted the situation and set himself to rehearsing the new orchestra for the start of the 1948–1949 series on November 1.

Much was expected of that opening. Kurtz knew it, and so did the sponsors. There was an extraordinary attendance, a brilliant and curious audience, and the ceremonies were quite unusual. Hugh Roy Cullen had been persuaded to introduce the new conductor and orchestra; he heard himself hailed by the chairman of the board, F. M. Law, as "the savior of the orchestra" and its most magnanimous friend. Roy Cullen's remarks were not long. They commemorated such leaders of the movement as Dr. Joseph Mullen and Walter Walne, both recently lost, and included a warm tribute to Hoffmann. The audience made Mr. Cullen fully aware of its own affectionate gratitude; and then Efrem Kurtz took his position before an orchestra representing a different day, fifty-seven of whose eighty-four members were new.

The program began with the *Red Pony* fantasia of Copland, a premiere dressed up by the presence of the composer in one of the stage boxes. It was not his privilege to hear one of his more distinguished creations. The potpourri from his movie score was a slick, hothouse evocation of pastoral scenes. But some of it galloped nicely at any rate, and in this atmosphere it received a modest audience blessing. (Kurtz put it away and it never reappeared in the repertory.) The evening moved then to its symphony, which seemed rather a curious choice for so festive a moment—Tchaikovsky's Sixth, the *Pathétique*, a work that haunted this building as persistently as the rats in the fly-loft. The other selection was Ravel's *Daphnis et Chloé* Suite No. 2. And as the various beauties of these creations were traced, the question to be pondered was what exactly had happened to the orchestra.

The critical listener found what he might have expected. It was evident that Efrem Kurtz, taking advantage of a much more generous budget, had made certain improvements in the band. The ensemble he brought to the stage was more glossy and virtuosic than the one it replaced, especially its strings and woodwinds. The brass tone was no longer the one Hoffmann had favored; by the substitution of French trumpets its timbres were brighter, but it lacked the same mellow romanticism. At the heads of the various sections were very competent leaders; a good deal of individual brilliance appeared in the soloistic material of this program. On the other hand, the new company was not thoroughly welded as a unit. Though obviously a collection of good players, it lacked the simultaneity of execution that is largely a matter of instinct, and the tonal results of this occasion were often uneven in quality. The old organization, fully developed in its own character, had often played with a sort of cohesion and expressive consistency not found in the first work of its more costly successor.

The opening had attracted a number of critics from other cities, one of whom wrote back to his paper that Houston had "gone dizzy over its new 'miracle' orchestra." He was a man well acquainted with dizziness, but this time he misjudged its degree. The local criticism was not rapt. Writing in the *Chronicle*, Eleanor Wakefield reported a decidedly "cold" performance of the *Pathétique* and said of Kurtz's work as a whole, "His music neither sears nor freezes, but it is tasteful and suitably balanced." Paul Hochuli of the *Press* was satisfied to discuss the "latent power" of the new ensemble and to mention that "Mr. Kurtz seems a worthy choice to lead the orchestra to bigger and better things." The substance of my own review for the *Post* has been given above; it took note of the orchestra's changes and dealt with its need for integration and more firmness of style.

Except by the foolish, there was nothing more to be said for the moment. The important fact was that the Houston Symphony Society, with this increase of the orchestra's funding, had accepted the full challenge of such an endeavor, the challenge to do the job complete. It was the first organization of the Southwest to establish an orchestra on that footing, and remains the only one that has done so.

In this honeymoon season it was pleasant to await further results. Kurtz was eager to please and surprise; he exerted his full charm in the hall and in other contacts with the city. His spirit was high. He amused hostesses by slyly discussing the latest scandals of Riviera society; it seemed that he knew everybody. He obliged the newspaper photographers by getting Dandy to pose at the piano (the poodle was also musical). Or he himself was photographed at his knitting, one of his chief forms of relaxation. He likewise dutifully went about speaking to luncheon gatherings and ladies' committees; he spoke with a thick accent, leaving guesses as to what he had said. Altogether the city found him good company and was in a humor to enjoy the incidental delights of his presence. Meanwhile he worked hard with the orchestra, which began to show the effects in its second appearance on November 15, especially in Brahms's First Symphony and in a sensitive reading of Debussy's *L'Après-midi d'un faun.* Kurtz had devised a new seat-ing arrangement by having the Auditorium's orchestra pit bridged over. The band was moved forward, which improved the stage picture, whether it had any effect on sound or not.

There was a brilliant procession of guest artists, centered by the ap-pearance of Igor Stravinsky as conductor of the January 31 concert. He put the orchestra through a program of his own works—*L'Oiseau de feu, Apollon Musagète, Le Baiser de la fée,* and the String Concerto in D. Two other composers, Roy Harris and Harold Shapero, attended premieres of their compositions under Kurtz's direction; the Harris piece, entitled *Elegy and Paean,* was a dialogue for viola and orchestra, with William Primrose as the excellent soloist. Among the other solo performers were Alexander Brailowsky, Eugene Istomin, Ginette Ne-veu, Tossy Spivakovsky, Erwin Laszlo, and Frances Yeend. (With the Primrose concert came a change in the orchestra's critical lineup; Ann Holmes succeeded Eleanor Wakefield as the *Chronicle*'s music review-er, beginning a valuable service that has come down to the present day.)

In its final event of the season, on April 11, the orchestra recognized the work of one of its members, Alfred Urbach, a splendid musician who had joined it as a cellist after leaving the army in 1946. As a hobby he had set about organizing a singing society, the Houston Chorale, and had quickly brought it to a membership of 150, which responded well to his diligent coaching. The choir now combined with the orchestra in a production of Beethoven's Ninth Symphony (the imported soloists were Paula Lenchner, Kenneth Schon, Margery Mayer, and Irwin Dillon) and acquitted itself with high credit. Thus began an association that has added much to the orchestra's interest.

One feature of the season had failed. Kurtz's idea for reviving the "pops" had been a series known as the Prom Concerts, which were put on in the Music Hall. Aimed for the college and younger married con-tingents, they attracted neither the young nor the old in large numbers, and this venture was dropped.

Orlando Barera had resigned as assistant conductor to accept a musi-cal offer in Baton Rouge, Louisiana (which incidentally deprived Dandy of a walking companion). Kurtz brought in as replacement a young violinist, Andor Toth, turned over to this gentleman what duties remained for the summer, and himself left for New York. He conducted some of the concerts of the New York Philharmonic in Lewisohn Stadium. Then he went to California and later to the Berkshire Festival at Tanglewood, Massachusetts, looking for players or pleasure. Houston would not see him again till the middle of October.

Kurtz had a three-year contract, and during this period of his service in Houston he worked under conditions approaching the ideal. He had generous sponsors and an eager audience, and his managerial aides were exceptional—the powerful Arthur Judson of New York City, who was his personal representative, and the very canny and resourceful Tom Johnson. For his second season the Houston society, on the recommendation of Johnson, instituted a major expansion of program. The 1949–1950 subscription series was enlarged to twenty concerts, the budget increased to $400,000 (a leap of $89,000 over the previous season), and the orchestra's first long tour beyond the borders of Texas was arranged, including twenty cities and ranging as far north as Chicago.

Kurtz did some recording with the New York Philharmonic in this summer, under a contract which he held with Columbia Records. When this became known certain supporters of the Houston orchestra asked why, since Kurtz was now its conductor and receiving a generous salary, he should not have recorded with his own group. It was a fair question—and was never satisfactorily answered. The conductor replied that he had gone to New York with the hope of rearranging his Columbia agreement, but had run into difficulties due to a sudden recession of the record market. This hardly made sense to his critics. But by the time he got back there were other matters to talk about, and the record question was conveniently bypassed. Efrem Kurtz was an excellent showman.

In general the new season repeated the flavor of the first. It had grace and a better polish in its musical yield, and it offered two guest conductors of exceptional interest—Sir Thomas Beecham and the New York Philharmonic's Dimitri Mitropoulos. Both were surprised by the organization they found. The sarcastic Sir Thomas had an easy time with the band and made not an invidious comment; indeed he decided to like Houston itself, which was later to have much meaning. Mitropoulos was altogether delighted. "It is the playing equal of the New York Philharmonic," he said of the new ensemble. Other little diversions turned up. Among them was a visit from Virgil Thomson, music critic of the *New York Herald Tribune* and in that position the darling of the *avant-garde*, who conducted a snip of his own music, part of his score for the film called *Louisiana Story*.[1]

In late February the tour began. Having first covered the grapefruit circuit, the orchestra arrived in Chicago on March 5, with pianist Rudolf Firkusny along to play Beethoven's C Minor Concerto as companion to Prokofieff's Sixth Symphony. The turnout was good, and the orchestra won praise from Claudia Cassidy, the fickle fury of the Chicago *Tribune*, and then accounted the terror of Midwest criticism—which proved that Kurtz knew where his friends were. On the whole it had been a good season.

The season that followed had a still more prosperous look. When all bookings were in for the 1950–1951 course, the orchestra found itself with a schedule of 103 public performances: 20 subscription events, 5 free Henke and Pillot concerts, 10 student concerts, 26 weekly broadcasts, 40 out-of-town dates, and 2 "specials."

Kurtz had again been away for the summer and returned only in time to rehearse for the opening concert on October 30, which had the Schumann-Glazounov *Carnaval* and César Franck symphony as its principal items. He was in form and now directed his handsome and increasingly flexible orchestra with a proud and confident lordship. It likewise answered him proudly. And there was certainly a considerable element in the symphony's audience—smart, fashionable, influential, and knowing, itself apt to move much in the international set—which found nothing but high virtue in the work of this glamorous leader. These stylish and traveled adherents, citizens of a world suddenly altered by new marvels of transport, formed a definite cult and were the strength of the Kurtz movement in Houston. To them he was "dear Efrem," and priceless.

---

[1] Further, at a concert in February the Duke and Duchess of Windsor were present, and for one of the few times in its history the Auditorium afforded a sidewalk canopy and a red carpet (borrowed from the Shamrock Hotel).

But the general audience for symphony music in any city is a varied group; its informed and regular members are not necessarily glamorous, witty, or fascinated by the latest whims of society. Some visit the temple with small concern for its social attraction or more strictly theatrical interests; and the judgments of this element, like those of the more volatile public, are there to be weighed by providers of the symphony art.

During the season there was a certain falling off in the audience. It was the more to be noted because of the very full houses for the two seasons before, and because there was certainly no absence of additional lures this time. The series had soloists galore, indeed, so many violinists that the favorite concertos for that instrument hardly covered the needs. Piano virtuosos were almost as abundant. The chief vocal occasion was offered by Kirsten Flagstad, in a Wagner program which included the *Wesendonck Lieder*. On March 19, Elaine Shaffer, the orchestra's siren of the woodwinds, was the featured performer in Bach's Suite No. 2 for solo flute and string orchestra, which she dispatched with high technical skill and musicianship.

The guest conductors were again eminent: Leopold Stokowski, who appeared on December 4, and Eugene Ormandy on January 15. Stokowski did a Wagnerian first half and then did the expected (though lightly) in his role of Discovering Spirit; he introduced Carl Ruggles's *Organum*, seventy-eight measures of grinding atonality by a fervent disciple of Webern. Ormandy brought no surprises; he was satisfied with a program of the Brahms First and the Beethoven Seventh.

As for Kurtz, now that he had to provide eighteen concerts a season, a certain strain on his repertory was indicated by the frequency with which some of his favorite items returned to the program, though he did his best to distract attention from that. Aaron Copland's *Quiet City* and Bartok's *Concerto for Orchestra* were among his departures from the canon in this winter; he performed Hindemith's *Mathis der Maler*, added Strauss's *Don Juan* and Berlioz's *Symphonie Fantastique* to his Houston catalogue, and finally got around, in the penultimate concert, to the music of Charles Ives, his Symphony No. 2. The season closed with the Verdi Requiem—another effective use of the Chorale. Kurtz had not coasted, nor had anything been spared to give the season

a respectable program. The orchestra had often responded with exceptional beauty. But the audience problem, if not a crucial matter, had
been a nagging and obvious telltale. The season had not done what its
sponsors had hoped for. The orchestra's luster and reputation were
growing, but so was the cost of operation. Maximum earnings were
essential to the new policy scheme.

The problem of great orchestra maintenance had been closely engaging the board; its committees had gathered a mass of data and had
made certain projections. At the start of this season Miss Hogg had laid
stress on the need for a new hall to give fuller advantage to the orchestra; it was an argument to which the city's officials were beginning at
last to respond. The vision of such symphony leaders as F. M. Law
(a veteran banker), Maurice Hirsch, T. E. Swigart, and Gus Wortham
had resulted in a broadening of methods for supplementary support
of the orchestra, both by enlargement of the annual maintenance fund
campaigns and by the setting up of an endowment fund plan. A committee had also begun work on a pension plan for the players.

When this series of concerts ended in April, 1951, the trustees were
sufficiently gratified but not in a humor to make hasty or sweeping commitments. They were asked to reconsider the position of Kurtz, and
they were cautious. In the end it was voted to renew his contract, but
this time only for two years. Kurtz had apparently expected a more
positive stamp of approval, but he quizzically smiled, said nothing,
and went his way for the summer. He was strictly a seasonal man. Indeed, though it hadn't quite dawned upon everyone yet, the day of the
settled, resident orchestra conductor was over.

For the 1951–1952 season a small change in the concert policy went
into effect. The twenty subscription performances, which had been
from the first in two series, were now divided between Monday and
Tuesday evenings, instead of being given entirely on Mondays. Otherwise there was the same generous booking of soloists, the same plan
with respect to guest conductors, the same "extras," and same effort by
Kurtz to give his programs the dressing of novelty. His devices included a Latin-American evening with music by Revueltas, Villa-Lobos,
and Oscar Fernandez, and performances of Honegger's Fifth Symphony, Shostakovich's Fifth, and the little known Symphony in B-flat

Major of Ernest Chausson. He gave Prokofieff's *Lieutenant Kije* Suite and Khachaturian's Cello Concerto (with Edmund Kurtz as soloist), and introduced minor contemporary works—Howard Swanson's Short Symphony and a mélange under the title of *Texas Suite,* by David Guion, which somebody had ordered for the orchestra.

The season's principal guest conductors were Vladimir Golschmann, of the St. Louis Symphony, and the eminent Bruno Walter. Dr. Walter was seventy-five, but age did not cause him to spare either himself or the audience. His program opened with Beethoven's *Egmont* Overture, followed in order by Mozart's G Minor Symphony, Wagner's *Siegfried Idyl,* and not one but two of Richard Strauss's voluminous tone poems, *Don Juan* and *Death and Transfiguration.* When the concert ended, about eleven o'clock, most of its listeners were perhaps more benumbed than exalted.

Kurtz's idea for the seasonal close was a Beethoven cycle—and no marvel of planning as such things go. It was set off in March by a drowsy performance of the Violin Concerto with Erica Morini, and thereafter was never fully awake. It was the tamest seasonal finale in a good many years and left everyone rather glad to be gone.

In this summer of 1952 there was a hopeful incidental development. Government restrictions on certain types of building, left over from wartime, were set aside, and the way was open to resume the campaign for a better orchestra hall. Miss Hogg led a committee that met with city officials, and the matter was pressed with all energy. Out of these sessions came a plan to modernize the Music Hall and the Coliseum, redesigning the former completely. Hermon Lloyd, one of the city's imaginative young architects, was selected to develop the project. But it would take time to see whether this compromise scheme had significant benefits for the symphony.

Meanwhile, in October, another orchestra season began with a rather desperate effort to impart a look of improvement to the City Auditorium. The change consisted of a movable, terraced floor, devised to cover the flat parquet section on symphony evenings, so that, as the program book put it, patrons seated in that section could "have the privilege of seeing as well as hearing the orchestra." (What some of the first occupants saw was a large rat that came out of the wings and, with Kurtz unaware of its presence, capered at length on the rim of the footlight trough in good time with the music under performance.)

This winter did not have such a lavish provision of soloists, though Francescatti, Isaac Stern, Guiomar Novaes, and Brailowsky were present in full brilliance. Stokowski also was returned, conducting the performance on January 27 (his contemporary tidbit this time was Herbert Elwell's *Ode for Orchestra*). The other podium visitor was Alexander Hilsberg, associate conductor of the Philadelphia Orchestra, who hauled out *Mathis* again. Kurtz's own programs added more or less current musical thought, including Hindemith's *News of the Day* Overture, another overture by William Rice, a Houston composer, the Ninth Symphony of Shostakovich, and a bolus entitled *New Frontiers*, by Thomas Beversdorf, also of Houston, conducted by the composer. Kurtz ended his season by resurrecting Monteverdi's celestial and seldom performed *Magnificat*.

Throughout most of this course of music, however, there were persistent signs that audience interest was slipping. Again average attendance had fallen below the anticipated level. Like the season before, this one could not be accounted a failure, but neither had it been successful enough on the new scale. The nights under Kurtz had developed that kind of monotony which gives the unhappy impression that every concert is the same one. Perhaps he was a little discouraged or sullen.[2] The events following the 1952–1953 season were not surprising.

Warren S. Bellows was now chairman of the orchestra board. He had been elected to succeed F. M. Law at the society's annual meeting in January. Head of a major construction concern, Warren Bellows, like H. R. Cullen, was a big man who believed in direct methods and independence of action. In April, as the conductor was preparing to leave town for the summer, Mr. Bellows called Kurtz to his office and in effect fired him as head of the orchestra, with a year's grace to make other arrangements. Meanwhile, Kurtz was told, there would not be a renewal of his contract; he would work under a letter of agreement that his New York manager had requested.

[2] Miss Hogg, who made it a point to attend every rehearsal, thought that Kurtz became bored and a little lazy about preparing the orchestra in this season.

The musical public was told nothing of this at the time; neither were some members of the orchestra board. The board as a whole was not informed until a meeting in September, when the Kurtz matter was thoroughly aired. Mr. Bellows's action was then ratified, with one of the twelve board members dissenting. The reasons officially given for dropping Kurtz were his disinclination to live in Houston, his failure to straighten out his phonographic arrangements and do more recording with the Houston organization, and the falling off in attendance at concerts. It was argued that the orchestra needed closer and more aggressive conductorial guidance.

But there had also been official concern of another kind. The private life of an orchestra leader is not quite private, and the late absence from Houston of Katherine Kurtz had not gone unnoticed by some of the symphony's sponsors. Neither had rumors that she and the conductor were separated. New York gossip columns had insisted that Katherine Kurtz was about to file suit and would name as corespondent a member of the Houston ensemble. The claim was not wholly incredible. There were some lovely girls in the orchestra, and one of these had become a frequent companion of Dandy on walks in the neighborhood of the Shamrock. The public was beginning to notice and ask questions, and the board wanted no extra-musical worries added to its other considerable problems. Social propriety was still a point to consider in 1953.

In any case, plans for the 1953–1954 season emphasized guest conductors, rather than a company of soloists; and of the five men booked, four could be regarded as having possible interest in such a post as the Houston conductorship. Those summoned were Hugo Rignold, conductor of the Liverpool Philharmonic Orchestra, Ferenc Fricsay, Maurice Abravanel (for two concerts), Erich Leinsdorf, and Ernest Ansermet. It amounted to another guest season, and only Ansermet, because of age and his peculiar connection with the orchestra of Geneva, could be considered entirely out of the competition.

Meanwhile, in August, the orchestra lost a valuable member. Elaine Shaffer resigned. She was in Europe and had lately given recitals with altogether successful results. It was not strange, for in addition to being a fine flutist and a musician of exceptional gifts, she was a person of much beauty and charm. She had found herself in demand as a solo artist and decided to remain in Europe. From Switzerland Kurtz endorsed her request to be freed.

Kurtz himself came back to a changed working arrangement. Faced with the problems of the City Auditorium for another season at least, Tom Johnson had been using his imagination again; the result was a new frame for the orchestra. It was a quite elegant shell with platforms, a curving roof, and clever lighting devices; it filled the auditorium stage, and its handsome decor gave a touch of theatricalism not earlier known by the orchestra.

But this season proved awkward to handle. Efrem Kurtz, a stubborn man, had not entirely accepted his situation. His sensitive ego was affronted. He took great pride in the orchestra, which he looked upon as his own; he was not in a humor to surrender the franchise meekly. He set himself to give a season that would sharply challenge the audience interest (not to mention the invading cavaliers, perhaps), and the programs were his best in three years. Rather pointedly, the first opened with Verdi's *Force of Destiny* Overture. It ended with the Beethoven Seventh, which he considered his particular forte among the creations of that master. But, although he was fully aroused and determined to impress himself on the audience all over again, the seasonal pattern was against Kurtz. It kept him from gathering momentum. Too many stage callers were popping in and out of the hall; and there was a further distraction in the form of a Christmas production of Menotti's short opera, *Amahl and the Night Visitors*, which was turned over to Andor Toth.

Significantly, the visiting podium stars came early. The first arrival was Hugo Rignold, who appeared on November 17 with a program commemorating the recent coronation of Elizabeth II. The music was all British and, not for that reason but because of its mixture and style of delivery, was unexciting. Mr. Rignold, a quiet and reserved young man, was not an impressive stage figure. The next conductor, however, who arrived a week later, was a man of high temper and exigent manner. This was Ferenc Fricsay. In his thirty-ninth year, Fricsay was on his first visit to the United States. His coming had been marked by an intensive publicity campaign, which proclaimed him the finest of the younger conductors elevated in the European theater since the end of the war. He was chiefly identified with the Radio Orchestra of the American Sector of Berlin (RIAS), which he had created in 1948 and had since headed. For the same period he had been musical chief of the Berlin Municipal Opera and had taken a hand in the Salzburg Festival management. This native of Budapest seemed to be ubiquitous. His American visit would be brief, allowing only three professional dates. He had begun with a week of conducting the Boston Symphony; he came directly from that city to Houston. His other engagement was in San Francisco. These were all orchestras whose conductorial situations at the moment were rather unsettled.

For whatever reason (an odd name can be helpful in such cases), the public of Houston was disposed to be curious about Ferenc Fricsay. There was an unusual turnout for his concert on November 23, a program consisting of Mozart's *Haffner* Symphony, Bartók's *Divertimento for String Orchestra* and Tchaikovsky's Fifth Symphony. There was likewise a touch of that form of excitement, generated by clever publicity writers, which brings the susceptible into the show with a firm predisposition to find wonders. Certain elements of this audience managed to find some where cooler heads in the gathering could discover no executional miracles. It was apparent, however, throughout most of this music, that some peculiar, fanatic intensity was at work on the orchestra. Fricsay's style had a curious flavor. Everything came out white-hot, overprojected, superclarified. When the music was quiet, it still carried a strange feeling of tension, and when it was nervous the climaxes were whipped up to such degree as to be painfully cutting—at least in the windstorms of Tchaikovsky. That the orchestra was made to yield some of the best of its beauties was not to be denied by the critical listener. That a rather crude order of podium showmanship was on display at other points in the evening was equally clear. Fricsay was a strange mixture to deal with.

In any case, for this concert he was voted exceptional laurels by the audience, swept away by the heat of his finish. Indeed the symphony's public seemed to have exhausted itself by this outburst; it had little enthusiasm for the next podium guest, Maurice Abravanel, though his two performances in December were more impressive for balance and insight.

Ansermet and Leinsdorf (then conductor of the Rochester Philharmonic) were not due until late in the season, and after Christmas Kurtz returned to the platform with the look of a man grimly determined. He had been salting his programs with the touch of the times; he now added to that seasoning the flavor of Gottfried von Einem's *Capriccio*, Samuel Barber's *Souvenirs*, and further items from the local composers: Merrills Lewis's *Symphony in One Movement* and William Rice's *Music in Memoriam*.

But the play had been taken from Kurtz; the talk was of other men and of possible change. And with little more than two weeks of the new year run, on January 16, the society did the expected, announcing the appointment of Ferenc Fricsay as principal conductor of the orchestra for the 1954–1955 season. He had been engaged ("in view of his impressive performance as a guest") to direct sixteen of the twenty subscription performances; the others would be assigned at a later time. The announcement made no mention of Kurtz.

Whatever his feelings may have been at the time, he kept them concealed and said nothing. His manners were always immaculate. He was getting up a production of Mendelssohn's *Elijah,* and the oratorio was delivered on March 8, with a massing of high school choruses. The next program concluded the season, and Kurtz acted with sentimentality—Russian style. He ended his term with a playing of Tchaikovsky's *Pathétique,* the symphony with which he had begun his adventures in Houston six years before.

But though the curtain was down and the conductor departed, the cult was not ready to give up. Some of its members were indignant and not to be reconciled. In late summer there was a meeting of half a dozen of its wealthier souls at the Tejas Club. They sent a message to the symphony board, proposing that, if the board would reconsider its action and keep Kurtz on, they would subscribe his full salary. The board naturally turned down the proposal. The society's thoughts were in other realms, and Kurtz returned to his guest conducting in Europe. A short time later, he and Miss Shaffer were married.

Chapter 10

The postwar epoch had a feverish pulse and brought remarkable changes of custom. Among these was a revolution in the methods of building. Great structures now rose with astonishing speed, and because of this general acceleration the work of remodeling the Music Hall went much faster than anyone had expected. It was announced that the hall would be ready in time for the orchestra's 1954–1955 season, and this was taken as a very favorable omen. It seemed fitting that new quarters should be occupied for the installation of Ferenc Fricsay and a fresh start for the symphony venture. Anticipations were very high this summer, and so were the seasonal ticket sales.

In late October the new conductor arrived on a wave of enthusiasm and hay fever. He brought with him a stylish and beautiful wife (she was of Rumanian and Austrian extraction), the same tension that had been noted on the other occasion, and a disposition to play the role of the prophet. Asked at the airport for his feelings about the Houston position, he replied with a snap: "It is exciting—and dangerous." As matters turned out, this remark proved sufficiently accurate.

Ferenc Fricsay (the name was pronounced Free-*shy*) was not one of those orchestra leaders endowed by nature with the look of authority and who, if they had not been musically gifted, could have been expected to find successful careers as revival preachers or faro dealers. He was not physically striking; he was of average height and beginning to be a little fat. He was also a little bald, with a fringe of reddish hair that accentuated the roundness of his face. He might have passed for a comfortable Bavarian friar, had it not been for the nervous play of his features. He seemed never to be in repose, and his face sometimes flushed when he talked. His dress was ordinary and careless; and possibly because he spoke English with difficulty, his manner seemed abrupt, ejaculatory, and dogmatic. All in all he was a far cry from the social grace and suavity of Efrem Kurtz.

Most status conductors, taking over the leadership of an orchestra, feel obliged to demonstrate their authority by the number of insignificant but exacting demands they can think of to be made upon players and managerial aides. This is all part of the show and is patiently suffered by the victims. As might have been guessed, Fricsay had the afflatus in full measure; his demands, as he went into rehearsal with the orchestra, were acute. But everybody cheerfully went along with these experimental cadenzas, and meanwhile the last strokes were applied to the Music Hall. The timing was close, but on the evening of November 2, with a splendid audience present, the reign of Ferenc Fricsay began in the new temple.

What the audience found, in advance of any music, was a very happy surprise. Nothing in Houston's theater experience had encouraged much faith in the possibilities of transforming the Music Hall. Other attempts of the kind, including some with the City Auditorium, had left things little improved or added problems as vexatious as the ones they were intended to cure. But Hermon Lloyd had applied a theatrical instinct as well as much practical sense to his effort, and it turned out to be the lucky exception. By using the hall's original stage and redesigning its other particulars, the architect had converted a drab tabernacle into a very handsome and tasteful theater. Entered through a beautiful, glazed foyer, which commanded a dramatic view of the city's skyline, the hall was now sumptuous and charming. In this setting the orchestra became something of a new spectacle also. The restyled building, though having nearly the capacity of the City Auditorium (it seated 3,024), by its sweep and excellent lighting gave an intimate feeling to the stage; the old quarters had given one of remoteness. It remained only to discover the sound of the orchestra under the high dome Mr. Lloyd had supplied. This test was accomplished by a program that opened with Haydn's *Clock* Symphony and went on to provide Bartók's *Dance Suite for Orchestra* and the Second Symphony of Brahms.

Again the results were gratifying. Nobody had quite hoped for perfection; the acoustically perfect orchestra hall is still a beautiful dream in this country. But by the end of the evening it was clear that this building had qualities as a resonator that were more than a fair exchange for the ones of the orchestra's old home.

Ferenc Fricsay had conducted with the same sort of intensity displayed in his work as a guest a year earlier, and again with uneven results. The better ones came in the Haydn and Bartók music, very cleanly delivered by the orchestra; the Brahms D-Major Symphony incurred oddities of stress and phraseology that were hard to accept as in the logic of this serene document. In any case the podium manners affected throughout this program had aggressively thrust themselves on the attention. Fricsay's style was exceedingly gymnastic, without having the grace that some podium figures impart to that method. With him, it gave an impression of hot struggle. And there was among its effects an especially unhappy peculiarity—a pronounced squat to indicate a *diminuendo*. It was a grotesque habit, and in this hall was more embarrassing than it might have been in another.

Still, the opening was judged a success of considerable measure. The newness of things had assured that. When all had been said in the press and elsewhere, the society congratulated itself. The next concert a week later repeated the results of the first, from the standpoint of attendance and audience attitude. On November 13 a "pop" was given under Fricsay in the new hall. When this proved to be profitable also, making it seem that the "pop" jinx was at last fading in town; official satisfaction increased, and the board members began thinking ahead.

They knew very little about Ferenc Fricsay beyond what they had learned from the stage. Although there had been a considerable stir over his coming, with the usual receptions, dinners, and other social affairs, these had not been as revealing as they generally are. Fricsay was a poor guest at a party. In the first place, his English was limited, which made it hard for him to speak freely with most of the company; but more than that, he seemed little inclined to participate. At such gatherings he was apt to appear either impatient or bored; and Mme Fricsay, whose copper-blonde beauty was striking, set a model of reticence on her own part. At a question about music from some official, however, Fricsay might burst into a torrent of words, and then his remarks could be curious. For although he had been in town only a few days and knew little or nothing of the city, he undertook to discuss the whole musical situation in Houston. He did not ask questions about it; he gave out sweeping opinions, sometimes of a very critical nature. This was offensive to some of his listeners, who had trouble in remaining entirely polite. For they knew that often his statements, so emphatically made, were absurdly in error, and they could have given him stiff answers.

The orchestra manager had also found that he had this dogmatism to deal with. It appeared in Fricsay's work with the band and in his contacts with the symphony staff. Tom Johnson, cheered by the good public reception of the Music Hall, was attempting to make the most of the opportunity; it was hardly helpful to have a conductor who went about taking every chance to condemn the new hall as "impossible." Fricsay's contempt for the building was a mystery, since he had begun to malign it with the opening concert—surely no adequate test of its possibilities.

There was an effort to soothe him. By the time of the third subscription affair, on November 16, Tom Johnson had had the stage shell from the City Auditorium altered and given a new finish. It now fitted into the Music Hall stage and conformed to the other decor. The orchestra was thus settled a little deeper into the platform, with a roof between itself and the fly-loft, and there were definite acoustical gains.

On this evening (chiefly a Mozart program with Elisabeth Schwarz-kopf as the vocalist) the orchestra's tone emerged beautifully blended and had frequently thrilling results. Fricsay was the chief beneficiary of all this, for the audience took the new setting to be an idea of his own and applauded him vastly. In view of the attitude he had actually taken, he should have blushed to accept the advantage. But he said nothing, and the public never knew of his lack of enterprise in the matter.

Now came a more curious turn. The contract with Fricsay covered only the 1954–1955 season. He was being paid by the concert; the total would come to about the same figure Efrem Kurtz had received for a season. The arrangement called for two terms with the orchestra, each of eight subscription events. A midseason vacation would allow the conductor to make a visit to Europe; the Fricsays had four children in Swiss schools and desired to spend Christmas with them. Another clause bound the society to give Fricsay notice, by December 1, of what intentions it had for the future. This made for tight guessing, since the season had hardly got under way when the time for this notification was at hand. And as they were asked to make a decision concerning the leader, the society's officers found themselves dealing with a number of quizzical factors.

The season had opened with a fine rush to the hall, and nobody could argue with that, but the new building had had something to do with this exceptional interest. Artistically the early results had been mixed. There was no serious fault to be found with the music making of Ferenc Fricsay; what concerned the officials more keenly was a personality problem. Apart from his work, the impression the conductor had made in Houston musical circles was not altogether reassuring; and, although nobody demanded social charm as a necessary qualification for his office, the abruptness and dogmatism of his manner had been resented by more than one valuable friend of the orchestra. Some of his statements they regarded as greatly intemperate. "If I come to Houston, I must be second only to God," he was reported to have said in an interview that received particular notice. There was another outlandish demand. On this visit the conductor and his wife were occupying as guests the luxurious apartment of Gus S. Wortham in the Warwick Hotel, one of the building's most beautiful suites. It now seemed that these quarters were not enough. Having visited briefly in some of the mansions of the town, Fricsay let it be known that he would expect to be furnished by the society with "a house as big as that of Miss Hogg or Mrs. Ledbetter" (Mrs. Paul V. Ledbetter, whose establishment matched the palatial dimensions of Bayou Bend), and a staff of servants to tend it, cost free. The officials who heard this absurdity gave it the name it deserved and then tried to believe they had not heard it.

But though the cultured public of Houston was lacking neither in tolerance nor a sense of humor, it had to be reckoned whether that public could be expected to take Ferenc Fricsay on his own terms. Another point to consider was whether the orchestra could expect again to have a truly resident conductor of rank, or whether, because of the world's changing conventions, its future development must be entrusted to a series of more or less visiting leaders dividing their time between continents.

The board turned over the questions and in mid-November instructed Tom Johnson to ask Fricsay for the terms upon which he would consider an extension of his contract. What came back was a jolt. The conductor replied in the form of a "Five-Year Plan" (itself a rather unfortunate term at this juncture of history); the "plan" looked more like a manifesto and again the tone was *ex cathedra* and brusque. Fricsay decreed the creation in Houston of "one of the world's great orchestras," and laid down the conditions for this. Principally they were nine, as follows:

1. A new orchestra hall must be constructed at once, seating not more than two thousand (the Music Hall was again described as "impossible").

2. Enlargement of the orchestra from eighty-five to ninety-five players, with replacement of about a quarter of the personnel.

3. Extension of the season from twenty-four to twenty-eight weeks, with a generous increase of rehearsal time.

4. Complete replacement of the orchestra's stringed instruments by a matched set, which the conductor proposed to obtain from a manufacturer friend in Europe for about forty thousand dollars.

5. Immediate entry of the society into the production of opera, by giving at least three operas a season.

6. Guarantee of a full European tour by the orchestra in the fourth year.

7. Guarantee of a transcontinental American tour in the fifth year.

8. The establishment in Houston, with symphony funds, of a branch of Deutsche Grammophon (with which Fricsay had a recording contract), in order to allow him to make records with the orchestra under this label—though his contract with the German firm held him to two American recordings a year.

9. A salary for himself of between fifty thousand dollars and eighty thousand dollars per season.

Nor did the prescription end there. Fricsay went on to overhaul the society's policy of support. The orchestra's budget for 1954–1955 was $407,000. He proposed to increase this to $525,000 for the next season, to be followed by other increases that would bring the budget to $700,000 a season for the fourth and fifth years.

This document was presented to the society's executive committee, of which Harmon Whittington was chairman; the other members were Miss Hogg, Gus Wortham, F. M. Law, Warren S. Bellows, Max Levine, and Russell L. Jolley. These were realistic appraisers. The new hall idea was of course foolish; the society had no way to erect buildings, and the municipal government had just spent about two million dollars to remodel the Music Hall for the orchestra's benefit. It was not suffering for quarters. The other proposals, however, were at least considered with reasonably straight faces. There was no disagreement with the ambition declared by Fricsay—building an orchestra of the first classification. On the other hand, he knew nothing about the problems of financing this particular orchestra, nor had he troubled himself to inquire about them. The committee's conclusion was that he had asked for too much too soon, and that any such absolute time guarantees as those he demanded were quite out of the question. Instead, the committee sent him an explanation of its position and an alternate offer. It proposed to renew the existing contract for another season. Thus Fricsay would have a chance to become better acquainted with Houston and all conditions affecting the orchestra enterprise, and both parties would be better equipped to make judgments concerning the future.

When Tom Johnson presented the board's letter, however, Fricsay was upset and indignant. He professed to be unable to understand why the society, if it so fully approved of his professional aims, should hesitate about putting them into effect simply because of the cost. "What is money to a city this rich?" he demanded with great heat. And he let it be known that he was not at all flattered by the counterproposal.

A few days later the situation gave cause for another kind of official concern. Fricsay's criticisms of the board were apparently being repeated to the orchestra members. When this leaked out and got into the papers, the conductor seemed eager to carry his campaign into that medium. His remarks to the press followed the line he had taken with Johnson: it was made to look rather as though he were a musical deliverer who had come to lead a region of darkness into the light, and whose efforts to do so (with consequent benefit to its downtrodden musicians) were being unreasonably frustrated.

The society looked on with embarrassment. It felt that its hospitality had indeed been poorly repaid. Fricsay's first term was to end with a concert on December 20, and that day Mr. Whittington addressed a letter to all members of the symphony board, enclosing copies of Fricsay's "plan" and the action taken upon it. Mr. Whittington's letter continued:

> The counter-proposal of the Executive Committee was made as an indication of the Society's attitude. Subsequently, matters had to be laid before Mr. Fricsay's manager, where such negotiations belong according to ethical business procedures.
>
> Mr. Fricsay, however, could not wait for these procedures. He preferred to make his possible contract a public issue and endeavored to disrupt the morale of the musical employees of the Society. Mr. Fricsay was brought to Houston not on contract as a regular conductor, but as principal guest of the Society. After your study of this report, we shall be happy to have an expression of your approval or disapproval.

Fricsay left for his holiday while the Whittington letter was in the mail. His manager was a New York agent, Andrew Schulhof, and the conductor stopped for a few days in that city. Before he departed for

Europe, Schulhof handed him a message from the Houston society: it stated that, if he so wished, the society would be pleased to release him from his obligation to return for the second half of the season.

Fricsay's immediate answer was angry. He told the agent to say he would be back. The society, however, thought otherwise. A few days later it sent another letter, prepared by its attorney, direct to Fricsay, who had then reached Ermatingen, Switzerland. It notified him that if he chose to return, contrary to its wishes, the society would not be responsible for any complications that might follow. There was no immediate answer. But on January 14 Fricsay cabled that because of an illness he would be unable to complete his season in Houston. The reply to his message was prompt: it wished him well and informed him that "all obligations between you and the Houston Symphony Society are mutually satisfied." So ended a minor digression for the orchestra. Fricsay had conducted eight of its regular concerts.

Whimsical chance plays a part in any orchestra's rise to unusual position and, as earlier mentioned, the Houston venture has been one of the lucky ones. The contretemps in its history have generally turned out in some way to its benefit, and this incident was another example. Facing the possibility of an awkward gap in its season, the society had moved without waiting to know whether it was altogether rid of Fricsay. Tom Johnson had been quietly dispatched to Seattle. The orchestra of Seattle was under the direction of a young American artist, Milton Katims, who had already been booked as a guest conductor for Houston when the midwinter vacation of Fricsay was arranged and who was also to be the spring tour conductor. The purpose of Johnson's trip was to hear Katims with his home orchestra and to ascertain whether, if the situation demanded, he could spend more time in Houston. This proved to be possible, and one problem was out of the way.

The first subscription concert of the 1955 series, on January 4, was taken by Andor Toth. Katims arrived for the second and remained to conduct two more subscription events and a "pop." He was in town through January 24—an interesting guest who had learned his trade under Toscanini as solo violist of the NBC Orchestra. Then the tour began, which occupied him for another three weeks as the orchestra visited West Texas and points in New Mexico.

Meanwhile, a special committee of the society board had been appointed to make recommendations for filling the chief conductorial post. In naming this body, Miss Hogg had suggested a close study of young American talents; she felt it might be a good policy if such a man were now chosen and had a chance to "grow along with the orchestra." Bearing this advice of the president in mind, the committee had paid special attention to Katims, but had learned that he considered himself bound to Seattle by "moral" and other unbreakable ties. The other young man (not a native American) in whom particular interest had been shown was Antal Dorati, who had once conducted in Dallas and now headed the Minneapolis Symphony. But while the committee was engaged with these cases, and one or two others, the factor of luck intervened. It changed the angle of vision and brought about a significant alteration of policy.

Andrew Schulhof, a veteran musical agent, was a conscientious and principled man, also persuasive and clever. It had embarrassed him that a client of his should have caused an unhappy situation in Houston; he was anxious to make amends and to hold the society's good will. Having kept in close touch with the Houston developments, he advanced an idea of his own. Schulhof had another exceptional client, then in England with a bit of time on his hands. He asked whether the Houston society would perhaps be interested in a chance to obtain this gentleman for the rest of the season. The offer was greatly alluring. Since the client in question was the legendary Sir Thomas Beecham, with all he represented in prestige, authority, and attraction, the society leaped at the opportunity. Beecham saw fit to accept and all details of the booking were quickly arranged and announced before the orchestra got home from its tour. No tidings could have done more to revive the interest of a somewhat faltering season.

The directors, however, were obligated to keep looking ahead, for some settlement of the principal conductorship was expected by the orchestra's public. The younger men given consideration had not proved very impressive, and the nominating committee was a little puzzled as to where to turn next, As a matter of fact, it turned away from its original idea and began thinking in terms of the more established and prestigious podium authority. But where was such a talent available? Every senior and eminent conductor in the nation seemed bound to a job.

In early February Miss Hogg went to New York to see what she could find in its halls that might offer some promise for Houston. She found very little of interest. But at last, when she was ready to abandon the search, an idea struck her that produced a dramatic result. She went to the phone and called Andrew Schulhof.

"What is Stokowski doing these days?" she asked him.

"Not very much," answered the agent, who stood in position to know; he was also Stokowski's representative.

"Do you think he might be interested in acting as a guest conductor for us?"

"I don't know," said the startled but ever-solicitous Schulhof. "We could find out."

"I would be pleased if you would."

It was done with very little delay. Leopold Stokowski was filling a guest engagement with the Detroit Symphony Orchestra; it was lucky that this illustrious master already knew something about the musical situation in Houston. His manager got him on the phone. In consequence, Ima Hogg returned home the next day with a matter of great interest to place before the executive committee. The result was that Tom Johnson was dispatchd to Detroit. He went with an offer and the powers of an agent plenipotentiary. His trip was entirely successful, and on February 20 produced musical news of the grand pitch. The announcement was that Leopold Stokowski would become principal conductor of the Houston orchestra with the start of the 1955–1956 season. He had been signed for three years. Under the contract he would direct at least ten of the twenty subscription performances each season and act also as the orchestra's musical supervisor with full power to determine its membership. Instead of a young conductor, the society had engaged one of the world's most celebrated patriarchs of the calling.

This item had a very wide echo as strict news, and was also widely "interpreted." What it simply and actually meant was that the Houston society had again demonstrated its readiness to accept the full challenge of orchestra building and to go beyond the limits of other such organizations in the region.

Meanwhile, however, there was the interregnum with its equal celebrity interest. When Sir Thomas Beecham arrived for his stint with the orchestra, which began on March 14, 1955, he was approaching seventy-six, another birthday being due in a month. There was never a more colorful orchestra chief. This world is a somewhat cynical place, and Thomas Beecham was one of its children who passed through it with a critical eye.[1] He was as famous for his barbed wit as for his musical brilliance. But he and Houston had once before got along well in spring weather, and now he returned in another March that was dressed like April. Sir Thomas again was charmed out of all malice, and what happened was probably no little surprising to the old gaffer's well-crusted soul. For this affair with the orchestra turned out to be anything but a casual accommodation on his part. It became instead a sort of swift, poignant romance between an aging conductor, who mocked at himself, and a young organization that roused, beguiled, and refreshed him. In his eyes it was doubtless a verdant and as yet not thoroughly tested assembly; and maybe he was a little bit right. The new orchestra could still be touched by the wonder of discovering itself. In the hands of Efrem Kurtz, who had put it together, it had been somewhat coddled. Under Fricsay it had been more distracted than otherwise. Beecham gave it another kind of experience. The orchestra was exposed to the rich, sunset glow of a vital personality, imparted with a unique style and a greatly masculine attitude toward the art. There was no fooling around. The orchestra was put to the making of a brave, joyous, keenly nerved, and soaring music. Such was the nature of Thomas Beecham at seventy-five, after a quixotic career of fifty years in the world's music halls.

The audience hugely enjoyed what he presented, which had to be so because Sir Thomas was having a grand time of his own. He forgot his gout in the process; his famous mannerisms were exercised. These included the habit of shouting so loudly as a long crescendo came to its

---

[1] He once said, when threatened with a strike in another orchestra: "Musicians have no cause to be stuffy: I have seen an orang-outang play the flute."

climax that he could be heard in every part of the auditorium. His programs were not novel; they offered the staples of the art. He played Rossini, Haydn, Mozart, and Handel (especially his own transcriptions of Handel), Beethoven, Bach, and César Franck; he accompanied soloists in other works of the canonical literature. What mattered was that Beecham was at the top of his form, so that the audience, listening to a course of familiar repertory, was made aware of unsuspected delights in a good share of the items.

The series was all too soon at an end. It closed with the Verdi Requiem, using the Chorale and an excellent solo company, given in Galveston on April 3 and for the home public on the two following evenings. Sir Thomas had spent only a little over a month with the orchestra, but the value of this union was not to be measured in terms of its span. It resulted in a very special kind of rapport, and few would deny that Beecham's spirit and method did much to mature the ensemble.

A souvenir of this episode remains in the form of a critical study of the orchestra, written by Sir Thomas on the day before his departure for England. It was written at Tom Johnson's request. It is more than a mere diagnosis of the organization; it goes on to discuss the whole musical situation in Houston, as Sir Thomas observed it. He had very high praise for the Chorale, recommended opera as an orchestra project, and closed with the following lines: "The most fortunate thing that could happen to Houston would be the acquisition of a musical director who would take a really serious interest in the artistic life of the community. I regret that both my preoccupations elsewhere and my years are too numerous for me to undertake a task which should be the pride of any younger man of ability to attempt."

Chapter 11

In Atomic Age civilization the price of good music was soaring with everything else. Since 1950 the orchestra's maintenance cost had risen sharply. Though earnings continued to cover about 50 percent of the outlay (a better than average record for such organizations), annual deficits well above $200,000 were now to be dealt with. It was a testing time for the nation's orchestra movements. In the ten years after the war's end, many that had sprung up in the 1930's and '40's, unable to adapt, either vanished or by their methods of compromise indicated their acceptance of second rate aims.

Having worked hard at improving its supplementary support plan since the days of Walter Walne in the presidency, the Houston society was in good position to meet the new pace, though its margins of victory gave no cause for complacency. The 1954–1955 season had cost $415,000. For 1955–1956, the budget rose by another $47,000 to a total of $462,280. The summer was spent in efforts to raise a sizable portion of this in the form of donations, and in August these labors were given a certain dramatization. Stokowski paid a brief visit to town to look over the orchestra setup. This was an unexpected development, and he came with the celebrated charisma in full glow.

The maestro's exact age had of late years become a mystery, but according to the best records available he was seventy-three when he arrived, like Lohengrin towed by a swan, to be invested with the orchestra's headship. Whatever the count, he was a splendid example of preservation and maneuverability, ramrod straight and of vigorous carriage, the famous aureole apparently of a natural and luxuriant blondness. As he stepped onto the sweltering platform of the railway station that afternoon, he presented the picture of Augustan authority in a unique mold—the vision that for more than a generation had been one of the major fascinations of the world's musical public.

Though Houston had been under this spell on other occasions, it it was a little different to be receiving Stokowski as the orchestra's own, and the ceremonies of this visit were unusual. In the following days they revealed, among other things, some of his small idiosyncrasies that caused interest. His neckties ravished admirers of high taste in that form of adornment. Others were taken by his accent (since he had lived in the country for most of fifty years), and found it an oddity that he chose to pronounce Houston "Hooston." The master was after all famous for his delicate ear.

He had two young sons by his late marriage to Gloria Vanderbilt, who were then in New York. Apparently as anxious to impress the lads as to finish the other concerns of this trip, he asked to be introduced to "a real Texas cowboy." As the last such specimen had disappeared from the Houston vicinity when Stokowski himself was a boy, the symphony staff was a little baffled. The best they could think of was to take him to meet a deputy sheriff at a pony-ride in a local amusement park, where he gravely accepted the badge of an honorary member of the sheriff's brigade and seemed satisfied.

Meanwhile he was acquainting himself with the orchestra's situation in general. He consulted Miss Hogg, met various members of the board of directors, and had daily discussions with Tom Johnson. Stokowski was perhaps readjusting his own habits of thought. For twenty-five years, beginning in 1912, he had been the resident conductor of the Philadelphia Orchestra, building it into one of the world's most celebrated musical organizations and himself into a legendary interpreter. Since leaving that position in 1936, however, he had led chiefly the life of a guest conductor in many parts of the world. He had formed a youth orchestra in New York City, but had not otherwise troubled himself greatly with administrative affairs. Now, after nineteen years thus spent, he was pledged to an effort more in the nature of the old Philadelphia assignment. There was much curiosity as to how he would go about this, but no one learned much at the time. Stokowski spoke of his plans for the Houston organization in generalities. Then he went back to New York for another six weeks.

Though rumors insisted that great changes would now be made in the orchestra's membership, this did not happen when Stokowski returned in October to begin work for the 1955–1956 season. Most of the old players remained, and the maestro's rehearsal demands, though strict, were not punishing. His criticism took another direction; he set in on the Music Hall. As a still new and comparatively untested facility, it seemed to offer conductors a peculiar temptation to sniff; and while Stokowski's exceptions were not as violent as those of Fricsay, he decided the building had certain acoustical failings. The more abstruse regions of physics were thus entered upon, and discussions of the hall's rate of vibration were soberly held and reached exquisite refinements of measure.

Likewise the maestro began by suggesting that the orchestra society should get into the presentation of opera, a form which he felt to be badly neglected in Houston. This was an indication that he hadn't been reading the papers very closely. The news sheets would have told him that the Houston Grand Opera Association had been formed that summer, chiefly through the efforts of Mrs. Louis G. Lobit, and that it was ready to get into production in January and had already arranged to take the orchestra into its scheme. But that was a side dish for the moment.

The great prestige of Stokowski would count much for the orchesrta in this inaugural season, and one of the benefits came promptly. On the day before the seasonal opening, Sunday, October 30, a portion of the final rehearsal was telecast on a national program, NBC's "Wide, Wide World." The orchestra thus made its debut on network television. One of the pieces played was likewise a premiere, Alan Hovhaness's *Mysterious Mountain*, commissioned for the Houston opening as a token of Stokowski's regard for contemporary musical thought.

The concert of the next evening was extraordinary indeed, its attendance and audience enthusiasm a fit tribute to a great musical figure. Stokowski could never have been more warmly or expectantly greeted; thus hailed he produced the magisterial style in a program that included with Hovhaness's composition the *Meistersinger* Overture, the second of Ravel's *Daphnis et Chloé* suites, and the Brahms Symphony No. 1. Hovhaness was present in the audience, and the plan of this concert was the one Stokowski would much favor in his Houston connection. He liked programs with new works to display; he liked the composers to be present. Few of his evenings would lack a premiere, or at least a first performance for Houston, and the airlines did a brisk business hauling to and from town a procession of musical spirits intent upon hearing their creations performed by a grand patron.

The slight personnel changes for this event were hardly noticed in the general excitement. Stokowski had installed new occupants of the first viola and cello stands (they were Robert Slaughter and Margaret Auë), and that was the turnover. He had altered slightly the disposition of forces, seating the woodwinds outside, placing the cellos and basses on parallel arcs, so that they faced the auditorium, and slightly changing the layout of the battery. What all this did was to give very much the arrangement that had been in effect when Ernst Hoffmann was conducting the orchestra twenty years before.

But a sort of alchemic phenomenon did occur, a transformation due to the character of the podium sorcerer. At his bidding the orchestra seemed to play with new beauty and elevation of style. The Hovhaness composition, rhapsodic in form and evoking certain ancient devices of Oriental music, was unfolded with dreamlike delicacy (the piece went on to considerable popularity), and everything else was dramatic. In the *Meistersinger* Overture and in Brahms's C Minor Symphony the greater poetry was fetched with a masterful ease, and often with that peculiar, velvety, and voluptuous sonority recognized as "the Stokowski tone." In all, it was a beautiful opening.

The next five programs were examples of the policy noted above. In his second concert Stokowski introduced Thomas de Hartman's dances from his opera *Esther*, and gave the first Houston performance of Charles Ives's quiddity, *The Unanswered Question*, before proceeding to the Beethoven Seventh. The third program included Henry Cowell's Sixth Symphony (Mr. Cowell was present); the fourth had Howard Hanson's G Major Piano Concerto, with Rudolf Firkusny as soloist; the fifth concert offered the world premiere of Khachaturian's *Festive Poem*, along with two other firsts for this series—Shostakovich's Tenth Symphony and Wallingford Riegger's *Dance Rhythms*. The sixth Stokowski occasion, on December 6, an all-Sibelius program commemorating the composer's ninetieth anniversary, used the Chorale for the first American hearing of his *Hymn to the Earth*.

All this, happening in a little over a month, had given the season's first part a distinctly contemporary flavor. It had also done other things. For while Stokowski was emphasizing his hospitality to the latter-day musical rhetoric, often with little speeches in behalf of the new items presented, his enthusiasm was not quite as contagious as he seemed to believe. Some of these works had stuck hard in the craws of some of his listeners.

There was now a relaxation of this pattern. Stokowski closed shop and went East for the holidays, leaving the orchestra to guest leaders; the ones who immediately followed were Max Rudolf and André Kostelanetz. Then Maurice Bonney, the associate conductor (appointed by Stokowski to replace Andor Toth) took over the stand for an evening and was followed in turn by Bernard Herrmann, who did two concerts. The master would be gone until late January.

Meanwhile the musical situation in Houston was altered by two important developments. Five months prior to the start of this season Miss Hogg had notified the directors of her wish to retire from the presidency at the end of the year. She had held the position since 1946 and, including her term during the early years of the orchestra, had served fourteen years in the office. She felt she was now entitled to turn over the burden and enjoy with a little more leisure the beauties of the orchestra she had helped to create. In December she again mentioned her wish to the other officials, and although they protested, her resolution was firm. They were left to select a new president, and the annual meeting was postponed to allow time for a nominating committee to consider the possibilities. When the meeting was eventually held on February 24, the committee called upon Gen. Maurice Hirsch to assume the society's leadership. When he accepted, the plan of organization that had been in effect since 1946 was modified and the office of board chairman eliminated. Thus opened another chapter of remarkable administrative performance.

The long connection of the Hirsch family with the symphony movement has been earlier noted in this record. Theresa Meyer Hirsch, the mother of Maurice, was a member of the original board of directors; his sister Rosetta, a violinist, was the first instrumental performer to appear with the orchestra as a soloist. Another sister, Josie, was an excellent pianist and favorite pupil of Rudolph Ganz. Such was the atmosphere in which Maurice developed his instincts. Music was a way of life with the family.

He took with him a natural affinity for the art when he entered the law to make a brilliant career of his own. It was twice interrupted for military service—for two years at the time of the First World War, and five years during the second. In the latter case, serving in the Judge Advocate General's department and then as a member of the General Staff Corps, his rank was that of a brigadier general; his chief duties were as vice-chairman and later chairman of the Renegotiation Board in Washington, a group directed to eliminate excessive profits from war work during the emergency. The board was empowered to renegotiate contracts not only of the army and navy departments but also of many other government agencies. Under General Hirsch it was credited with having saved the government over thirteen billions of dollars, without destroying incentive in private enterprise. For this achievement the Distinguished Service Medal was conferred upon him, among other official recognitions.

It was not only his rare gifts as a mediator, however, that had influenced the nominating committee. The general was sought because of a combination of other traits that especially suited the symphony cause.

He was a lifelong and generous lover of art, a true and discerning cosmopolite, a patron of the rare and exotic. As a young man he had been one of the city's most charming and eligible bachelors; it was not until his Washington service that he ended that state by marriage to a beautiful native of Arkansas, Winifred Busby, and made her a present of the fascinating and various world. For Maurice Hirsch's great pleasure was travel; his habit was to circle the globe each summer as casually as most people would go to the seashore, and he traveled by unusual routes; his romantic wanderings had taken him, as a seeker of beauty, to some of the earth's greatly remote and mysterious places. He was, in short, a lover of life, a student of the endless variety of human nature, and a social spirit of exceptional culture, manner, and tact. As a director of the orchestra society for nineteen years, Maurice Hirsch had helped form its philosophy. He took over the presidency with affectionate interest, and as chief spokesman and host of the enterprise found himself with a public function so happily suited to his characteristics that it became his absorbing concern.

While the Symphony Society was thus rearranging its official organization, Stokowski returned from his holiday, just in time to observe the other incidental development of this 1955–1956 season. He arrived back in the city on January 18. On the following evening the Houston Grand Opera Association delivered its initial production in the orchestra's temple, thus settling a number of questions concerning its own aims.

There had been periodic attempts to supply regular seasons of opera in Houston since the early days of the city, including one by the symphony association itself. None of the schemes had gone far. Having that record of failure to consider, plus the fact that the Metropolitan was now making spring visits to town, if only for two or three days, the musical public had regarded the prospects of the new venture with a rather skeptical glance—which may have been shared by Stokowski.

But this time the promoter was no dilettante and the planning had not been dreamy. Mrs. Louis G. Lobit, who had fostered the idea, was a woman of means and sound practical judgment, with a great love for the operatic form and a very wide company of friends. She had recruited the services of Walter Herbert, a conductor trained in the German theater, who had lately been a producer of regional opera in New Orleans, and they had decided to begin with a version of Strauss's *Salomé*, to be followed a week later by *Madame Butterfly*. The Strauss opera had never been given in Houston and thus offered the chance of a rather spectacular start—or a deadly debacle if the company's resources were not adequate.

There was in fact a victory sufficient. The Music Hall curtain went up on a well-handled production of *Salomé*, staged with professional skill and imagination, the dramatic values of Strauss's morbidly fascinating score firmly in place. There was little for the critics to land on. Brenda Lewis, a young soprano from the New York City Center company, was the competent Salomé; the other chief singers also were imported; the rest had been principally drawn from the Chorale and fitted into the scheme quite ably. Walter Herbert had selected an orchestra highly responsive to his touch—and this was no wonder, since the opera conductor had wound up with the bulk of the symphony personnel. The public was fully excited. And when the company added the next week a very winning production of *Butterfly*, theatrically as effective as the other piece and with Nancy Swinford an excellent prima donna, there was a new burst of enthusiasm. Mrs. Lobit's venture had the look of a winner. (A little more time was to show that this public approval was well placed. In its second year the company began expanding its program, and at the time of this history its seasons consist of five operas, which are given some twenty performances. It has entertained an exceptional roster of singers and continued to present staging of a quality highly unusual among organizations of its kind. The note belongs to this record because the way for the opera venture was opened by the presence in Houston of the fundamental need of good opera—a ready and eloquent orchestra. On the other hand, by contracting for the full orchestra on a seasonal basis, as it has long done, the operatic society has added both to the symphony's revenues and to the artistic refinement of the older organization.)

With *Salomé* out of the way, Stokowski opened his first spring season in Houston with more new works. They included Olivier Messiaen's *The Awakening of the Birds*, which the audience seemed to agree was strictly for the creatures named in the title. This curio was in fact laughed out of the hall, to the maestro's obvious vexation. But on January 31 he delivered, with great heat, a sort of answer to the late opera excitement in town. His stroke *drammatico* was the first local production of Carl Orff's *Carmina Burana*, and Stokowski turned it into a fireball. There is room for some doubt as to whether the German composer, who called his creation a "scenic cantata," had in mind quite such an effect as this performance achieved. The choral matter of the work consists mostly of chant, and Orff's expressive design hardly suggests a massive singing assembly of 150 performers. But such was the body Stokowski supplied by enlisting the full Chorale, and he arranged the dynamics of Orff's primitivism to suit this force. The results were overwhelming, and the show as a whole became one of Stokowski's memorable evenings in Houston.

The master had divided his time with the orchestra this season into three periods, and once more he returned to New York. There was another procession of guest conductors, beginning with Heitor Villa-Lobos on February 6, who delivered a program of his own works. The evening of February 14 brought a very gratifying reunion, when Sir Thomas Beecham returned to the rostrum. Though the physical strain under which he now worked was apparent, it was nowhere to be felt in the music he made. The orchestra hailed him, and his readings of Mozart's *Jupiter* and Beethoven's *Eroica* symphonies were models of spirit, vigor, and clarity. Milton Katims conducted the next two concerts, then left with the orchestra on a tour of a month, chiefly through Florida, Georgia, and Tennessee.

Stokowski was back for the last two concerts of the season, and again stressed new works. The occasion of April 2 was largely devoted to another Orff creation, entitled *The Triumph of Aphrodite*. This extended eroticon, after the manner of *Carmina*, was supplied with a vocal company as generous, but the music held little excitement. Orff's idiom seemed to have lost its surprises in this hall. A week later the season closed with a splatter of contemporaneous styles. Three items of Stokowski's program were heard for the first time in the city: Camargo Guarnieri's *Danza Negra*, Oscar Espla's *Don Quixote Verlando las Armas* (a North American premiere), and Paul Holmes's *Fable*, which had won the society's Texas Composers' Award. But as none of these was exactly arresting, and as the evening further included two famous anaesthetics of the repertory, Ravel's *Bolero* and Tchaikovsky's F Minor Symphony (both as reliably narcotic in the hands of one conductor as another), the concert ended with a goodly part of the audience either drowsy or half way home.

The master had demonstrated a policy. That winter no American symphony orchestra could have been more hospitable to contemporary musical ideas. But this had proved costly in one way. A considerable element of the orchestra's public, though willing to listen to experimental music in a certain degree, considered that Stokowski had exceeded that reasonable limit. These subscribers had found little of interest in the new music presented; it had left them more often bewildered, irritated, or bored. Although they respected the lordly conductor, they felt they had been badly imposed upon; and now that the course was finally over, these patrons began letting the management hear their complaints. Whether or not their objections were passed on to Stokowski, his next move was conciliatory. When he issued part of his plan for the 1956–1957 season (to go along with the membership campaign), the design seemed temperate enough. He would conduct fourteen of the twenty subscription performances, and he let it be known that eight of his concerts would be devoted entirely to a Beethoven cycle. Given that promise of a pillar of orthodoxy at the center of things, the discontented subscribers slept better and more easily signed their renewals. Stokowski gave no plans for his other six programs while the ticket committees were busy.

His second season in Houston began under the new administration, which dedicated the opening concerts, on October 30 and November 5, "with profound appreciation and affection" to Miss Ima Hogg. Stokowski's music for these occasions was discreet, generally familiar, and most charming. The first concert opened with Handel's D Minor Overture and went on to include Brahms's Second Symphony, the *Tannhäuser* Overture, and two brief novelties—the *Solemn Melody* of H. Walford Davies and a concerto for wind and percussion by the Houston composer William E. Rice. A week later the main items were

Mozart's *Jupiter* Symphony and Tchaikovsky's *Swan Lake* music, with just a touch of the modern in Michael Tippet's dance suite from his opera, *The Midsummer Marriage*.

There were then two concerts launching the Beethoven cycle. They covered the first three symphonies, the Triple Concerto in C Major for piano, violin, and cello (with Lois Banke, Raphael Fliegel, and Marion Davies as soloists), and the G Major Piano Concerto with June Stokes as the keyboard artist.

Meanwhile came another sign of Miss Hogg's benevolent interest in the orchestra—a new shell for the Music Hall stage, including a "sound reflector" built in accordance with the latest acoustical theories. This device was a recommendation of Stokowski; Miss Hogg had supplied it as a Christmas gift to the orchestra. Along with it Stokowski ordered the hanging of four acoustical panels on the theater walls. It was a delicate matter to decide whether these fittings (which later came to be known as the range cover and biscuit boards) made a difference in the orchestra's sound. At any rate, they gave the audience something to talk about. More obvious, as this 1956–1957 season developed, was that Stokowski had the orchestra working at the peak of its form. The noble sonorities he repeatedly coaxed from the instrument were examples of the genius of his own talent.

On November 27 he interrupted the Beethoven series to give a Russian program consisting of Glière's narrative Symphony in B Minor (*Ilya Mourometz*), Prokofieff's G Minor Violin Concerto, and Borodin's Polovtsian Dances from *Prince Igor*. There was a curious contretemps. Fredell Lack was the beautiful soloist in Prokofieff's vehicle, and she and Stokowski disagreed about a passage near the end of the work, where the changing meters of 4/4 and 5/4 are involved. The result was that the orchestra finished ahead of the violinist. Who then was at fault? It was a curious question to come up in a concert of Stokowski. Whatever the case, he calmly turned back in the score, consulted the passage, and proceeded to have his soloist and ensemble repeat that part of the coda, which ended this time as it should. The audience appreciated his gallant aplomb, but did not thank him as warmly for his introduction of Glière's bloated creation of 1911, whose "humid earth" wanderings are endless.

The concerts closing this phase of his season were in the spirit of Christmas and were lovely. On December 17, and again two nights later, Stokowski offered a program beginning with Alan Hovhaness's idyl, *As on the Night,* followed by Berlioz's *L'Enfance du Christ,* both heard for the first time in the city. Lois Townsend, a Houston soprano, sang beautifully the very difficult material of the Hovhaness creation; the Berlioz oratorio had excellent soloists in Audre Lokey, Philip Maero, Jack Waggoner, and Yi-Kwei-Sze, supported by the Chorale at its best. Stokowski deserved great credit for the conduct of it all, but much of the poignant beauty of these evenings had been assured by the earlier work of Alfred Urbach in preparing the choir.

Stokowski now left for his midwinter retreat, leaving the orchestra to guest conductors. There were six this season, with a concert each: Sir Malcolm Sargent, Walter Herbert, André Kostelanetz, Maurice Bonney, Victor Alessandro, Jr. (conductor of the San Antonio Symphony Orchestra), and Pierre Monteux. All except Sargent were familiar to Houston. He appeared on January 14—a striking theatrical figure who made vivid and interesting music. It was certain that he would be asked back.

Stokowski resumed charge of the series on March 1, with four concerts left. The first was a part of his Beethoven cycle; the next two, however, brought in the contemporary note and one offered the presence of a lady composer, Natasha Bender of New York, who showed up in the hall, very glamorous and frieghted with ideas, to hear the performance of her *Soliloquy* for oboe and orchestra.

The season's finale was what it had to be. On March 25 and 27 Stokowski offered productions of Beethoven's Ninth. Again there were excellent soloists with the Chorale; the maestro presided with all drama, and the reactions, both public and critical, were the ones always induced when the Ninth Symphony closes a season. People then feel they have rendered their cultural surtax for the year and are glad to go home and undress.

For the 1957–1958 season there was a policy change. The orchestra's schedule was expanded from twenty to twenty-four concerts, but these would be given in pairs (the same program on successive Mondays and

Tuesdays) instead of in two separate courses. This plan was the work of the clever Tom Johnson. It had an economy value, for while it meant a gain in the actual musical traffic, it also meant that Stokowski's duties and seasonal cost would be reduced. He was receiving $2,500 a program. He now had only eight programs to get up, as compared with fourteen for the previous season. Stokowski accepted the change without argument, mainly because it would not require him to spend as much time in the city and he welcomed the chance to remain close to his young sons in New York. On the other hand, with fewer programs he could no longer be as lavish in hosting the new musical fashions. He nevertheless managed to pass out favors enough to composers, and in this season again they produced a certain audience backlash, most felt when he presented a cello concerto by Ernst Krenek, with Margaret Auë as the sacrificial performer. A case of aggressive atonalism, the work affected the hall like an east wind seeping under the doors. But most of the audience bore with good humor, and occasionally with some profit, a collection of small innovations by Rodion Shchedrin (*The Humpbacked Horse*), Panufnik (*Sinfonia Elegiaca*), José Serebrier, Peter Mennin, Sylvestre Revueltas, and others, which Stokowski scattered among traditional items before closing his part of this season with another production of *Carmina Burana*.

There had been only three podium guests in midwinter: Villa-Lobos and Stravinsky had an evening apiece, and Walter Susskind, conductor of the Toronto Symphony, presided for two concerts and then headed the orchestra on its tour in February. This arrangement of touring under temporary conductors had now become a regular policy, but it was an unsatisfactory plan. Other orchestras with prestigious leadership were offering that leadership to their bookers.

The cost of this 1957–1958 season had been $488,968. Stokowski's three-year contract ended with the season itself, and the directors paused to take stock of their bargain. The general feeling was one of gratification. The conductorial scheme had not worked altogether in the ways some had expected, but Stokowski's presence had been a powerful influence. The orchestra stood in a new bracket of interest, and optimism prevailed in the board room. An increase to thirty concerts was decreed for the season to come, and there was no doubt as to what the society's next gesture would be. The maestro was invited to renew the connection on a season-to-season arrangement; he was pleased to accept.

When Gloria Vanderbilt separated from Stokowski in 1955, she said in an interview that for ten years she had been treated "like an Arab wife." By this she apparently meant to suggest that the maestro had been rather remote on his mountain top. At any rate, that had been the case in his late union with the Houston Symphony Orchestra. This connection, though generally pleasant, remained formal. Stokowski was a visitor to his organization; he spent little time in the hall when not strictly engaged in music making, and seemed neither to feel nor to invite that sentimental affection which often develops between a great orchestra leader and his force. His "orchestra-building"—if such was the name for this service—was not quite of the kind that some people, including some of the players, had expected.

The truth was that Stokowski had found in Houston an already excellent orchestra; in the sense of actual construction there was not much left to be done. At the start he had refilled a few spots in the band; the later changes had been the normal turnovers of any such organization, and he had left them to be handled by Alfred Urbach, the personnel manager, and Tom Johnson. It was another kind of building that he was now peculiarly fitted to do. This naturally concerned the orchestra's style. There was no doubt that Stokowski's effect, in that special regard, had been felt. To the players, however, he often seemed coldly remote, a self-centered and unapproachable figure. They felt they were much taken for granted. At rehearsals the master had an air of imperial gravity, but if he was irked, could be melodramatic in his tantrums. He did not wear glasses at any time in the presence of the orchestra. This was impressive, but some players complained that they were reprimanded for errors of reading, mostly in new scores, that actually had occurred at the main desk. Their complaints were necessarily private.

Stokowski's program policy, too, though never a great issue, continued to nag some of the audience. This was a delicate matter. The patrons in question were perfectly willing for music to be treated as a continuing art, with due notice accorded the output of the day, but they felt the conductor to be over-playing his role as a propagator. Because their own interest was not chiefly in matters of style, they saw no virtue in listening at such length to experimental music that generally bored them severely. The first magic of Stokowski had worn off, and after his third season this fact became increasingly evident. He no longer automatically drew full houses.

The more these signs of unrest were manifested, however, the more he seemd bent on his course. During the 1958–1959 season he organized (with Mrs. R. R. Dean) the Houston Contemporary Music Society, for the giving of small ensemble concerts in other quarters of town, and these he conducted without fee. He was thus in a way fighting his own shop at the Music Hall. The symphony officers made no objection to that; they only hoped the competitive venture would channel off some of the new-day bagatelle from the orchestra programs. It was not to do so. The contemporary thrashings continued in the regular concerts, and this season included a quite generous survey of the younger Soviet school. Meanwhile the declining attendance (especially among season subscribers) was becoming a genuine worry. At last it had to be quietly suggested to the master, by a circumspect member of the board, that with audience behavior what it was at the moment, perhaps a slight modification of his repertory scheme would be the course of wisdom. Stokowski was ruffled but seemed to give thought to the hint. Soon afterward he announced for the season to come a Brahms cycle that would occupy most of his time. But a cool draft had blown over his relations with the Houston society, and its effects would be felt in the working conditions of the next winter.

For that winter—the season of 1959–1960—Stokowski's connection with his "home" organization became casual indeed. He opened the course on October 19, remained in town less than a month, and was not again present till the middle of March. Meanwhile the season took on a wide mixture of values.

In the opening weeks two of Stokowski's four programs were devoted to his Brahms enterprise. Between these, however, he inserted a virtually all-contemporary occasion, the strange items of which were a symphony for strings and percussion by Harold Faberman and Henry Cowell's *Variations for Orchestra*, the latter involving a piano player who is called upon to do part of his playing with a stick. Both composers were on hand; their obeisances to the master were rather effusive; and a good part of the audience, again finding itself bored by the ceremonies as well as the music, gave signs of its lack of enthusiasm for this particular pattern.

The orchestra also was becoming a rather disturbed body—not because of anything it was asked to perform, but because of the loose working arrangement from season to season. The players felt there was really no leadership very greatly concerned for their welfare, and this had its effect on morale. There was no longer an assistant conductor, Maurice Bonney having departed, and Ezra Rachlin, conductor of the Austin Symphony Orchestra, was brought in to direct three of the mid-seasonal pairs. Other programs were handled by Vladimir Golschmann, Walter Susskind, and a sort of protégé of Stokowski's, Georges Sebastian, from the Paris Opera, who used only his last name in the billing and for rather mysterious reasons (for he had never before been heard of in the city) attracted a phenomenal audience. But the cardinal dates were in February. They brought a conductor of extraordinary capacity. He handled the orchestra with a singular freedom and delicacy, and the rich play of imagination in every work it performed left a spell that carried a touch of the mystic.

In this winter the most widely discussed visitor to American symphony podiums was a British authority, Sir John Barbirolli, on leave from his duties as conductor of the Hallé Orchestra of Manchester. The name of Barbirolli was well known to most American musical listeners, for in 1937, at the age of thirty-eight, he had succeeded Arturo Toscanini as head of the New York Philharmonic Orchestra. He had led that body for seven years when the radio broadcasting of fine music was at the height of its vogue. But few Americans other than New Yorkers were familiar with his work in the hall. He had left the Philharmonic in 1943 to take over the Hallé, England's oldest symphony organization, then crippled by the rigors of wartime. His labors in rebuilding that instrument, and restoring completely its prestige, had made him an extraordinary position in British music and won him a knighthood in 1949. He had returned briefly to America in the season of 1958 to conduct the Philharmonic as a guest, a reunion that proved highly impressive. The excitement resulting from that appearance had brought him on another trip to the country, and this 1959–1960 visit allowed for a short tour. There had been a great many more demands for Barbirolli by American orchestras than he had time to accept. Tom Johnson, with his canny judgment and instinct for the right moment, had made one of the bids that were taken up.

So it was that on February 1 and 2, 1960, the Gospel According to Sir John was first heard by the Houston musical public in its own hall. The evenings were to be noted in rubric, for their revelations were dramatic and spellbinding.

The texts that Barbirolli employed for the meetings were a suite of Elizabethan airs, in his own arrangement for strings and four horns, the Eighth Symphony of Ralph Vaughan Williams, Fauré's *Pelléas et Mélisande* Suite, and Debussy's *La Mer*. They were made into concerts of great beauty and poetic distinction. Many listeners declared they had never heard the orchestra play in that manner before, and in a way it was so. The effect on the Houston organization of this slight, wiry, and greatly seasoned conductor (in his sixtieth year) was indeed transforming enough. The music passed in a dreamlike way. He worked with a beat wonderfully supple and flowing; and though his direction resulted in the highest precision of execution, the memory left in this case was of exquisitely veiled colors and mysterious interchanges of shadow and light. The musical listener recognized a profoundly developed technique and a master of the orchestral palette; the rest was a matter of temperament working in mysterious ways. Barbirolli had made music of a glowing romanticism in a style of the fullest maturity.

The critical commentary was excited and grateful. In the *Post* this reviewer reported that Sir John had imparted a magnificent lesson to the orchestra at a very desirable time. Ann Holmes said in the *Chronicle* that "the thrill came back into Symphony Hall last night," and T. V. Thompson, writing in the *Press*, also declared that the evening had been "a lesson in pure beauty." The thrill was of a kind that had lately been little aroused in Houston musical quarters.

An hour or two after his second performance Barbirolli was off to continue his tour. The circuit that he and his wife, Evelyn, were making had been oddly arranged. The stop following Houston was Toronto. From there they were shuttled again to the deep South; the place this time was Atlanta. And in Atlanta they found a surprise.

This American visit of the British conductor had set off the inevitable rumors. Most of these claimed that he was ready to part with the Hallé, feeling his work there to be done, and that his second trip to the States within a couple of years was not due to his interest in the scenery alone. Tom Johnson had looked into the rumors and knew where they were false. But also he had made a few other discoveries that put his imagination to work. Nobody had studied the Barbirolli rehearsals in Houston as closely as he did. He had studied them as a musician himself, with great interest in what he saw done, but also because he enjoyed the association. The Barbirollis were frank, warm, and unassuming; between sessions of work at the Music Hall they had enjoyed chatting with an easy companion; and Tom Johnson had listened carefully to their impressions of Houston and to Barbirolli's opinions of the orchestra. By the time of the concerts an idea had begun to form in his mind, but he said nothing about it for the moment.

Barbirolli was not due in Atlanta for three weeks. In the meantime there was a meeting of the Houston society's finance committee to consider various matters of policy. It included a discussion of the conductorial situation and the question of what further could be expected of the working arrangements with Stokowski, who had spoken, if somewhat vaguely, of his intent to retire from this office. When the regular business of the committee was finished, Tom Johnson asked three of its members—General Hirsch, Gus Wortham, and Harmon Whittington—to remain, and to these friends of the movement he confided his late idea. It was a long-shot possibility, but it took firm hold of their interest. As a result, Tom Johnson was authorized to explore further by making a trip to Atlanta.

What he knew and had told his officials was that Barbirolli would never consider a break with the Hallé, to which he was deeply devoted. On the other hand, Sir John was now assuming a supervisory office in Manchester, shortening his home season and allowing himself more freedom to work elsewhere as he chose. Johnson went to present him with an invitation to spend most of that newly gained time in Houston, putting himself astride the Atlantic as conductor-in-chief of both orchestras. This dramatic plan was in the pattern of the new conductorial custom. And it could be greatly lucky for Houston. Few men in the world could be expected to follow the grand "act" of Stokowski, and the officers were agreed that Barbirolli was one of the few. Thus when the British couple arrived in Atlanta they found the Houston manager waiting, and the proposition was in due course presented. Barbirolli received it with obvious pleasure and interest. He could offer no immediate answer, which nobody had hoped for; but Tom Johnson had marshalled his arguments well and was encouraged by the conductor's line of discussion and the questions he asked about Houston. Sir John was returning directly to England. He left with a promise to consider the matter, and Johnson came home to report to the committee of three.

All this had been handled with the greatest discretion; the orchestra season went on with no hints of unusual things in the wind. Stokowski returned in mid-March and began his spring course with a miscellaneous program that ended with Beethoven's Sixth Symphony. The Pastoral was a timely reminder that the fields and wildflowers were putting forth again—and so was the grapevine, it soon proved. In late March some hint of the transactions in Atlanta had leaked out. The press began sniffing, on both sides of the water, and a few days later a story was published that Houston had made Barbirolli an offer.

The society found itself in an uncomfortable spot. It was in no position to deny the report, and thus had to explain that Stokowski had indicated a disposition to wind up his arrangement with Houston. This in turn forced the master's hand—or he seemed to feel that it did. Whatever the case, at the final concert of the season on April 4, he dramatically stepped to the footlights and announced to the audience that for reasons connected with his "personal life," the next season would be his last with the orchestra. He then led a performance of the Brahms Requiem, whose solemnities seemed fully in order. Clearly the ties between Stokowski and the Houston organization were under serious strain as the Music Hall series concluded.

The administrators, however, did not at once answer his public announcement. They expected Barbirolli to act. But Barbirolli had not said when he would make his decision, and the wait for his answer became long. In Europe again he had plunged into a heavy program of work. It made him a poor correspondent, and his agent in England seemed little disposed to advance this particular matter. Months passed and there was nothing to report to the board. Tom Johnson became increasingly fretful, and early in August, under cover of taking a brief holiday, he flew to England and surprised the conductor in London.

This gesture was another case of the right thing at the right moment; it appealed to Barbirolli's theatrical instinct. He responded by inviting his Houston friend on a picnic. While they were driving from London into the country, Johnson had a chance to present a carefully worked out plan, and eventually the moment arrived (during lunch in a Sussex field) when Barbirolli could no longer put off a decision. A week later the Houston manager was back at his post and handed over to General Hirsch and his committee a signed contract.

The announcement would have been simpler to make if Stokowski had not chosen to dramatize the idea of a farewell season. It would be an embarrassment now to center attention on another conductorial personage. Out of consideration for Stokowski's position, as well as for other practical reasons, the contract matter was kept quiet. Attention was invited instead to preparations for the 1960–1961 season, which had been planned in the usual arrangement, Stokowski having the opening and closing divisions of four concerts each, Sir Malcolm Sargent being listed for most of the others. As it happened, however, the season was not to follow its format.

Stokowski returned with full panoply, opening this farewell course on October 17 with a program that had Beethoven's *Eroica* as a centerpiece. The program books carried solicitous greetings, and all other arrangements were fitting. But three weeks later, between the second and third of Stokowski's concerts, the drama suddenly went out of this show. The society announced the appointment of Sir John Barbirolli as conductor-in-chief of the orchestra, with the start of the 1961–1962 season, and this official confirmation of all the rumors and hints struck with a powerful impact. It was as though a switch had been pulled, reversing the lighting in the Music Hall. Inevitably audience interest was directed ahead; Barbirolli became the excitement. And as usual in such cases, the public impatience to get on with the new was not entirely concealed.

Stokowski said nothing, but thereafter his manner said much. His concert of November 8 was a chilly one. He left as soon as he could for New York. Shortly before leaving he had asked the society to book a choral group in which he was interested; the request had been considered and turned down. Stokowski seemed to grow indignant about it. The result was that when he had been in New York a few days, he notified the officials that he would not return for the rest of his season. They were hardly surprised. The board's expressions of regret were formal, and Tom Johnson was left to fill a gap in the orchestra's schedule. This was cheerfully done, the season being finished by Sargent, Golschmann, Laszlo Somogyi, Georges Sebastian, and Erich Leinsdorf.

The chapter should not end thus. Stokowski's term had meant much to the orchestra, aside from the mere glow and prestige of his name. The organization had absorbed his style well, and while it was doing so, had gained a new sense of position. It had learned to live at the top of the mountain, and having become fully accustomed to that rarefied air, was left a more polished and confident body. Its coverage of new music had been considerably widened, and its stylistic facility sharpened by the volume of this rhetoric it had dealt with in five years. Stokowski had made a number of phonographic recordings with the orchestra (among them *Carmina Burana*, Shostakovich's Eleventh Symphony, Gliere's *Ilya Mourometz*, and a *Parsifal* album), and these had a certain publicity value, if the profits were otherwise modest. On the other hand he had not been of help as a touring attraction (because of his refusal to fly), and except for the records had done little to connect his name other than locally with the enterprise. He had often baffled or irritated a good share of his listeners by what he presented, but some of this irritation was healthy, and in the rest of the repertory he had made for that audience, in ways wholly his own, a great deal of very beautiful music.

His real feelings about Houston, the city itself, were never quite clear. They could not have been very inclusive. Although he appeared at a good many social affairs given by the orchestra's patrons, his visits were apt to be brief and his conversation was general. To Miss Hogg, who was often his hostess and who attended every one of his rehearsals in Houston, Stokowski seemed rather a figure of tragedy; he impressed her as "a very lonely and unhappy man." It may have been so. He made no close friends in the city. When not at work with the orchestra he had kept much to himself in his Shamrock suite, working on the transcriptions that have been his principal contributions to the great orchestral literature. If in social connections he seemed to lack warmth, it was not strange. Many a great artist, musical or otherwise, has been ironically isolated from close personal ties by the very characteristics that enabled him so easily to communicate with large masses of people. Stokowski's marriage to the Houston orchestra had been one of convenience. That being the case, both parties had perhaps got from the union everything it was possible to get. Stokowski had been paid about $150,000.

Chapter 12

The particulars of Barbirolli's contract had come out with the formal announcement. It covered a three-year term, allowing for Sir John to divide his winters about equally between the orchestras of Manchester and Houston. These facts were rather spitefully noted in some columns of the British press. The writers seemed to imply that England should be jealous about sharing her chief orchestral artists. They pretended to wonder that Barbirolli should consider "wild Texas" a working place equal in interest to the pulpits offered at home, suggesting that the motive could hardly be other than mercenary. There were efforts to find out what the conductor would be paid, and the speculations were exceedingly foolish. None of the British journalists thought of an explanation so simple and obvious as that Barbirolli had accepted one of the most attractive musical platforms in the United States, and that he had chosen this adventure for reasons perfectly clear in his character.

After all, the conductor was not so British as he might have been. Giovanni Battista Barbirolli (for so he was christened in December of 1899) was a man of rather curious blend. Son of an Italian father and a French mother, he was a native of London, born within sound of the bells of St. Mary-le-Bow and thus, among other endowments, an authentic and unalterable Cockney. He took up his father's trade as a cellist, worked where he could ("I have made music everywhere but in the streets, and I may yet do that"), and branched into conducting in the London theaters and eventually with the Scottish Symphony Orchestra. His characteristics as a leader included Italian passion, French *délicatesse*, and a British downrightness about matters of labor and craftsmanship. From Glasgow he had gone to the New York Philharmonic, bringing to that post the style of a natural and impulsive romantic.

Some American commentators were puzzled when in 1943 Barbirolli abandoned that safe, comfortable New York berth for the starved life of the Hallé and the grimness of wartime England. (Winston Churchill was likewise puzzled when he was asked to approve passage for the hometurning conductor on a British warcraft: "If he's that big a damned fool, let him come," was the prime minister's comment.) The young romantic had acted on impulse. It was a lucky hunch, and his labors in restoring the Hallé against serious odds made him a great name. After seventeen years in Manchester Barbirolli was perhaps a little tired of the routine.

In any event, his brief visit to Houston in 1960, a matter of chance, had developed into a strange sort of experience. His meeting with this orchestra had had a curious feeling of recognition and generated a quite mystical spell. Everybody who listened had felt it, and certainly Barbirolli had felt it. He could hardly have failed to remember it when the offer was made, or when Tom Johnson surprised him in England. The explanation of Barbirolli's agreement with Houston seemed thoroughly clear: the young romantic had grown into the older romantic, who was still ready to act on impulse. The apostle is led to his labor by curious means. Of course, the salary was quite handsome—if that had to be taken into consideration.

The summer passed and in September a friend of the orchestra, visiting in London, encountered the Barbirollis at a social affair. Thinking to be helpful, she asked what they would like as to living quarters in Houston. "It doesn't really matter," the brisk Evelyn replied; "we're not at all stuffy about it. Just an apartment with a fridge and a window, you know." This reflected the spirit of the new artistic administration. It was to minimize the ceremonious fuss of the medium. When the Barbirollis arrived for the season in Houston on October 11, 1961, they avoided most of the usual formalities and then seemed to have taken up residence in the Music Hall. They were there early and late. There was work to be done, and for some time the place of work was the only feature of Houston of which they appeared to take more than a momentary notice. This change of attitude was refreshing; it had been fifteen years since the orchestra had experienced such a modest approach by a podium figure of celebrity. An atmosphere of camaraderie and understanding prevailed in the hall, and it helped in large measure that Evelyn Barbirolli, a professional oboist of high skill and a person of great good humor, could enter into this beginning adventure with such relish. She knew how to be jolly in ways that made the harder rehearsals seem fun.

Barbirolli had less than a week to prepare for his opening concert. As on the previous visit, his practice sessions were models of economical method and concentration on the strict point of the matter, a technique of rehearsal that no conductor acquires without a long and greatly various labor. His manner was sympathetic and coaxing; his ardor was that of a zealot. But while his style was impulsive, his detection of error was deadly; and failure of spirit was the deep, unforgiveable sin. At the end of the week he knew the orchestra inside out, and the players recognized an authority that, although it could give painful rebuke, was essentially benevolent and thus to be trusted as having the whole interest at heart. They gave back more than respect at the union rate of respect. They began to give back their affection.

The results became beautifully evident in the concerts that inaugurated this 1961–1962 season, the orchestra's forty-eighth, on the evenings of October 16 and 17. "Sir John and Lady Barbirolli are warm, friendly individuals who like Houston and Houston people," said a welcoming note in the program book. The music was certainly of the friendliest and most benevolent kind. There was nothing in it to startle, but much to display the riches of an orchestra fully illuminated and controlled with inspired grace. The list opened with Berlioz's *Roman Carnival* Overture, followed by the intermezzo from Delius's *Fennimore and Gerda*, Kodaly's *Peacock Variations*, and the Second Symphony of Brahms. In the shorter selections the orchestra's textures were luminous; in the Brahms symphony the colors were exquisitely shaded and the poetry complete. The romantic spell that Barbirolli had produced in his first meeting with this organization was cast again, and with these concerts a wonderful ease came into the listening at the Music Hall.

The season consisted of sixteen pairs; Sir John had twelve to conduct. The first six kept him engaged through November 21, and the next morning he departed for Manchester. He took up his Hallé duties the moment he landed, put in two months of intensive work with that organization and with London ensembles, and was in Houston again for the second part of his Music Hall series beginning on February 12. There were people (including his agent) who felt that this program, attempted at sixty-two, could be nothing but a ticket to a quick physical breakdown; but except for added travel it was no great change from the pace to which Barbirolli had long been accustomed. He was not living on his nerves to the point that most people supposed. He was stronger than he looked, and this winter he found the adventure exhilarating.

While he was gone the orchestra had played under three guests— Izler Solomon (from the Indianapolis Symphony), André Kostelanetz, and Ezra Rachlin—and a fourth week of this interval was used in another way. The managements of the three principal Texas orchestras had worked out an exchange visiting plan, and the evenings of January 29 and 30 were given over to concerts by the Dallas Symphony. It came under the gingerly charge of a visiting conductor of its own, the familiar Laszlo Somogyi, and, although it was clear that this gentleman and the Dallas contingent were not welded by intuitive ties or any other kind, their efforts were politely received by the audience. (The visiting plan was not followed again.) In the other off weeks the Houston organization worked for the opera company.

Sir John's first season had a number of excellent soloists—Sidney Harth, Leonard Rose, Jacques Abram, Berl Senofsky, Gina Bachauer, and Phyllis Curtin among them. The great interest, however, was Barbirolli himself, as week by week he enchanted both players and listeners with his own order of musical necromancy. There are conductors who convert music of the greater dimension into a series of fresco paintings; the landscape is perhaps grand, charming or highly dramatic; it remains nevertheless at a distance. It has an Olympian formality. There are other conductors who, working with the same elements, give a different effect, and this difference is as though they had gone down into the beautiful fields, taking the listener along; he finds himself somehow under the trees with the warm scents of the earth and the sun patterns around him. This evocative power was the genius of Barbirolli, and the Houston public responded to him with increasing delight.

Some of this public had quarreled with the program schemes of Stokowski; there were few criticisms of Barbirolli's designs, though in fact they were not too much different from the typical lists of his predecessor. They had a fair, if not quite equal percentage of what is commonly called modern music, including the strictly contemporary. They took in about as much of the twentieth century. If the audience tolerance seemed to be higher than before, it must have been that the stranger musical styles, when they did turn up, were more judiciously set against the other material, or maybe more persuasively played. Barbarolli's first season included Bernard Herrmann's *For the Fallen* (a 1943 product of Hollywood's musical culture), Malcolm Arnold's *Tam O'Shanter* Overture (likewise the work of a movie composer), William Walton's Violin Concerto (with Senofsky), Carlisle Floyd's motherhood song cycle, *The Mystery* (with Phyllis Curtin), and Walter Piston's *Symphonic Prelude*, a work partly commissioned by the Women's Committee of the Houston society. Among more or less standard repertory selections that Barbirolli introduced to the series that winter were Bruckner's Symphony in E Major (No. 7), and Mahler's in C Minor, *The Resurrection*, which ended the course on March 19 and 20, having Frances Yeend and Elena Nikolaidi as soloists with the Chorale and University of Houston Choir.

In his second season Sir John's innovations took in the Third Piano Concerto of Bartók (with Leonard Pennario), Carl Nielsen's Fifth

Symphony, Elgar's Cello Concerto (with Marion Davies), Arnold Bax's *Tintagel*, Paul Creston's Third Symphony and Mahler's philosophical Ninth. There was a sort of novelty also in the fact that this 1962–1963 season, though it offered a dramatic production of Verdi's Requiem Mass, managed not to conclude with that famous solemnity. It ended instead with a program chiefly devoted to the full score of Ravel's *Daphnis and Chloé*, a first Houston performance of this famous creation with its choral matter included.

The lasting importance of these two seasons was the orchestra's assimilation of another strongly individual style; the characteristics of Barbirolli were stamped more and more deeply upon it. The playing had become more profound, richer, more imaginative in blend; and as this happened the truth about Barbirolli himself had become more striking. It was a very clear truth. When he played the Romantics and Impressionists with this organization well attuned to his spirit, the Music Hall had a unique value; when he worked in any style of composition whatever, the product was of rare elevation and finish. It was music that flowed with a wonderful ease and variety of coloration. No other conductor had made the orchestra sing in exactly that manner.

Barbirolli had accomplished his changes with little revision of the ensemble. He had refilled a few places and made several additions to the strings, but essentially he had worked with the organization he found. If his music had mystery, there was none as to the way in which he had heightened the executional sensitivity of the band. This had been done by intensive rehearsal and the cultivation of pride. He had won the devoted respect of the players and had given the city an inspired orchestra.

And as though to acknowledge this excellent service, one of the city's great funds was now opened to the musical cause. In 1937 Jesse H. Jones, one of the orchestra's first patrons, and his wife, Mary Gibbs Jones, had established a foundation called Houston Endowment, Inc. It had passed under the administration of John T. Jones, Jr., a nephew of Jesse, and on June 1, 1962, this gentleman paid a call on the city council of Houston bringing an offer. The foundation proposed to demolish the old City Auditorium and to erect on the same ground a magnificent hall for the city's chief theater arts. For this it was ready to spend six million dollars. The offer was a stunning surprise. It was accepted with all speed and a few months later, when the architect's first plans were submitted, the council voted to name the new structure in honor of Jesse H. Jones. Meanwhile the orchestra had few wants. All the gods seemed to be looking after its welfare.

Art is a jealous mistress, as the poets have said, and G. B. Shaw put it more bluntly by remarking that nothing makes a man so selfish as work. It has to be so with the artist, at least, and Barbirolli in Houston illustrated the maxim. Few conductors could ever have been more immersed in the business of music making itself and less concerned with the incidental affairs of the office. He was not a gregarious soul—certainly not at the hours that most people consider appropriate for the exercise of gregarious instincts. Although he had spent most of two winters in town, Houston did not know him as it had known most of its other conductors. It knew only what could be learned from his work. Of course that was a great deal, if the listener had imagination himself. To others, Barbirolli was a mystery. He did not speak at businessmen's luncheons; he did not delight ladies' committees by appearing at teas, full of drama and interesting anecdotes; he was not photographed in the act of receiving plaques, citations, honorary police whistles, and such, nor quoted in long interviews dealing with matters of very little concern to anybody. He seemed always to be in the Music Hall, completely absorbed by the musical problems of the moment.[1]

A small number of Houstonians had chances to know him in rather homelier ways. The Barbirollis had an apartment and lived simply. It was accordingly not unusual for residents of the neighborhood to encounter them in one of its stores or supermarkets, taking a distinct pleasure in shopping. But to strangers the vision could be startling.

At some time during his travels in Italy Barbirolli had impressed a musical hatmaker whose proud claim was that his father had catered to

---

[1] An instance of Sir John's rather total absorption with matters of art: After his second season in Houston he stopped off, en route to England, to conduct the New York Philharmonic. It was April and the time limit for United States income tax renditions was near. He suddenly realized this. The result was a long-distance telephone call to the Houston orchestra manager. "Tom," said Barbirolli, quite casually, "I'm doing me income tax. How much do I make in Houston?"

the great Guiseppe Verdi himself. This craftsman had conferred upon the conductor a beautifully made hat, which he attested to be an exact copy of the model Verdi had worn. It was black and expansive. Sir John was greatly attached to this headpiece, if hardly of a stature to balance the wide spread of its brim. It gave him a look about midway between that of a resurrected pre-Raphaelite painter and a Javanese rice farmer—especially confusing when the rest of the costume consisted of an old sweater and baggy gray slacks, flat sneakers with red socks, a sort of Inverness cape, and a walking stick. Even in Houston the vision of an elderly gentleman dressed in this manner and shopping for fish is a little out of the usual.

The spectacle meant two things—that Sir John had just left a rehearsal at the Music Hall and that he was his own favorite cook. In matters of food the Italian side of his temperament ruled, and those lucky enough to be invited to the Barbirollis' small parties had soon found that his talent for *culinaria* equalled his skill with the baton. He cooked in his undershirt. The parties were late, for the maestro was a poor sleeper and paid little attention to the hour; and after the coffee he enjoyed talking far into the morning with musical friends. Often his commentaries were droll. At such a gathering he explained how he prepared for his first performance of Bach's celestial B Minor Mass by memorizing the score while he was getting over an illness, and how he had since kept it in mind.

"There's quite a bit of it, you know, and it's not given every day in the year. It easily slips out of the head. But I'd bothered meself to learn all of the fugues by heart, and now every morning when I'm scrubbing me teeth I go over 'em."

"Johnny!" protested his wife.

But the revelation was worth twenty rhetorical lectures on the art of conducting. By such means is great music preserved.

As time passed, however, it was evident that the work schedule Sir John had set for himself on two continents, with no chance to relax between crossings, was a serious drain on energy. Sometimes in these winters in Houston he was bitterly tired, and sometimes he was ill. For a while he had a racking cough and a fever, but he was scornful of Tom Johnson's proposals to get a relief man.

"Don't worry yourself," he would say to the manager as he stood in the wings, very pale. "I'll be all right when I get on the box." And he always was.

Sir John had won loyalty from the orchestra by the measure in which he bestowed it. He stood ready to do anything for the "troops." At the close of his first season there remained the Dallas orchestra call to return. He had not fully recovered from his illness, and certainly knew nothing about Dallas; but he had become enough of a "Texian" to infer that a certain rivalry was involved in this cultural exchange. He would not hear of a substitute and himself went with the orchestra. In Dallas he conducted one of his most beautiful concerts, and never seemed to be prouder than when he said to the band after it ended: "I fancy we stuck up Houston's flag tonight!" That was certainly the agreement in Dallas the next day. By the end of his second season the orchestra would have followed Sir John to the moon.

He went to Europe in this summer of 1963, spending the first part with the Hallé and later conducting the great organizations of Berlin, Vienna, and Rome. Meanwhile a significant date passed for the Houston organization. On June 21 it became fifty years old. The anniversary would not be officially marked till the start of the new season in October, and Sir John spent much of the late summer in planning his third course for Houston.

While he was absent there was another dramatic reminder of time passing: the demolition of the City Auditorium began, and proved harder than anyone had expected. The building had been put up in 1910 to endure, its framework of massive steel girders and its walls thicker than those of a fortress. It was a proud old landmark, shabby though it appeared, and now it resisted the wreckers like a living thing. They fell behind with the work; it was pushed into the nights, and in the garish and flickering illumination of searchlights, with the din of destruction and laborers darkly silhouetted and gnomelike, the scene was fantastic and hellish. It suggested a compound of all the operatic cataclysms the old building had ever contained.

This project represented a scheme to transform an entire neighborhood, obliterating other venerable relics. Jones Hall would become part of a Civic Center development whose total outlay for artistic and entertainment facilities would be forty million dollars or more. It seemed that the whole city was being made over again. The ever-expanding and more complex freeway systems had turned it into a maze; and now, with its population well over a million and a quarter, people who remembered the appearance of Houston in 1940 were beginning to think of themselves as pioneers. There was hardly time to look back any more. The Nuclear Age had compressed time, and events of a week ago, swept into the past, seemed as remote as though they had occurred in another century. The drama of change was devouring, and old-timers stepped lively so as not to invite the glance of the wreckers.

In turning this point of its history the orchestra found itself with a winter "pop" venture that seemed stable. It too had resulted from enterprise shown and support furnished by the Jones interests in Houston, which included a newspaper, the *Chronicle*. In 1960 the paper had underwritten and set out to promote a series of one-dollar concerts to be given in the Coliseum, adjoining the Music Hall and providing ten thousand seats. The idea was a modification of the Summer Symphony plan which had operated for twenty years and would furnish the same order of programs. Extensively publicized by the sponsor, this experiment had begun with a concert conducted by Arthur Fiedler; the attendance was large, and two other concerts in the winter of 1960, directed by Golschmann and Malcolm Sargent, had established the idea as a hit. In each of the following seasons Barbirolli had taken one of the series.

The success of this course was in its way a profound victory for Orpheus, since the vast, noisy, barnlike building was unsuited to the needs of a fine orchestra. If the Coliseum was inviting of any concert music at all, it was that of a double brass band; when the orchestra played in this cavern it sacrificed much of its beauty, drama, and delicacy. But there is no satisfactory way for symphonic music to be played to a gathering of eight or ten thousand souls; and that being the case, the merits of this venture were doubtless equal to those of any other attempting the same thing. The concerts supplied interesting conductors and soloists, and at the date of this history the Coliseum endeavor is still popular.

Chapter 13

As a prelude to the anniversary season the orchestra's budget took its annual rise. This time it went up by $117,000 over that of the previous year, which meant that the estimated cost of the 1963–1964 season would be $715,000. As earnings could not be expected to produce more than half the amount, there was need for some $315,000 in donated support.

It was a sign of the movement's maturity that the campaign for this help was a matter of routine, carried out by a well-trained organization, and that the public of Houston in general understood the requirements of the orchestra. Thirty years of good planning and labor had gone into the making of these favorable circumstances. In 1934, Joseph S. Smith, the society's fifth president, had outlined the support pattern the orchestra would require as it grew; in the years between 1936 and 1942 his successor in office, Walter H. Walne, had done much to establish the idea that the city's business community should contribute to the symphony's upkeep. Since the end of the war, the plans urged by these leaders had been fully developed, and a visitor to Houston in 1963, looking into its cultural characteristics, would have found the setup of its orchestra movement an especially interesting study.

The administrative core of the symphony enterprise is a five-member finance committee that determines broad policy lines. The chairman of this body in 1963 was Gus S. Wortham, one of the state's most powerful financiers and executive talents, who had served since the committee was created in 1947 and in all was to spend twenty-three years in that office. It is a record unique for the venture. Mr. Wortham's contributions to the symphony cause, both material and advisory, have been vital, and the orchestra has not known a more faithful or generous friend.

At the close of each season the finance committee receives from the orchestra manager a projected budget for the season to come and, when it is approved, sets in motion the operations designed to provide for the indicated deficit. The obvious method is by solicitation of outright gifts, and the general maintenance fund campaign is undertaken in either April or May.

Under its own chairman appointed by the finance committee, the maintenance drive is in three parts. There are men's and women's divisions for the solicitation of special gifts, the first consisting of about eighty prominent business men, the second of forty or more women active in civic affairs. The third soliciting body, known simply as the women's division, is much larger in number, having four or five hundred participants. Potential subscribers whose donations would be expected to exceed one hundred dollars are assigned to the special gifts organizations; all others are canvassed by the women's division. Its members accordingly visit a great variety of firms and individuals; they will accept gifts in any sum whatever (the average number of contributions from this canvass is over 3,500), and they are spreaders of the symphony doctrine. About 20 percent of the orchestra's deficit is made up by the women's division.

The work of the two special gifts organizations is not so concentrated in time. It is carried on over the whole year, or until the required total is reached. Some extraordinary performances have been achieved by the ladies and gentlemen of these echelons; and every victory they win is a monument to the spirit of F. M. Law, who in 1945, while serving as chairman of the board, showed the way by personally taking to the downtown streets and raising fifty thousand dollars in an afternoon from his hard-headed confreres of the business world.

Harmon Whittington, serving as chairman of the fourth maintenance fund campaign, had made the plan solid in 1948 by leading his forces to a quick triumph. Other chairmen who had helped set the tradition of this office were Stanley W. Shipnes, 1949; James L. Shepherd, Jr., 1950; Max Levine, 1951; Russell L. Jolley, 1952; Robert W. Kneebone, 1953; Charles L. Bybee, beginning with 1954; W. Leland Anderson, 1955; Frank C. Smith, 1958; Leon Jaworski, 1959; William G. Farrington, 1960; and Michel T. Halbouty, 1961. Among these leaders, Charles L. Bybee was of particular note. Repeatedly called upon to take charge of the maintenance campaigns, he had directed, in addition to the one mentioned above, the efforts of 1956, 1957, and 1962; he would likewise preside over those from 1963 through 1967; a record of service that stands high in the society's list. (In 1968 Mr. Bybee was succeeded by Frank A. Watts, and Mr. Watts by Max Levine for the 1969 campaign.)

During this span there had been years when the campaign goals were not fully attained and money had to be borrowed for immediate needs, against the prospect of later donations. And there had been and would again be critical times when the movement was threatened and magnanimous friends would absorb the accrued deficits, well up into six figures, and thus give fresh life to the venture. These benefactors had never made known their assistance. For that reason a comment of General Hirsch, supplied as a note for this record, has significant meaning:

Not merely chapters, but volumes, would be required to recount the names and activities of the many individuals and organizations which have supported the Symphony movement throughout its years. However, the aid of some of them has been so great that it can truly be said the Society could not have continued without their help, not only financially but from the standpoint of inspirational encouragement and personal dedication. Outstanding among them, in addition to those mentioned at some length in this volume, are Mrs. W. S. Farish, Mr. and Mrs. Harry C. Wiess, and Mr. Gus Wortham, each of whom has given most generously of time, service, and funds, but always with the insistence that their participation be anonymous.

Others whose signal generosity must be commended are Mr. and Mrs. Leonard F. McCollum, Mr. and Mrs. H. Gardiner Symonds, Mrs. Richard M. Sheridan, née Cecil Blaffer; Mrs. Flora Isabel Johnson, Mrs. Kenneth Dale Owen, née Jane Blaffer; Col. William B. Bates, Mr. and Mrs. Oscar S. Wyatt, Jr., Judge J. A. Elkins, James A. Elkins, Jr., Alfred C. Glassell, Jr., the Humble Oil and Refining Company, and Sears Roebuck and Company.

So had the venture been nurtured, and so it continues to be.

Indispensable to the maintenance fund campaigns is the Women's Committee of the Symphony Society, which supplies part of the personnel for these annual efforts. But although it considers this its chief reason for being, the Women's Committee, with a membership of about five hundred, has an almost bewildering number of other interests and aims. There are few avenues of orchestral propaganda and service in which this body is not active. When the orchestra came to its fiftieth year, the Women's Committee was marking the twenty-sixth year of its own history. It had been organized in 1937 under the administration of Walter Walne, who took his idea from a similar auxiliary of the Boston Symphony Orchestra. Thinking of a leader for such a model in Houston, he turned to Miss Ima Hogg; the organizational meeting was held in her home and she became the committee's first chairman. Its purpose was stated in the by-laws; "To aid and assist in all feasible ways in promoting the interests of the Houston Symphony Society."

The committee found an immediate way; it began by accepting a challenge to sell $26,000 in season subscriptions for the orchestra's 1938–1939 season, which was to open the original Music Hall. Among leaders of that effort were Mmes. Walter H. Walne, C. A. Chase, W. P. Hobby, Andrew Rutter, Ralph Conselyea, Guy B. Bryan, Alston Clapp, Jr., George Bevier, W. L. Russell, J. D. Walker, and Jesse Andrews. Work of importance was likewise done by Mrs. E. G. Maclay and Mrs. John F. Grant—work that led to the linkage of this organization with the maintenance fund campaign. Ever since, the committee has shown a restless and practical energy. Apart from assistance given to the general support campaigns, its activities are chiefly related to the orchestra's student educational services, to regional promotion of the symphony cause, and to the furtherance of music appreciation in general. The committee has a large part in arranging the orchestra's student auditions, which are open not only to young musicians of Houston but also to those of the Southwest area; it sponsors an annual exhibit of student art, inspired by musical subjects; it operates a seasonal transportation service, providing conveyance for handicapped children to and from the orchestra's concerts for young people, and supplies volunteer ushers for these events.

Among other affairs, the committee arranges for the entertainment of guest artists who appear with the orchestra; it gives an annual appreciation party for the players, and arranges protocol when distinguished visitors are present in the audience. It has added to the orchestra's repertory by commissioning various new musical works, and its study groups follow closely all ideas in connection with orchestra promotion and administration. And its ladies look lovely at concerts, which also is a service to art.

The twenty-fifth anniversary of the Women's Committee had been commemorated on November 13, 1961, with a reception given in the home of Mrs. Gus S. Wortham. The observances included a handsome brochure, which Miss Hogg prefaced with the following words: "This souvenir edition is dedicated to the members of the Women's Committee and to the thousands of past members who, throughout the years, have given self-effacing and dedicated service to the fostering of a great and beautiful instrument for the enjoyment of our community, regardless of age, nationality, or faith. The true and beautiful are monuments to the spirit of man." It was the grace of the day that nearly all the fine workers to whom Miss Hogg's message referred were in attendance. The committee had much reason for joy.

Among other historical data, the brochure listed the chief administrative officials of the committee since it was formed. Miss Hogg had acted as chairman from 1937 to 1939. Other chairmen, from 1939 through 1949 (some serving for more than one year) were Mmes.

John F. Grant, J. R. Parten, Andrew E. Rutter, Aubrey Leon Carter, Stuart Sherar, Julian S. Burrows, and Paul V. Ledbetter. In 1949 the title of the chief office was changed from chairman to president. Those holding the presidency, through 1962, were Mmes. Albert P. Jones, Ben A. Calhoun, James Griffith Lawhon, Olaf La Cour Olsen, Ralph Ellis Gunn, Leon Jaworski, and Garrett R. Tucker, Jr. Since 1962 the committee presidents have been Mrs. M. T. Launius, Jr. (1963–1965), Mrs. Thompson McCleary (1965–1967), Mrs. Theodore W. Cooper (1968), Mrs. Allen Carruth (1969–1970), and Mrs. David Hannah, Jr., (1971–).

In 1946 the committee appointed its first chairman of the women's division for the maintenance fund campaign, Mrs. Charles L. Bybee. Others who have held this important responsibility, to the time of this history, are Mmes. Davis Faulkner, George E. B. Peddy, Harvin Moore, John Hamman, Jr., J. G. Lawhon, Edward L. Flowers, Jr., Proctor Thomas, Karl Hasselmann, Leon Jaworski, William T. Fleming, Jr., Garrett R. Tucker, Jr., Marvin T. Launius, Jr., R. R. Dean, William G. Bowen, R. Lee Chance, Theodore W. Cooper, Thomas H. Bearden, Edward W. Kelly, Jr., Joseph L. Levin, Fred Landry, David Hannah, Jr., and Robert B. Wall.

Each year since 1938 the Women's Committee has drawn into its membership a new company of young and intelligent spirits. They have been trained in a tradition of service that has done much to ensure the orchestra's future.

Chapter 14

When the summer of 1963 began burning itself out on the plains of south Texas, the printer for the Houston Symphony Society received a small change in his usual orders. He was handed a new cover design for the program books, which carried the superscript, "Golden Anniversary Season." The semi-centennial was now to be formally marked. In September there was a sprucing up of the Music Hall, the symphony office was hard put to take care of its reservation demands, and finally, in early October, ten days in advance of the seasonal opening, Sir John came back in his hat. There was a sort of poetic justice in this. The famous headpiece of Barbirolli, much weathered and triumphantly plain, was a suitable token of the unaffected approach to the anniversary observance. There would be no extravagant ceremonies. General Hirsch, Miss Hogg, Tom Johnson, and a brace of committees had planned the few special affairs that seemed called for. The feeling had been that an orchestra of such record should make itself heard at the center of the nation's musical life, and the season's tour had been arranged to include New York City after a visit to Washington, D.C. Under Sir John, the tour would start in mid-February and continue for three weeks, with eighteen other dates to be played. The New York concert would be the first ever presented there by a symphony orchestra from the Southwest.

Except for one feature, the home season was laid out in the usual pattern. There were sixteen concert pairs, Sir John having the first six and the last. Four visiting conductors at midseason would direct a pair each; they were Carlos Chavez, Georges Tzipine (conductor of the Victoria State Orchestra of Melbourne, Australia), Frederick Fennell, and Charles Munch. The added feature was a special program that would bring together Sir John and one of his most eminent friends of the pianistic fraternity, Artur Rubinstein—an event promptly sold out to the doors.

The season began on October 21. Letters had been sent to many early-day friends of the orchestra, now scattered to other parts of the nation or world, asking them back for the ceremony, and more than a few of them came. Invitations had also been sent to the better known music critics of the newspapers and magazines of New York, Washington, and other cities. There was not such a rate of acceptance among these, but Miles Kastendieck of the *New York Journal-American*, Harriet Johnson of the *New York Post*, and Irving Lowens of the *Washington Star* were in attendance and, from the magazines, Millie Considine of *Diplomat* and Christie Barter of *Cue*. The rest would wait to learn what they would learn. On opening night the visiting journalists and other friends of the society were entertained with a dinner given by General and Mrs. Hirsch in the Petroleum Club. It was a clear and beautiful evening and the dining hall of the club, forty stories above street level, afforded a magnificent view of the city, its myriad patterns of colored lights flung to an infinite distance.

Sir John's opening program had a rather fairy-tale quality too: it began with Elgar's *Cockaigne* Overture, followed by Ravel's *Mother Goose* Suite; the other numbers were Strauss's *Death and Transfiguration*, and Beethoven's Seventh Symphony. Perhaps the mixture was a little odd, considering the extra meaning attached to this opening—or perhaps it was perfectly right. Barbirolli was at his elegant best in this music, letting his fancy run free; and though the local criticism found the orchestra a little under its very best form, the visiting inspectors were much gratified.

Time's report of the concert offered a curious comment: "Sir John's touch has made Houston the finest orchestra in the Southwest—and, more important, a better one than Dallas."[1]

Other reporting of this anniversary season suggested that Barbirolli had extensively overhauled the Houston organization in order to bring about his results. Such writing was highly imaginative. As earlier noted Barbirolli had made few changes, adding only six players to the company. He had made his significant gifts as a teacher—an ardent perfectionist, a refiner of talent, an imparter of style in the great line. The 1963 orchestra had a complement of ninety-two players, sixty-one being strings in the disposition of sixteen first violins, fifteen second, twelve violas, ten celli, and eight basses. Though fifty years old, the orchestra was still essentially a young organization; the average age of its members was under forty. Only four players had served in it for twenty-five years or longer: its greatly resourceful concertmaster, Raphael Fliegel, Benito Alvarado and Irving Wadler, violinists, and Kittrell Reid, trumpeter. They were recognized at the fifth concert of the season, on November 18, and presented with medals by General Hirsch in a ceremony much approved by the audience. But others were still in the band who had played under Ernst Hoffmann in the days before 1940, among them Joseph Gallo, Louis de Rudder, Joseph Karcher, and Leonard Manno, all of the string ensemble. Twenty-six of the players were women, including one principal, Shirley Trepel, who headed the celli. It was not in the least a tired orchestra, but there

---

[1] But this was an interesting comment from a publication which had long seemed to delight in misrepresenting the characteristics of Houston, cultural and otherwise. One of its typical claims: that the Houston orchestra, anxious to please Hugh Roy Cullen when he was its chief sponsor, often played *Old Black Joe*, his favorite song, in its concerts. Nothing of the kind was ever done. But supposing it had been, why would the solecism have been so strange? Stephen Foster's *Old Black Joe* is now accepted as American folk music. Much of the world's great music is indebted in some way (often by direct quotation) to folk tunes which are no more authentic or respectable as music than Foster's song.

were in it enough gray heads to remind one of its respectable history. It was a proud organization.

Barbirolli had once stated his professional philosophy as follows: "The success with which the conductor inspires eagerness and willingness in the men of the orchestra (who must follow him anyway) determines the conductor's powers. The happiest relationship results when the conductor regards the men, not as employees to whom he has a right to dictate, but as co-workers, with whom he comes together for the common purpose of joyous music making. The men should be willing to follow him, not through fear or duty, but through affection and respect." These thoughts were not spoken in Houston; they were part of an interview given by Barbirolli in 1938, when he was in process of assuming full charge of the New York Philharmonic Orchestra. As a young conductor of thirty-nine, he was then stating an ideal. As a veteran of sixty-four when this anniversary season in Houston began, he had long since become fully the model of his own theory. It no longer required formal expression; it was expressed by his presence. He did indeed have the complete affection and respect of his "men."

Because that was the case, the orchestra pulled into its best form for the second concert of the season, causing many to wish it had been the first. This program began with a contemporary item, Ron Nelson's *Savannah River Holiday*, and moved on to Béla Bartók's suite of *Roumanian Dances*, Tchaikovsky's Violin Concerto, with Henryk Szeryng as soloist, and the Fifth Symphony of Shostakovich. The new music was charming; the performance by Szeryng, who was new to the audience, was one of full brilliance and character, and the orchestra's whole work was a joy. The business proper to the anniversary season had begun.

The next two programs of Barbirolli were miscellaneous and had excellent solo artists (the Gorini-Lorenzo team in Poulenc's double piano concerto and Milos Sadlo in Shostakovich's Cello Concerto), and then came a special affair. On November 18 and 19 the concerts were all Wagner, commemorating the 150th anniversary of that creative titan. They opened with the *Flying Dutchman* Overture, followed by the *Siegfried* Idyll, then offered the Prelude and "Liebestod" from

Tristan and three generous episodes from *Die Götterdämmerung*—the Rhine Journey, Funeral March, and Immolation Scene. Elinor Ross was the visiting soprano, singing with passion and high beauty the "Liebestod" and farewell of Brunnhilde, and this latter left strong in the minds of all listeners the grim vision of Valhalla collapsing.

Two days after the second performance of this program the president of the United States, John F. Kennedy, was in Houston. He came to speak at a dinner of his political party and spent the night in the city. It was his last. A few hours after he left the next morning, he was assassinated in Dallas, and with this shock a grey curtain fell over the life of the nation.

The sixth concert of the anniversary season, which has been scheduled for Monday, November 25, was postponed because the day had been designated by President Johnson as one of national mourning. The orchestra played on Tuesday and Wednesday evenings instead. Sir John had reordered the original program, placing on it, as a memorial to the late president, the calm and lovely ninth episode of Elgar's *Enigma* Variations ("Nimrod"), which in England has come to be associated with occasions of state mourning. It was introduced by the conductor as "in homage to one of the most beloved and glorious warriors in the cause of peace that the world has known." He asked the orchestra and audience to stand for some moments in silent prayer, after which, as though it grew naturally out of the stillness, Elgar's deep tribute to friendship was played with ineffable beatuy and feeling. It surprisingly closed into a drum roll, sustained, muffled, and distant, and then, with a drama that wrenched every heart in the gathering, *The Star Spangled Banner* was heard in the noblest of its own pacing and sound. There could not have been a more fitting service of its kind in the nation. It mattered little what other music was played for the evening (the chief items were Richard Strauss's *Don Quixote*, with Shirley Trepel and Wayne Crouse as the cello and viola protagonists, and Tchaikovsky's F Minor Symphony). All emotions had been drained by the prelude. These concerts were the saddest of the orchestra's history.

Carlos Chavez was a fitting choice to open the anniversary guest list. Mexico's principal orchestra chieftain had conducted the Houston ensemble at intervals almost since its beginning. He could always be counted upon to inject a contemporary element into his programs, and in that respect was in form when he presided on December 9 and 10. He gave his own transcript of a Buxtehude chaconne, Hindemith's *News of the Day* Overture, and Stravinsky's *Symphony in Three Movements*, along with Rimsky-Korsakoff's *Scheherazade*—all music to show off his high brilliance and personality as a podium artist.

A week later Georges Tzipine was a pleasant visitor, with a standard program and Jorge Bolet as soloist in Tchaikovsky's B-flat Minor Piano Concerto. Frederick Fennell brought with him another pianist, James Dick, to play Khachaturian's lively concerto, and offered Samuel Barber's *Symphony in One Movement* (movements were getting scarcer this year), among other selections. The closing concerts of the midseasonal series were delivered by Charles Munch, who conducted the Love Scene from Berlioz's *Romeo and Juliet*, Honegger's Fifth Symphony, and the César Franck symphony—a program of high finish and expressive distinction.

Honoring custom, there had also been a "gala" on New Year's Eve, with Arthur Fiedler conducting and the pianist Earl Wild in an all-Gershwin list. The hall had been filled, but this year there was little holiday spirit on either side of the footlights. It was a time of sober reflection. The young public took the orchestra for granted among the pleasures of Houston; the older public remembered how it was put there and wondered whether the younger one understood. The veterans recalled work that would never be officially celebrated. They remembered the first efforts to link the orchestra movement with the educational system of the city, and thus honored the labors of Miss Hogg, Mrs. Ray L. Dudley, Mrs. Albert P. Jones, Mrs. A. M. Tomforde, Miss Helen Saft, Miss Mildred Sage, Mrs. Aubrey Leon Carter, Mrs. Joseph S. Smith, Mrs. Walter A. Walne, Mrs. McClelland Wallace, Mrs. Robert Maroney, and many others.

The fruit of these efforts was now to be found in the splendid student concerts of the orchestra—eighteen per season, with a total attendance of more than sixty thousand from the city's elementary and high schools. For twenty years the society had given direct aid to the region's musical young: one plan was an annual competition for instrumentalists, the winner receiving a prize of two hundred dollars and the right to appear with the orchestra in a student performance. This contest had discovered the exceptional gifts of Van Cliburn, a native of Kilgore, Texas, who at nine had made his orchestral debut with the Houston ensemble. Another phase of the plan supplied scholarships providing for study with various players of the orchestra. There was much to remember in this season, and older patrons recalled, with particular warmth, the unsung labors of E. E. ("Joe") Stokes, a percussionist in the organization for many years and likewise secretary of Local 65 of the American Federation of Musicians, whose wisdom and good judgment had smoothed many a rough spot in the long road.

Meanwhile there had been another highly gratifying development. On December 13, the symphony office had announced the conclusion of a new contract with Barbirolli, which meant that Sir John would continue as conductor-in-chief for at least three more years, through the 1966–1967 season. "It has been mutually agreed that the financial terms of the contract will not be divulged by either party," the bulletin stated. But a good guess would have been that a hundred thousand dollars or more was involved.

Tom Johnson had made a second visit to England in the previous summer to work out the arrangements for this pact, which made certain significant changes in Barbirolli's relation to Houston. The society acquired a wider claim to his services, with the right to determine the number of concerts he should conduct with its own organization; the agreement further provided that henceforth Sir John's bookings as a guest conductor were to be handled exclusively through the Houston Symphony office. Although the agreement did not otherwise affect his connection with the Hallé, its meaning was emphasized by the fact that Sir John's personal agent, Kenneth Crickmore, had left England and taken up residence in Houston. As Crickmore put it, he had realized that his client had "entered on another effort of full dedication"—a rather evident fact. There had been from the first a sense of unique rightness in this union between Sir John and the Houston organization, and in the spell they produced for the audience. But the practical advantages of the situation were likewise obvious. In addition to the very handsome emolument, Houston offered Sir John every measure of understanding and official support. The working conditions could hardly have been more tempting, and the possibilities of this adventure were fascinating. General Hirsch, whose friends had long called him the Great Persuader, had used the best of his own arts to influence the conductor's decision.

When Barbirolli returned from England on January 23 to resume charge of the orchestra, the anniversary tour was uppermost in his mind. He had only four days to prepare the program that would open the second part of his season, and it was evident that he was a tired man. That was the penalty of his transatlantic commuting, and the serious strain of this double life would continue to be felt on both sides of the water, especially in opening performances. It was somewhat to be noticed in this concert, but not in the playing of its chief number, which resulted in a strange drama indeed. The work Barbirolli had chosen for the principal spot, and on which most of the rehearsal time had been spent, was the Sixth Symphony of Ralph Vaughan Williams. Although the conductor had not given his reason for this choice, no professional observer of the orchestra could be in doubt as to what he was up to.

The word *unique* is so loosely employed in this day as to have lost most of its meaning, but the Sixth Symphony of Vaughan Williams is rightly to be described as a unique and enigmatic work. Its effect is like that of no other piece in the repertory. Written in 1947, it represents the ripest maturity of a very great English composer, who was then seventy-five. Because Vaughan Williams was one of the finest musical craftsmen of the century, the expressive devices of the work are superbly designed and manipulated. But this is the craft that forgets craft. The symphony is a deeply philosophical tract, and the four movements, which are played without pause, form a drama whose spell is entirely uncanny. The last movement is the work's singular feature. It consists of one long, veiled, gradually weakening pianissimo, lasting some ten or twelve minutes. Though it gives the impression of lasting much longer,[2] it never loses its hold on the listener's attention; and becoming fainter and fainter, as thread after thread of the sound is

---

[2] After one early performance of the symphony, which he conducted, Vaughan Williams soberly thanked the ladies and gentlemen of the orchestra "for having played *pianissimo* for three hours."

abandoned, the music seems finally to vanish into infinity. Yet it is not gone; a haunting ghost of it remains. Is it a sound or a memory? One cannot be sure, for it seems to come now from a dreadful, measureless distance, as though something far greater than music had dissolved beyond any recovery. The listener is more likely to shudder than to offer immediate applause.

When the symphony was first given in London in 1948, under Sir Adrian Boult, the critics and public were left puzzled and strangely disturbed. They felt they had heard one of the most powerful art works of the century; and it was the last movement that shook them. The symphony had no "program." What then was the meaning of that section? Surely it was no expression of a personal resignation to death. The scale was too wide to suggest that. Bearing in mind the date of the work's composition—so soon after the shock of the atom bomb— both critics and public concluded that Vaughan Williams had uttered a prophecy. He was sought out by reporters and asked to explain. He refused. "Take the music for what it is," he replied. They continued to press him, however, and finally the grim old veteran referred them to a speech of Prospero in the fourth act of Shakespeare's *The Tempest*. When they went to the text they found this:

> Our revels now are ended. These our actors,
> As I foretold you, were all spirits, and
> Are melted into air, into thin air;
> And, like the baseless fabric of this vision
> The cloud-capp'd towers, the gorgeous palaces,
> The solemn temples, the great globe itself,
> Yea, all which it inherit, shall dissolve,
> And, like this insubstantial pageant faded,
> Leave not a rack behind: We are such stuff
> As dreams are made on, and our little life
> Is rounded with a sleep.

Was more program required?

Vaughan Williams lived on to compose other music, and his Eighth Symphony is dedicated to Barbirolli, whom he nominated "Glorious John" on the title page. They had long been intimate friends. But neither to Barbirolli nor anyone else did the old man ever confide more as to the meaning of his Sixth Symphony, which the public of Houston heard for the first time on January 27, 1964.

The audience that night was affected as the London public had been. It felt a mixture of fascination and unease. The rest of the program did not very much matter; it was dutifully played. But sensitive listeners, realizing what had gone into the symphony's rendition, understood that Sir John was preparing one of his chief works for the road. And they now knew what to expect.

There were three more programs to be given before the tour began. They were beautifully chosen and played. The first of these pairs, on February 3 and 4, brought Rudolf Serkin to give a masterful dramatization of Beethoven's C Minor Piano Concerto; its companions were Allen Trubitt's *Overture in D*, which had been written to commemorate the semi-centennial of Rice University in 1962; Fauré's *Pavane*, with voices from the Chorale, and the Sibelius Symphony No. 1. There was a deep and infectious joy in the making of all this music—another example of Barbirolli's regenerative powers. The week before he had seemed to be driving himself. One could hardly believe he had taken time for a good meal or a full night's sleep since arriving in town; but as always when he came back to this organization he was uplifted in spirit. Every conductor worth hearing has in him a touch of the actor's flamboyance and egoism. The more theatrical side of Sir John's nature was brought out by the special conditions of this season, and he acted with great relish the role he felt was expected by the audience.

In the next concerts Leonard Rose, the excellent cellist, performed a contemporary piece, William Schuman's *Song of Orpheus*, along with Tchaikovsky's *Variations on a Rococo Theme*; the other principal items were Brahams's Third Symphony and Ravel's *La Valse*. For the "going-away" program of February 17 and 18, Hans Richter-Haaser was the solo performer, fitly heroic, of Brahms's D Minor Piano Concerto. There was another new work, Theron Kirk's one-movement symphony, and Sir John offered a richly characteristic performance of Rimsky-Korsakoff's *Coq d'Or* Suite, the colors of it prismatic and fascinating.

These three weeks had let everyone know that he had his "troops" fully prepared. The orchestra packed for the journey and on the morning of February 19 left in a chartered plane for its longest course of concerts in other parts. Sir John had contracted to direct all twenty performances to be given, and nobody doubted that he would.

The tour led eastward to Florida (in Miami the orchestra found itself advertised jointly with a heavyweight prize fight), then north through the cities and college towns of the seaboard states. Traveling by plane, rail, or bus, the tourists arrived finally in Washington on February 29, in the teeth of a blinding snowstorm. They were met by a chattering delegation of Texans (some of them just arrived from Houston), and that afternoon the Barbirollis, the orchestra members, and these friends were entertained at a White House reception. A few hours later the orchestra played in Constitution Hall for an audience of three thousand, whose distinguished patronage included the president of the United States and his family.

After the formalities of a stage welcome and the national anthem, the program consisted of the *Corsair* Overture by Berlioz, Delius's tone poem, *In a Summer Garden*, and two symphonies, the Vaughan Williams Sixth and the Beethoven Seventh. The evening had the air of a state function, and for that reason the reporting was concerned chiefly with its social particulars. A great deal of space was expended on the listing of parties and titles, on descriptions of hair styling and splendid couture, and what was said by somebody to somebody. But in small corners of their papers the Washington music critics were heard from. They became chiefly involved with the Vaughan Williams symphony; and in attemtping to explain the effects of that mystical work, they left themselves not much time for estimating the separate qualities of the evening's conductor and orchestra. What they said was enough, however; and the orchestra had accomplished one of its principal aims. Washington was rather a warm-up.

Three days later the main point of this journey was reached. On the morning of March 3, with a little less scud in the air, the organization was set down by its busmen at New York's new Philharmonic Hall, a unit of its mounting Lincoln Center development. The building had been in use only a few weeks and in fact was not thoroughly finished. There was time for a short brush-up rehearsal before lunch; afterward the orchestra rested. Its conductor might have been expected to do likewise. But the unyielding Sir John, delighted to be again in his old haunts, made use of the afternoon for a long, leisurely stroll with his lady and Tom Johnson for company, amusing himself by window-shopping the big stores along Fifth, Madison, and Park avenues. From that pleasure he went directly to Philharmonic Hall—and to the business at hand.

The audience numbered some 2,700; again it included many a long-time friend of the orchestra. Miss Hogg was among those waiting, indomitable at eighty-one in her loyalty to the instrument she had done so much to create. General and Mrs. Hirsch were present, with a fine representation of the board and the Houston audience generally; and there were other tokens of home. But chiefly it was a New York audience—the audience that attends any concert of quality music in that city. The program was the same one that had been presented in Washington.

It is a simple story to tell. As for the New York reaction to this concert, it is best to let New York speak for itself. On the next morning, or soon thereafter, the following opinions appeared in the critical press of that city.

Alan Rich, in the *New York Herald Tribune*, under the headline "Bravo Houstonians!": "The city of Houston has every reason to be proud of its orchestra. Its sound is light, flexible, and infinitely varied. It produces a striking mass of big sound, and also produces some wonderful, clean pianissimos. It is an orchestra that can do full justice to a well-balanced and demanding program. It was an evening of triumph all the way."

Louis Biancolli, in the *New York World-Telegram*, under the headline "Sir John and His Brilliant Texans": "One of the country's major orchestras and one of the world's major conductors teamed up for a brilliant concert in Philharmonic Hall. It is a first class orchestra and it has a first class conductor in Sir John. Barbirolli returned to New York a greater and profounder interpreter than ever. As for the Houston

Symphony, which he leads so magnificently, it would be the crime of the century if it waited another fifty years before coming to New York."

Harold C. Schonberg, in the *New York Times*: "The orchestra's playing was clear and detailed. It was spirited, too. Throughout the evening it proved itself to be a responsive, well-integrated orchestra. With this kind of interpretation [of Vaughan Williams's Sixth Symphony] and the playing he drew from his orchestra, Sir John is welcome any time."

Miles Kastendieck, in the *New York Journal American*, under the headline "Texans Outstanding in Debut Here": "Celebrating its fiftieth anniversary by making its most extensive Eastern tour, the Houston Symphony Orchestra made an outstanding debut in Philharmonic Hall last night. The brilliant quality of its playing not only placed it among the major orchestras of the country, but challenged them to look to their laurels. The musicians willingly give Sir John Barbirolli incisive rhythmic response, exceptional brilliance and remarkable pianissimos. The results assure audience interest and hearty applause. Philharmonic Hall came alive with a series of stunning performances."

Harriet Johnson, in the *New York Post*, under the headline "Houston Music Captures the East": "Sir John Barbirolli of Houston, Texas, and Halle [*sic*], England, is a five foot-two volcano transplanted to the biggest state in the Union. . . . Through the seeming enjoyment and energetic relaxation of its playing, the Houstonians performed more like a European than an American orchestra. They played as if their love of music and opportunity for expressing it were more important than the job, per se. Sir John apparently gets results through being beloved, not feared by his orchestra. It is just about a unique accomplishment. The program was played to a full, enthusiastic house."

Winthrop Sargent, in the *New Yorker*: "It surprised a good many people, including me, by the brilliance and virtuosity of its playing. The orchestra shone with a sort of aggressive spit and polish seldom encountered in the older ensembles along the Eastern seaboard. The works performed made for an unusual evening of listening, and they were all done with astonishing craftsmanship by both conductor and orchestra."

Irving Kolodin, in the *Saturday Review of Literature*: "This orchestra plays not merely with assurance and enthusiasm, but also with an intelligence that reflects Barbirolli's lifelong conviction that making music should be a communal affair. . . . The mood that was sustained through the long-drawn, quiet close of the Vaughan Williams symphony made one aware that a revaluation of the relative skills of American orchestras is very much overdue. Houston, clearly, has one of the best."

There was no one else to be heard from. That was the whole of the New York critical faction; the result had been a clean sweep of respect, approval, and enthusiasm. Smiling a little, the orchestra went on to its other business.

Nine days after the New York concert it reached home. When the tourists were met at the airport by Mayor Louie Welch, General Hirsch, and a delegation of two hundred representing the chief civic and cultural organizations of Houston, Sir John's response to the greeting was typical. "I must say that I feel very proud, privileged, and honored to have returned with my troops and our mission accomplished," he said. "I cannot say I'm surprised, knowing the troops I had under my command." Then he accepted a gold key to the city, put it in his pocket, and left the rest of the ceremony to others.

No banners were run up in observation of the orchestra's victory. It had done no more than its intelligent patrons had had reason to expect it would do. But there were two more concerts in the season, and at these affairs the conductor and players were made to feel, in quite wonderful ways, the great affection and pride of the whole city. Houston is often careless about evaluating its blessings and riches, but this was not one of the cases.

Gina Bachauer was a brilliant soloist in the first of these concerts, playing Rachmaninoff's D Minor Piano Concerto on a program with Mendelssohn's *Hebrides* Overture and Dvořák's Symphony No. 4. There was still a great effort to come. On March 23 and 24, the Golden Anniversary season concluded with productions of Sir Edward Elgar's oratorio, *The Dream of Gerontius*, which gathered an exceptional company of interpreters. The vocal soloists were Kerstin Meyer, soprano, Richard Lewis, tenor, and Donald Bell, baritone; the Chorale and University of Houston Choir were again merged with remarkable drama and grace.

"This is the best of me," the devout Elgar inscribed on the final page of his score. Barbirolli was a disciple of Elgar's, and his approach to this work was completely devoted and reverent. These performances were also the best of Sir John, of an eloquent orchestra, and of all who took part in this celestial anthem of regeneration and hope.

Chapter 15

The orchestra's next two years could be summarized by the title (taken from Goethe) of a famous musical work: Calm Sea and Prosperous Voyage. They extended the spirit and graces of the festival season. They gave a sense of completeness, of solid values assured, of a tranquil advance of the enterprise. Sir John and his company made music of an ideal unity; these years were the ones of their most evenly beautiful work. Meanwhile a change came in the view from the Music Hall. Ground had been broken for Jones Hall on January 9, 1964, and during these seasons the new building took shape and was visible from the foyer of the orchestra's home.

Sir John opened the 1964–1965 season with a broad masterwork, Schubert's immortal Symphony in C Major, and closed it with another, the Beethoven Ninth. The interpretations themselves were masterful; they showed the completeness of a style. In the months between, he was much engaged with the music of his two favorite impressionists,

Ravel and Debussy, of which he seemed ever to give more graceful and searching evocations. Among the works he introduced to the series in this winter were Elgar's First Symphony, Gerald Finzi's Cello Concerto (with Shirley Trepel), Bruckner's Third Symphony, Carl Nielsen's Fourth, a *Fantasy for String Orchestra* by Elmer Schoettle of the University of Houston faculty, and Joseph Kaminski's *Israeli Sketches.* And along the way came a memorable Sibelius evening, with Francescatti as soloist. The guest conductors at midseason were Laszlo Somogyi, Georges Tzipine (for two pairs), and on December 14 and 15 a newcomer to this podium, André Previn. Previn had begun his career as a pianist and arranger of film music in Hollywood; he had there headed his own small combo, which became well known for recordings in the popular field. As a piano performer he had appeared with the Houston orchestra in a "pop" program in 1956; since branching into formal conducting in 1960 he had been back to direct "pops" of the dollar series in the Coliseum. He now made his conductorial bow to the orchestra's regular patrons, who listened politely and went home to resume preparations for Christmas. Some of them may have reflected that few orchestras of the nation were better fitted to take the measure of conductorial interest than this one. It was an efficient, sophisticated, and highly sensitive instrument; it was also one of good will. But it was not automatically brilliant. It was accustomed to the grand touch at the helm and without having that challenge to enliven it fully was apt to be a little erratic.

But in the concerts of Sir John or in others, there were many occasions for the audience, newly enthralled by the organization, to delight in the qualities of its individual workmanship. It was a time to pay tribute to such of its artists as Raphael Fliegel and his associate concertmaster, George Bennett; to the woodwind principals—Raymond Weaver, oboe; Byron Hester, flute; Richard Pickar, clarinet; and Paul Tucci, bassoon—and to many another fine hand. In James Austin the orchestra had assuredly one of the nation's best trumpet performers, a splendid musician and superb tonalist. James Tankersley headed the horns most ably, and in Shirley Trepel, the solo cellist, Wayne Crouse of the viola contingent, Philip Edley of the basses, and its major percussionists, James Simon and David Wuliger, the Houston ensemble had players of exceptional stamp.

Best of all, at this point in its history the orchestra movement was guided by greatly able and generous administrators. The cost of securing such musical qualities rose steadily (it amounted to $845,000 in 1965), and the problems of administration were multiplied proportionally as all life was becoming more expensive and complicated. There was no faltering on the part of the orchestra board; the needs were in some manner provided. General Hirsch, Gus Wortham, and their fellow executives labored to open new channels of contributed aid, and the general had a number of gratifying announcements to make in these seasons. The most pleasing from his standpoint, because it exemplified an idea he had especially advocated, was delivered at the start of the 1965–1966 season. A series of subscription performances had been endowed—the first such benefaction in the orchestra's history. The donor was Joseph Mullen of New York City, whose father had been the society's third president; the series would be known as the Nazro Memorial Concerts, in memory of Underwood Nazro, Clara Wheeler Nazro, Wheeler Nazro, and Joanna Nazro Mullen. As the printed announcement explained: "In one of the most important and significant contributions ever received by the Houston Symphony Society, Mr. Mullen has agreed to defray each year the entire cost of one of the Houston orchestra's subscription concerts, by gifts during his lifetime, and thereafter by a bequest to the society's endowment fund adequate to provide sufficient income to continue the financing of these annual performances." The first Nazro Memorial Concert was presented on October 25, 1965, Mr. and Mrs. Mullen attending.

Most of the music delivered in this 1965–1966 season was standard repertory, whether the programs were those of Sir John or the visiting conductors, who were André Previn (for two pairs), Georges Tzipine, and Jussi Jalas. All offered their dutiful gestures to contemporaneous styles; but the snippets performed, if not already familiar, were such as demanded small notice. Sir John opened his course with Satie and Villa-Lobos, and along the way paid his respects to Menotti (Violin Concerto, with Fredell Lack), Bartók (Sonata for Two Pianos and

Percussion, with Gorini-Lorenzi), Mennin, Creston, Benjamin Britten, and Samuel Barber. Previn delivered opuscules by John Williams and Ned Rorem; Jalas produced an effusion by one Joonas Kokkonen, entitled *Opus Sonorum*, in the row technique, which did something to empty the hall. A far more ingratiating novelty (never before heard in these concerts) was Richard Strauss's Oboe Concerto, with Evelyn Barbirolli delightfully serving the solo part. And Sir John furnished no grander nights with the orchestra than on November 22 and 23, when his program was all Wagner with three very good soloists (Janice Harsanyi, soprano, Kolbjorn Hoiseth, tenor, and Malcolm Smith, bass) to give the first act of *Die Walküre*, the closing scene of that opera, and parts of the finale of *Siegfried*. The season concluded, *in nomine Domini*, with a moving production of Handel's *Messiah*, soloists and choir rising to heights of rare beauty on a rich and exultant orchestral performance.

There had been only one lapse in the harmonious course of these post-anniversary seasons. As a consequence of the nation's inflated economy, labor struggles were becoming common to American orchestras, and in 1964, when a new contract with the union was pending, the pressure was felt by this one. A players' committee asked rates of increase in the pay scale which the board felt to be quite unreasonable. Though the case was a matter of simple arithmetic, the demands were insistently plied. The tone of the argument was not bitter, but it was of a kind new to this organization and was finally pressed to the point at which nothing was left but to threaten suspension of the orchestra. Nobody could face that prospect. At the critical moment common sense and good spirit prevailed; compromises were struck and the situation was saved. The talents of General Hirsch as a patient arbiter held the movement together in these difficult days, as they were to do again when a similar crisis arose in the labor negotiations of 1967. It was a gentle but a firm hand in the pilot house.

In the autumn of 1966, to mark the beginning of a new theater season, Jones Hall for the Performing Arts was presented to the public of Houston. The city thus acquired one of the handsomest structures of its kind in the nation. Though various forms were to use the hall, the principal one would be the symphony, and it thus came as a crown added to the orchestra's other rewards. The dedication took place on the afternoon of Sunday, October 2, with a simple ceremony and music supplied by the Houston All-City Symphony Orchestra, an interschool body conducted by Harry Lantz, and by the Chorale under its founding director, Alfred Urbach. The entire season, however, had been designated as a festival keyed to the hall and memorializing its donors, and the following evening the building received its first standard orchestral performance when the Houston Symphony opened its fifty-third season, Barbirolli conducting. This concert, an addition to the orchestra's regular schedule, was a premium event and, at prices of a hundred dollars for box seats and fifty for those in the parquet, had been sold out long in advance. It drew a brilliant assembly, with many visitors of note from other regions, and exciting discoveries abounded.

Sir John's program began with a work by Alan Hovhaness commissioned especially for the purpose. Entitled *Ode to the Temple of Sound*, it was a piece of some eighteen minutes' duration, rhapsodic in form, devout rather than grand, scored with the taste and delicate mystery that are characteristic of its author. The rest of the program consisted of Elgar's *Enigma* Variations, Griffes's *The White Peacock*, and the two *Daphnis and Chloé* suites of Ravel, again with the Chorale to assist.

Except for the dedicatory composition, Sir John had selected from his favorite repertory to try the new Temple of Sound, and as he guided the orchestra through its whole range of effects, from the filmiest *pianissimi* to its grandest upheavals of sound, the test was indeed fitting and thorough. It was most impressive in the evening's finale, the Ravel music. With the chorus entirely hidden in the orchestra pit, its sounds rising from nowhere to be reflected by the vastly remote dome of the auditorium, the effect was uncanny, and this music, for once, acquired precisely the other-world mystery that its author intended.

Two nights later, on October 5, the Houston Grand Opera Association took over the hall with a version of *Aïda*; and the following day (dividing the opera performances) the building was used by the visiting Joffrey Ballet troupe. At the end of a week it had been well tried as to both theatrical and acoustical qualities. Small oddities had appeared, as in every great hall of the world, but the plant's technical rating was excellent.

The public rejoiced in everything. Jones Hall was indeed a magnificent gift, striking in aspect and of the greatest luxury in all its appointments. Designed by the firm of Caudill Rowlett Scott, after the most modern theater concepts, it had cost $7,400,000, exceeding the original estimate by a million and a half. Though it seated the same number as the Music Hall, three thousand, it did not offer the intimate note of that playhouse; the emphasis here was on the spatial quality. Nothing more stressed this characteristic than the grand loftiness of the auditorium ceiling, with its floating acoustical panels; the balcony seemed nearly in heaven; and the cavernous stage had a sixty-foot span and proscenium height of over thirty feet. Above the parquet the sweep of the box gallery was stunning. An elegant green room honored the name of Edna W. Saunders, who had done so much to encourage interest in the finer theater; and a floor below the main hall were luxurious offices for the Symphony Society, the opera company, other art groups, and the hall management. There was something to be festive about as this season proceeded. Insofar as facilities for the musical forms were concerned, every reasonable thing had been done for the public of Houston.

But although the new building brought on a new surge of attendance, the society's officers had a formidable complication of cost figures to turn over in mind. Jones Hall was expensive to live in. On concert nights the officials found their enjoyment a little chilled by recollections of the latest budget projections. For that reason the next turn of events seemed providential. Soon after the start of the 1966–1967 season, the Houston society was singled out for an offer of major support by the Ford Foundation of New York, which proposed to confer on it an endowment of two million dollars, provided the society could raise an equal amount by donation within five years. Meanwhile, for that period, the foundation would make grants of a hundred thousand dollars a year to the orchestra's maintenance fund. This offer was hailed with delight and accepted. William A. Kirkland was appointed chairman of a special committee, and the work of soliciting the two million required by local gift was begun without wasted time.

Sir John gave in the new hall's first season twelve mellow and beautiful concerts. They offered examples of contemporary styles—music by Piston and Tharichen, Alban Berg and Serge Saxe, as well as some by Houston composers, Merrills Lewis especially. But mostly they honored the deep-rooted and immutable classics of the repertory, and their distinction lay in the depth and poetic completeness of the renditions. The only other conductors of this winter were André Previn, brought back for two pairs, and A. Clyde Roller, the orchestra's associate conductor, who did one.

Sir John started the last phase of his sixth season (the final term of his second contract) on January 30, 1967, and closed it on April 3 and 4 with the massive challenge of Mahler's Third Symphony, the Chorale again giving a remarkable account of itself in this work. For the most part it had been a noble and nourishing season, a fitting climax to six splendid and enlightening years. The curtain came down, and the conductor was honorably tired. Barbirolli had made up his mind well in advance of this final event; he had asked to reduce his time with the orchestra. The strain of a double artistic administration, with an ocean between, had at last taken its toll; he wished for the relative ease of guest conducting in whatever part of the world might appeal to his fancy. Nobody could better understand such a desire than the world-roamer who headed the orchestra movement, and it was to General Hirsch that Barbirolli had made known his decision.

Sadly, but proudly as well, the society met the request of a grand leader. Sir John was moved to the status of conductor emeritus; the provision was that he should return to his Houston charge for a part of each season—whatever part he desired. The first year of this arrangement would give him six pairs of the 1967–1968 series of eighteen.

The officials, however, who had not wholly anticipated this turn of affairs, were now left with a vexatious decision of their own. The obvious difficulty in parting with a conductor of full stature is how to follow the act, and new conditions had complicated the problem. It was a changing public that American orchestras now sought to attract —a result of the world's so-called population explosion. Late studies had shown that the median age of the American population was well below thirty; the scientific advice was that the young, rather than the meek, were to inherit the earth. The Houston society had taken note of a certain conductorial trend elsewhere in the nation; its officials were also much conscious of box-office reports. Their deliberations were not long, and their action surprised some of their clients. They decided to try André Previn as conductor-in-chief, giving him his first chance of the kind. He was put under a two-year contract.

Though André Previn was thirty-eight, he appeared to have an appeal for the "new youth." Born in Berlin and educated in Germany and France, he had spent most of his professional life in America. Although he had lately been a guest conductor of standard orchestras in both England and the United States, his image remained principally that of a Hollywood motion picture composer and recorder of popular music. In these roles he had become well known to the younger musical public of Houston, which had turned out in considerable force when the orchestra had him as a "pop" leader. He himself had a youthful appearance. He was small, energetic, and agile; he wore his hair long, with extravagant sideburns, after the fashion much followed by certain youth at the moment, and this seemed to have meaning for young males who showed up in the hall with necks equally shaggy. As a visitor to town Previn had favored the haunts of the "mod" set, and there was small reason to doubt that in those quarters he was fully approved.

The orchestra management had other reasons for wishing to experiment with a younger conductor at this time. One of these grew out of the difficulties of touring. The spring journeys to other regions had become increasingly necessary in order to build up revenue, the competition for such bookings was increasingly keen, and in this scramble for dates the Houston organization had too often been under a handicap. For, although it had had status conductors since the days when Efrem Kurtz was in charge, it had rarely been in the position to send its regular leaders on tour. Except for Barbirolli, they had all refused to assume the full drudgery of travel, and Barbirolli had worn himself out at the grind. On the other hand, booking committees in the smaller communities, finding the orchestra more and more costly, were beginning to resist the custom of podium substitutes. If they were to help pay for the upkeep of the orchestra, they demanded to be given the whole package. More than most orchestras traveling the university circuits, the Houston needed a resident conductor able and willing to stand the strain of touring. Previn might furnish the answer. The opportunity to make a name for himself in his first conductorial post would be incentive enough, his youth should supply the enthusiasm required, and with his characteristics and professional background he should appeal to the general collegiate public as he apparently had to the local young. That had certainly been one of the considerations in taking him on. In any case, his appointment had been a gesture to youth.

The society's main public was not ready to make up its mind about Previn at once. That would have to be done in the hall. Though most of this public had heard him at least once as a guest of the organization, the more judicious subscribers now felt they knew little about him. Some thought it strange that at this point in its history the orchestra should be placed under a man who himself was not fully established in the symphony field. But these patrons were willing enough to be convinced that the policy move was a good one. Meanwhile there was a summer to get through. Previn spent it in California and elsewhere. He arrived back with just time to prepare for the start of the new season, and on October 2, 1967, he inaugurated the orchestra's fifty-fourth series by conducting a program of Brahms's *Academic Festival Overture*, William Schuman's Third Symphony (a 1941 composition), and the Beethoven Fifth. There was an excellent audience in Jones Hall, and this selective assembly, having rendered the indicated gestures of welcome, began the more critical study of André Previn.

The season of eighteen pairs was arranged in the usual pattern. Previn had the first eight, guest conductors would take over in midwinter, and he would return to direct the pair closing the season in April. The design of his first program was the one he would follow throughout. Each of his evenings was divided, as exactly as possible, between traditional music and the present-day styles of the art, with a careful avoidance of the too freakish or traumatic in the modern experiments. The scheme was an effort to gratify both sides of the musical house; it was the sort of approach to be expected of any ambitious conductor attempting to get on with a new public.

André Previn began with the more than generous blessings of the local press, which for some reason had chosen to treat him, before his arrival, not as a talent yet to be tested, but as if he were already a brilliant and established authority. The implication had been that he was making a quite gracious concession in accepting the post, and that not Previn himself, but the musical public of Houston would be on trial. The two critics now reporting the orchestra—Ann Holmes of the *Chronicle*, and Carl Cunningham, lately installed by the *Post*—were hardly exempt from this chimera in dealing with Previn's early performances, and altogether there was much passionate beating of wings in the journals. But that state of emotion was hardly repeated in the auditorium. Contrary to hopes, the Previn occasions were not stormed by the public, and as the season progressed the signs of indifference became plainer. There was a box-office decline, and it threw into question one theory upon which the society had made its experiment. Clearly there had been no great rush by the young as a consequence of the new podium rule. What appeared as a more embarrassing symptom, however, was a falling off in attendance by the orchestra's more settled and habitual patrons. Many of these were not making full use of their memberships, and empty seats measured the losses.

If this embarrassed or disappointed the management, the management had no right to complain; and there was certainly no mention of these matters to Previn himself. He might have thought to ask how the box-office was going (older and far more noted conductors had been known to do so, as a means of directing their own effort), but he was not obligated to show that form of concern. The stage was his province to handle; he did as he wished to do with the orchestra—or what he found himself able to do. He was clever, facile, or possibly brash, and he had supporters for whom these qualifications were enough. Among the more seasoned adherents of the art and of this particular orchestra, some felt they had been asked to accept a rather superficial order of music making, and these were the ones who had fallen away. When the season passed into the hands of guest conductors in January (they were all men of an ample artistic estate, Ernest Ansermet, Charles

Munch, and Barbirolli), the audience traffic at Jones Hall became nearer to normal again.

Previn was gone for four months. He spent part of this time with the London Symphony Orchestra and during his visit was named principal conductor of that organization, a cooperative endeavor. The arrangement was supposed to fit in with his obligation to Houston and thus give him a transatlantic commuting life similar to the one Barbirolli had led. He was back to finish the season on April 15 and 16, which he did with a program of Prokofieff, Benjamin Britten, and Brahms. Two days later the orchestra started its tour. It would again be on the road for three weeks, with visits to Washington, D.C., and New York.

The tour might at least have been a pleasant conclusion to an otherwise unexceptional season, but Previn returned in no humor to enjoy the experience. Whatever the reason, he now developed a temperamental afflatus of his own, which caused him to take a grudging or condescending approach to the journey. He was severely critical of some of its planning, especially the bus travel required, and implied that, except for its principal dates, the trip was a labor unworthy of his talents or time. As it turned out, this was ironic. The small towns on the route liked Previn and gave him enthusiastic reviews. In Washington the critics were no more than polite, and in New York he was soundly shelled by some of the press as a minor conductor who had put on a pretentious and quite tedious evening.

Although the home series was over, a pendant had been added that kept the conductor in town through the middle of May. It consisted of four concerts for young people, sponsored by Foley's department store, the program being split between the orchestra proper and a jazz combo with Previn as pianist. These "pops" were delivered in Jones Hall; there was a satisfactory attendance, and so the first season of Previn arrived at its ambiguous close.

Whether or not he had been prudent in criticizing the tour, there was no official reaction, and he was free to make plans for the season ahead, which he did between summer engagements with the London Symphony and other organizations. Meanwhile the Houston management booked four podium guests for the 1968–1969 series and, as all were composers of considerable note who could be expected to give some of their time to their own music, the season was assured of a strongly contemporary character. The composers were Sir William Walton, Morton Gould, Carlos Chavez, and Aaron Copland. Barbirolli would be back to conduct two concert pairs, and one was assigned to Clyde Roller. When the repertory was chosen, twenty of its fifty-five items represented the post-Mahlerian styles. Previn had twelve of these for himself.

But before the summer was over, Previn's personal manager, a New York agent, paid a visit to Tom Johnson to ask for certain revisions of Previn's contract. The conductor petitioned for an increase of his salary and a wider artistic authority, including the right to select the orchestra's soloists and guest conductors, as well as the repertory they were to give. The money request was rejected by the executive committee. With Previn's other demand, however, the society compromised to the point of conceding that the orchestra's guests and their repertory should be chosen by joint agreement of the conductor and management. This was a matter of formalization rather than a policy change, since that had been the usual procedure in past years.

A few weeks later Previn returned for his second season. This began on September 30, 1968, when he conducted a program of Weber's *Euryanthe* Overture, Walter Piston's Sixth Symphony, and Schubert's Ninth. He was cordially welcomed back to his duties by General Hirsch, whose remarks in advance of the concert included two other gratifying announcements. One was of an annual Young Artists' Competition to be held under the society's supervision, with generous cash prizes. The project would be endowed by a Houston corporation, Pennzoil United, through the efforts of its board chairman and president, J. Hugh Liedtke and William C. Liedtke, Jr. The other announcement was of a major gift from the Moody Foundation of Galveston, providing for two concerts yearly to be given by the orchestra in that city.

These were happy reminders of the symphony's status as it entered its fifty-fifth season. More and more it was considered a regional treasure. Its home public was very conscious of this on the evening that opened the 1968–1969 course, and André Previn was in a splendid position to benefit. Few conductors of American orchestras had before them a greater variety of opportunities.

His program designs for this season repeated the patterns of his earlier series. There was a sufficient mixture of styles. In his second concert he contrasted the music of William Schuman with that of Tchaikovsky and Rachmaninoff; in his third he got around to the Polish composer Penderecki, rated the leader of the hour among tonal experimenters, whose threnody, *To the Victims of Hiroshima,* was played. Some of the other items delivered by Previn were new to these concerts, and in most cases he found his novelty efforts well received by the critics and most of the house. On the other hand, this season presented the same audience problem that had haunted the previous series. In midwinter the management reported average attendance to be running about seven hundred per concert under the orchestra's normal, and the first of the guest conductors (Walton and Gould) did little to better the situation. The islands of vacancy in the hall were becoming a major concern.

There was a small episode in the Hollywood key. The presiding conductor had a wife and two children in California, the children being by a previous marriage. Mrs. Previn, a song writer, had come with him for part of his first season in Houston. She did not appear for the second. Shortly after it started, however, another Hollywood lady made a somewhat splashy appearance in town. This was the young cinema actress, Mia Farrow, lately divorced from Frank Sinatra. She became a frequenter of Jones Hall and the much-noticed companion of Previn.

As they went about over the city, they were often conspicuous because of their dress. No model of conventional Hollywood glamor, Miss Farrow appeared in the fashions esteemed by the "flower children" of California; the conductor was apt to wear faded blue jeans, an old sweater, and sandals without socks. The gossip columns were thus offered a feast, and took to it with relish, keeping a close record of the comings and goings of the couple, including an instance in which they were refused service by a fashionable restaurant because at the dinner hour they were barefooted. Photographers added their work to the journalistic melange, and loose tongues were invited to wag. A news magazine called the affair "a mad mod romance"; to other observers it seemed rather a clownish display.[1] Whatever the case, the Symphony Society looked on and was not flattered by the type of publicity generated.

Previn's ambitions in his Houston position had never been very clearly defined. But he made a point of his disrelish for the orchestra's method of touring. It had been his main theme when he went before the executive committee in September to discuss some of his ideas; he was quoted as having told the committee that these journeys, which took the organization to numerous small towns, were "artistically degrading" and backward. His recommendation was that the orchestra be sent only to the principal cities of the country or the musical centers of Europe. When he was reminded that such a policy would be very expensive, he replied that it need not be so; with proper planning, he argued, such tours could well pay for themselves. "I'm willing to stake my career on that," he had somewhat grandiosely concluded.

By such strictures the conductor seemed bent upon producing a contest of authority. The touring plan was the work of the orchestra's manager, Tom Johnson, who could properly feel that his judgment in such matters was a good deal riper than that of the podium occupant. Previn's attitude put something of a strain on relations at Jones Hall, but nothing was officially made of the situation, as further developments showed. He finished the first part of his season on December 3 with a program including a symphony by Oliver Knussen (a semi-twelve toner) and Stravinsky's *Symphony of Psalms* as the main items. He was then free until March, and he departed at once for New York. Four days after he left Houston, the society announced an offer to reengage Previn for two more seasons, with the title of musical director added to that of conductor-in-chief, implying a somewhat fuller artistic authority.

There was no immediate answer from Previn. The season proceeded under its podium guests, one of whom, the young Israeli conductor, Daniel Barenboim, made a brilliant impression in a program built

---

[1] The association continued. In February, 1970, Miss Farrow bore twins in London, and Previn, who had acknowledged the paternity, indicated he would seek a divorce from his wife, Dory.

around Beethoven's *Eroica* Symphony and Elgar's Cello Concerto with Jacqueline Du Pré (the conductor's wife) as the solo artist. Carlos Chavez and Aaron Copland took over in order, performing their own works for the most part, and Sir John returned for two programs, the memorable one being another production of Mahler's *Resurrection* Symphony. The series was pointing toward its close.

In late February there was still no indication from Previn regarding the contract, which remained in the hands of his New York agent, Ronald Wilford. Tom Johnson wrote Wilford to ask why there had been no action. The answer had a tone of complaint. Wilford wrote that he himself had held up the negotiations, and then added, "I have now become aware of a serious lack of communication between you and André, and unless this is cleared up, I don't see much reason for any agreement." This lamentation was hardly intended for the eyes of the manager alone. It could be expected that the letter would go before the directors, with its implication that somehow Previn was being willfully hindered. Then came another objection.

Among plans for the 1969–1970 season, the symphony office had booked a short, warm-up tour for the orchestra in advance of the regular opening. It consisted of concerts to be given in four neighboring towns—Clear Lake City, Baytown, Bryan, and Galveston. The bookings had been made before Previn departed, with the understanding that he was to conduct the performances. He now asked to be relieved of the duty, since the dates for these concerts, September 15 to 19, conflicted with those chosen for the opening of the London Symphony's season, which he had also agreed to conduct. He suggested that the Houston engagements be either rearranged or cancelled, indicating that he considered the tour project of very minor importance in any case.

The society was not of a disposition to argue that point, but neither was it inclined to have its policy dictated by the conductor. It had its own contracts with the four towns to consider, and these promised the orchestra with its titular chief. There was no reason why Houston should be expected to defer to Previn's London employers. He was notified by letter that he would be expected to keep the Houston commitments. This brought no immediate answer, and meanwhile there was no further communication concerning the new conductorial contract.

There were two more subscription concerts of the 1968–1969 series, and in late March Previn returned to conduct these. A curious situation prevailed. He did not report his arrival to Tom Johnson and largely avoided contact with the manager while the programs were under rehearsal. The last concerts were given on April 7 and 8, and two days later the orchestra was to leave for its spring tour. Tom Johnson would not be making the trip. He had kept his door open while the preparations were made, but the conductor had not called to discuss either the tour itself or the contract offer that had been in his hands for four months. A communication gap of a kind was indeed in effect.

The tour was made under the supervision of Carl Fasshauer, a managerial aide. There was the usual amount of bus travel. At various points there were concerts to present in what Previn had designated as "toilet towns," and as this duty appeared to bring on him so great a distress, the journey was hardly of high spirit. In Green Bay, Wisconsin, he missed an appearance, reporting himself ill, and Clyde Roller was flown in to deliver the concert. Previn had gone off to New York.

Meanwhile, in mid-April there had been a meeting of the executive committee to examine the results of the season and the orchestra's position and outlook. The directors reconsidered their bargain. As a consequence Tom Johnson was sent to New York to meet the orchestra when it arrived for its concert. He heard the performance in Philharmonic Hall on the evening of April 30; the next morning he delivered a message to Previn's agent. It was in the form of a letter from General Hirsch, fully detailed, stating that the Symphony Society did not wish to continue its association with Previn beyond the end of his seasonal duties in May. The principal reasons given were the loss of attendance at concerts and the fact that Previn's other connections, the London post in particular, conflicted with his obligations in Houston. There were other objections, but of these little was said.

The society would not quickly award its conductorial title again. An all-guest season had been voted for 1969–1970, and arrangements for this had been started before Johnson set out for New York. When the plan was complete it represented another considerable gesture to the younger conductors: Antonio de Almeida, forty-one and the former head of the Stuttgart Philharmonic Orchestra, was appointed principal guest, with six of the season's pairs to deliver. In addition to the usual programs assigned to Sir John and Clyde Roller, the leadership would be shared by Jussi Jalas, Hans Schwieger, Sixten Ehrling, and Hans Schmidt-Isserstedt, with Schwieger to take the organization on the 1970 spring tour. There was one other change in the operating arrangements for 1969–1970—a series of ten matinee concerts to be given on Sunday, the programs of which would be the same as for the night occasions of the following Monday and Tuesday.

The release of this plan by the symphony office coincided with the reappearance of Previn, who came back from New York for the purpose of conducting a concert on May 16, presenting the winners of the Young Artists' Competition, and four "pops" of the Foley's series extending through May 23. He now chose to declare in the press that he had been "inhumanly" treated and "fired" by a group of archaic administrators. The society pointed out that as Previn had not signed the contract he was offered, there had been no job to be fired from.

The conductor had no answer to that, but certain echoes of this argument lingered on to be heard in another context. The time had come for renewal of the players' contract, and the union made stringent demands, calling for a pay season of fifty-two weeks, as against forty-three under the old contract, and stipulating a three-year term. When this bid was rejected as wholly infeasible, the union took its turn at belaboring Tom Johnson, repeating the Previn charges of noncommunication on the part of the manager. It was not the manager, however, but his executive chiefs who had spoken. Their counter-offer to the players was a three-year contract graduating from forty-three weeks in the first to forty-seven in the third, with base pay rising by similar steps from $200 to $220 a week. The union rejected this offer, and the argument ended in a deadlock. General Hirsch had announced the society's position as "adamant." "There is no reason for further negotiations," he had told the musicians' committee on May 5. "There are no more plums. I honestly think we should perhaps just close down the Symphony. The struggle to raise money is too great."

Such was the climate in which the "pop" series had been given.

When it ended on May 23, so did the union contract. Legally, the orchestra was out of existence. No arrangements had been made for the start of the summer series at Miller Theater in June, and the city government, anticipating a possible suspension of the orchestra, held back its accustomed appropriation of $100,000 for that purpose. These were sobering thoughts for all parties, and the atmosphere became gloomy indeed. General Hirsch left town for a weekend, with the parting remark that if the union had any further communication to make, he would be in his office on Monday morning. When he arrived he was met by a musicians' committee. An hour later the society was happy to announce the acceptance of a compromise plan—a two-year contract that included the features of its own offer. All other things then fell into place and the business of music-making proceeded.

This summer of 1969 brought another reminder of Hugh Roy Cullen's devotion to the orchestra movement and the cultural wellbeing of Houston. It came in the form of a substantial gift from the Cullen Foundation to the society's endowment fund; the purpose was to establish a series of concerts in memory of Roy and Lillie Cullen, and of their daughter, Mrs. Agnes Cullen Arnold.

Chapter 16

The Houston orchestra's fifty-sixth season had extra-musical drama from the outset. It began on the evening of September 22, 1969, with Antonio de Almeida conducting before a brilliant assembly in Jones Hall. This inaugural concert was dedicated to the men of another adventurous enterprise largely generated in Houston: it honored the American astronauts whose collective efforts had landed the first men on the moon. Several members of space teams were the guests of Miss Ima Hogg in her box. It may have struck some of the audience as a curious thing that the music of Haydn and Schubert, so richly evoking the attitudes of the late eighteenth century, should find itself linked with the staggering wonder of moon travel. But nobody was startled; Houston is accustomed to paradox. More comment was undoubtedly spent on the visiting conductor, who was strikingly handsome, and on his style with the orchestra, pleasant if not greatly commanding. Older patrons, beginning this course of music, could dream a little and ask themselves what was ahead. Life had much changed in the period covered by this venture; the times had never before seemed as uncertain, distracting, or deeply disturbed. Traditional values, including those served by the cultured theater, were being bitterly challenged or ridiculed, and discord was the atmosphere of the day. In the social turmoil of the 1960's the nation's art movements had suffered. Most American symphony orchestras were in difficult straits. There was no reason to assume that the institution of the symphony orchestra, a cultural heritage from the Age of Reason, was necessarily assured for the future. The old patrons, if they were distressed by the outlook, could at least feel they had kept the faith well and that the Houston endeavor was in better condition than most.

In October of this season one of England's best symphony organizations, the Royal Philharmonic of London, was on a tour of the United States and paid a visit to Jones Hall for a concert. General Hirsch and most members of the Houston society's board of directors attended. The special interest, in their case, was that the orchestra was traveling not with a British conductor, but under the direction of a young American artist, Lawrence Foster. They had heard about Foster, who was twenty-eight. A native of Los Angeles, he had done most of his musical study in this country, had completed his training in Europe, and after brilliant achievements had gone on to become principal guest conductor of the Royal Philharmonic. His performance in Houston supported the fine things that had been written about him. He made a vivid impression on the audience, including the critics and the Houston society's delegates, who would keep this meeting in mind.

Meanwhile there was another change in the orchestra's line of administrators. In early December, when the society's annual meeting was closely at hand, General Hirsch asked to be relieved of the presidency. He had held it for fourteen years. They had been the most eventful and rewarding of the orchestra's history; their burdens had also been the most onerous and wearing. The society's debt to the general could hardly be measured. When the method of acknowledgment was decided upon, the other officers felt it would best come at the end of the season.

The board's immediate action was to call upon one of its most noted and widely experienced members, Dr. Charles F. Jones, president of the Humble Oil and Refining Company, to take over the society's leadership. The willingness of Dr. Jones to accept the responsibility, notwithstanding the already heavy demands on his energies, was further significant evidence of the status held by the orchestra movement at this point in its history. Again the policies of the organization would reflect the ideas of a brillint mind and a broadly humanitarian spirit.

The regular season concluded in April, and on May 12, 1970, the transfer of authority was recognized in a ceremony both splendid and touching. A banquet was given in honor of General Hirsch at the Shamrock-Hilton Hotel. More than seven hundred friends of the Symphony Society were present, including not a few who had seen the beginning of this venture. Miss Hogg, Gus S. Wortham, and Dr. Jones were the hosts who paid eloquent tribute to the "man of all seasons" who had given so greatly of himself and his means to the orchestra cause. Mr. Wortham read proudly the formal scroll which attested that the Houston Symphony Society had in gratitude conferred upon Maurice Hirsch the title of president emeritus. The general's response was in character—vivacious, witty, and charming. But although he avoided the sentimental and solemn, he contrived to let everyone know that whatever his title might happen to be, his work for the movement was not over. That was what they had wanted to hear. Altogether the evening was one of warm memories and gratifications, as affecting as a mellow and beautiful concert.

A little more than a month later a great blow fell. In his new office of conductor emeritus, Sir John had returned for two programs of the 1969–1970 series. The first had been given on November 23, 24, and 25, with Handel's Concerto Grosso in B-flat and Carl Nielsen's Fifth Symphony as the orchestral selections, and Lili Kraus as soloist in Beethoven's G Major Piano Concerto. The second program, delivered on November 30, December 1 and 2, was all Berlioz, beginning with *Harold in Italy* (which again had Wayne Crouse as the viola soloist) and closing with the *Symphonie Fantastique*. This occasion had a double anniversary significance: it observed the centennial of the passing of Hector Berlioz; it also included the birthday of Sir John himself, who became seventy on December 2. That anniversary had already been officially noted in England, Queen Elizabeth having added to Barbirolli's other distinctions the title of Companion of Honor. The program book happily mentioned the citation. Sir John was delighted to be in Houston again. The Berlioz evening was among his grandest deliveries with this organization he loved.

He was scheduled to return in February for two more weeks with the orchestra. But that meeting was not to occur. In midwinter Sir John was ill—too ill to persuade his physicians in England that he was able to travel. He had to cancel his Houston commitment, and the two programs were turned over to substitutes hastily chosen—Julius Rudel and Sixten Ehrling. The public that heard them was anxious. But a little later the news seemed to be better; Sir John was reported to be working again in Manchester and London, which allayed some of the Houston misgivings. He continued to work through the spring and on into the summer. But on July 28 the song ended. Death struck down one of England's most illustrious musical artists. It came while he was rehearsing the London Philharmonic Orchestra, which he was to have led on a tour of Japan. Gallant John! He had worn himself out in the service of beauty, a perfectionist spirit to the end. He was a unique character, a man of great courage and heart. Born into a quieter, more mannered, and orderly world, he had lived by the ideals of his own epoch. He was one of the world's last masters of romantic style in the musical form.

When the Houston orchestra movement had absorbed this shock, plans for the 1970–1971 season were somewhat changed and the season was advertised as an open competition for the leadership of the orchestra. Every conductor who appeared would be a candidate for the post—or so the public was advised in a booklet sent out by the symphony office. The brochure further announced that the board of directors, in considering the various talents on trial, would use audience attitudes as a primary source of judgment. The season was allotted to seven conductors, one of whom, A. Clyde Roller, was already the orchestra's associate leader. The others were Andre Vandernoot, Georg Semkow, Antonio de Almeida, Lawrence Foster, Hans Schmidt-Isserstedt, and Maurice Handford. Foster and Almeida were assigned four programs apiece; Vandernoot received three; the others two each, or a single performance.

While it lasted, the competition was lively indeed, for all these men were remarkably able and the ones who came early were throbbing with ambition and ideas. Vandernoot, from Brussels, surprised the audience by making his first concert largely a chamber recital, in order to show off his exquisite control of small groups and his rare coloristic finesse. Then he engaged the more massive romantics with great impulse. Semkow, a handsome Polish authority, gave the image of an iron disciplinarian; his chief bids were heroic performances of symphonies by Tchaikovsky and Scriabin. Lawrence Foster and Almeida divided the concerts left in the season's first half with a somewhat comic result. When the season arrived at that divisional point, with three competitors still unheard from, the contest was declared to be over.

Lawrence Foster had scored another major success in this hall, comparable with the one he had made on his visit with the Royal Philharmonic. In his first appearances with the Houston organization, which began on October 19 and continued through October 27, he had handled the orchestra beautifully. His programs had included the music of Prokofieff, Weber, Haydn, Elgar, Vaughan Williams, and other composers, and in all these styles he had shown easy and graceful assurance. His work had expressed a personality that was fresh, vigorous, and ingratiating; his personal style was all business, applied without podium quackery or brashness. The excitement it generated was real. He had won remarkable praise from the critics and did indeed seem to be the audience favorite as well, though perhaps the society read into the audience plaudits of this season what it wanted to find. From the start it had been clear that official sentiment leaned strongly to Foster— a revival of that yearning, long felt in the board room, for a young American genius appointed by destiny to lead the orchestra into its full glory. Whatever the case, the officials decided that no further deliberations were necessary. On December 12 the society's new president put an end to suspense in the podium contest by announcing that Lawrence Foster would be the orchestra's next conductor-in-chief. At twenty-nine, he was the youngest man ever entrusted with the leadership. On March 10, Foster was put under contract for three years. After the 1971–1972 season, he would carry the title of music director as well as that of conductor-in-chief.

One of the novelties that went into the closing phase of this 1970–1971 season, attracting a notable audience, was a sentimental gesture on the part of the Symphony Society. Some thought it was long overdue. The society brought back, for the first time in its history, one of its former resident conductors as a guest. Efrem Kurtz flew over from Switzerland to conduct for two evenings, March 15 and 16, the organization that he had done much to establish. It was a happy reunion, with most of the old cult present in its brightest regalia and spirit. Nor was Kurtz a disappointment to these loyal admirers of smartness. In the neighborhood of seventy, he was the same polished, immaculate, debonair figure, the same striking theatrical grandee, who had handled the orchestra twenty-odd years before. He was made to feel welcome in beautiful ways, and great beauty he gave back in a program that included Albert Roussel's Third Symphony and Chausson's little known *Poeme de l'Amour et de la Mer*, with Kerstin Meyer the excellent singer in the latter work. The party given for Kurtz after the final performance, in the home of Mrs. McClelland Wallace, was itself a *poeme d'amour* between the conductor and his former employers, for all the differences they had once had were forgotten amid greetings both happy and tearful.

There is no satisfactory way to conclude any history unless it is that of a dead venture. Then at least a stopping point is arbitrarily set for the writer, and a summing up of the story is possible. With living history he will ever be tempted to continue the record until his fingers are mashed in the printing press. Since the Houston Symphony Society is alive, active, and changing at the hour of this writing, two additional notes must suffice to bring the present account to an end. They seem appropriate because both are reflections of this venture's position and continuing growth.

On June 6, 1971, the society concluded a new two-year contract with the players' union, giving the musicians a full-year working arrangement, 52 weeks of employment instead of the 45-week season they had had under the previous contract. This meant that the minimum annual salary would be $10,400. Five weeks of vacation time were provided under the plan, and other benefits were included.

The second incident was of major importance from the standpoint of the society's welfare. On June 30, 1971, the last possible day and indeed almost the last possible hour, the society qualified for the grant of two million dollars which the Ford Foundation had offered it five years before. The condition had been that the Houston organization raise an equal amount by donation within the period specified. William A. Kirkland had performed a distinguished service for the orchestra by leading his solicitation committee to victory; they had raised $175,000 on the last day of the effort. Including gifts already made, the society now had within sight an endowment fund of some $4,250,000. The orchestra's budget for the 1971–1972 season was $1,743,192.

Thus did the enterprise stand at the mid-point of its fifty-eighth year. Having founded it well, the directors could await the next turn of the story with confidence.

APPENDIX

For its first full season of concerts, 1913–1914, the Houston Symphony Association had 138 guarantors, who pledged a minimum of $25 each in underwriting. They were listed as follows in the program book:

Mrs. Wm. Abbey
Mrs. J. L. Autrey
Mr. R. L. Autrey
Mrs. Frank Andrews
Mr. Lewis Anderson
Mrs. B. F. Bonner
Mrs. J. S. Bonner
Mrs. James A. Baker
Mrs. D. Burnett
Mr. Frantz Brogniez
Mrs. Bettie Bryan
Mr. R. E. L. Brooks
Mr. Gustav Berau
Mrs. Lucy Boyles
Mr. E. T. Barden
Mr. R. L. Blaffer
Mr. Bennie Brown
Mr. Chas. Boedeker
Mr. Julien P. Blitz
Mr. Bassett Blakely
Mr. Craig Belk
Mr. Geo. M. Bailey
Mrs. R. L. Cox
Mrs. S. F. Carter
Mrs. J. P. Carter
Mr. L. A. Carlton
Mr. Ennis Cargill
Mrs. W. B. Chew

Mr. J. S. Cullinan
Mr. D. B. Cherry
Mr. A. S. Cleveland
Mr. Jas. Crow
Mr. J. W. Carter
Mrs. J. T. Crotty
Mr. O. S. Carlton
Mrs. R. C. Duff
Mrs. T. J. Donoghue
Mr. F. F. Dearing
Mr. Lynch Davidson
Mr. S. B. Dabney
Mr. Jas. D. Dawson
Mrs. Amanda Dunlay
Mrs. H. R. Eldridge
Mr. Howard Figg
Mr. Henry S. Fox
Mr. R. M. Farrar
Dr. J. H. Foster
Mrs. H. B. Fall
Foley Brothers
Miss Blanche Foley
Mr. M. E. Foster
Mr. C. F. Franks
Mr. J. L. Freed
Dr. J. P. Gibbs
Mr. W. H. Gill
Mr. H. M. Garwood

Mrs. Fannie S. Green
Mrs. J. S. Goldman
Mrs. Jules Hirsch
Mr. Hugh Hamilton
Mr. W. C. Hogg
Miss Ima Hogg
Prof. P. W. Horn
Mrs. Pearl R. Hudson
Mr. H. T. Huffmaster
Mrs. J. C. Hutcheson Jr.
Mr. I. K. Harris
Mr. Fritz Heitmann
Mr. Frank Ireland
Mrs. M. T. Jones
Mrs. W. E. Jones
Mr. Jesse H. Jones
Rev. W. States Jacobs
Mr. Will Kendall
Dr. J. Allen Kyle
Mr. W. H. Kirkland
Mr. Ed. Kiam
Mr. G. E. Korst
Mr. P. Kalb
Mrs. Edgar O. Lovett
Mr. Abe Levy
Mrs. Z. F. Lillard
Mr. L. Lechenger
Mrs. Jonothan Lane
Mrs. I. S. Levy
Mr. Emil Lipper
Mrs. R. S. Lovett
Mr. H. F. MacGregor
Mr. Richard Maury
Mr. W. C. Munn
Mrs. H. Masterson
Mr. Jos. F. Meyer
Mr. Homer Matthews
Mr. Geo. Macatee
Mrs. Jos. Mullen
Mr. H. C. Mosehart
Mrs. Edna McDonald

Mr. John McCleary
Mrs. E. L. Neville
Mr. C. E. Oliver
Mr. Wm. Olschewske
Mr. C. G. Pillot
Mrs. Edwin B. Parker
Mrs. E. A. Peden
Mrs. J. E. Pierce
Mrs. W. G. Priester
Mrs. H. B. Rice
Mr. Wm. Rice
Mrs. Herbert Roberts
Miss Mary Rouse
Miss Stella Root
Miss Laura Rice
Mrs. J. M. Rockwell
Mrs. B. A. Randolph
Mrs. S. C. Red
Mr. J. W. Reynolds
Mrs. Rosine Ryan
Dr. W. H. Scherer
Mr. R. H. Swartz
Mrs. W. B. Sharp
Miss Ella Smith
Mrs. Jas. S. Stewart
Mr. Minor Stewart
Mr. Henry Stude
Mr. Arthur Saft
Mr. Jas. L. Storey
Mr. G. F. Sauter
Mr. Max Schnitzer
Mrs. J. L. Thompson
Mrs. Tom Taylor
Mrs. W. A. Vinson
Mr. R. W. Wier
Mrs. H. T. Williamson
Mrs. C. C. Wenzel
Mrs. Gentry Waldo
Mrs. C. R. Wharton
Mr. H. Waddell
Mr. J. F. Wolters

ORIGINAL OFFICERS

First officials of the Houston Symphony Association, elected in October, 1913, were as follows:

PRESIDENT	Mrs. Edwin B. Parker
FIRST VICE-PRESIDENT	Miss Ima Hogg
SECOND VICE-PRESIDENT	Frantz Brogniez
CORRESPONDING SECRETARY	Mrs. William Abbey
RECORDING SECRETARY	Mrs. Z. F. Lillard
TREASURER	H. F. MacGregor

Directors

Mmes. R. C. Duff, Jules Hirsch, Edwin B. Parker, William Abbey, Joseph Mullen, Will Jones, Z. F. Lillard, Turner Williamson, Bess Stewart, Gentry Waldo, J. L. Thompson, Misses Ima Hogg, Laura Rice, Blanche Foley, Ella Smith, Messrs. H. F. MacGregor, Ike Harris, Henry Stude, Abe Levy, Will Kendall, Jesse H. Jones, Frantz Brogniez, D. B. Cherry, J. S. Cullinan, Edgar Odell Lovett

Honorary Members

Rabbi Henry Barnstein, Mrs. Wille Hutcheson, Mrs. J. C. Carr, Prof. E. Lindenberg, Miss A. Cranford, Harry Warner, John Reagan, Dr. E. Blitz (New York)

Advisory Board

Rabbi H. Barnstein, Rev. W. States Jacobs, Mrs. W. B. Sharp, Mrs. C. C. Wenzel, Mrs. H. Masterson, Mrs. J. C. Carr, Prof. P. W. Horn

Signers of the Charter Application were Mrs. Edwin B. Parker, Miss Ima Hogg, Mrs. William Abbey, Mrs. Gentry Waldo and Julien Paul Blitz.

PRESIDENTS OF THE HOUSTON SYMPHONY SOCIETY

1913–1917	Mrs. Edwin B. Parker
1917–1921	Miss Ima Hogg
1921–1931	Mrs. H. M. Garwood
1931–1934	Dr. Joseph A. Mullen
1934–1936	Joseph S. Smith
1936–1942	Walter H. Walne
1942–1945	H. R. Cullen
1945–1946	Joseph S. Smith

1946–1956   Miss Ima Hogg
1956–1970   Gen. Maurice Hirsch[1]
1970–   Dr. Charles F. Jones

CHAIRMEN OF THE BOARD

The office of Chairman of the Board was created in 1946 and discontinued in 1956. Those who filled the position in that ten-year span were, in order:

1946–1948   Gus S. Wortham
1948–1950   F. M. Law
1950–1953   Warren S. Bellows
1953–1954   Harmon Whittington

CHAIRMEN OF THE MAINTENANCE FUND CAMPAIGNS

The Houston orchestra's maintenance fund plan was instituted in 1945. Chairmen of these annual campaigns have been as follows:

1945   F. M. Law
1946   Gus S. Wortham
1947   Gus S. Wortham
1948   Harmon Whittington
1949   Stanley W. Shipnes
1950   James L. Shepherd, Jr.
1951   Max Levine
1952   Russell L. Jolley
1953   Robert W. Kneebone
1954   Charles L. Bybee
1955   W. Leland Anderson
1956   Charles L. Bybee
1957   Charles L. Bybee
1958   Frank C. Smith
1959   Leon Jaworski
1960   William G. Farrington
1961   Michel T. Halbouty
1962   Charles L. Bybee
1963   Charles L. Bybee
1964   Charles L. Bybee
1965   Charles L. Bybee

[1] President emeritus.

1966   Charles L. Bybee
1967   Charles L. Bybee
1968   Frank A. Watts
1969   Max Levine
1970   Max Levine

CHAIRMEN OF THE WOMEN'S COMMITTEE OF THE HOUSTON SYMPHONY SOCIETY

1937–1939   Miss Ima Hogg
1939–1940   Mrs. John F. Grant
1940–1942   Mrs. J. R. Parten
1942–1944   Mrs. Andrew E. Rutter
1944–1945   Mrs. Aubrey Leon Carter
1945–1946   Mrs. Stuart Sherar
1946–1947   Mrs. Julian S. Burrows
1947–1949   Mrs. Paul V. Ledbetter
1949–1951   Mrs. Albert P. Jones
1951–1953   Mrs. Ben A. Calhoun
1953–1955   Mrs. James Griffith Lawhon
1955–1957   Mrs. Olaf La Cour Olsen
1957–1959   Mrs. Ralph Ellis Gunn
1959–1961   Mrs. Leon Jaworski
1961–1963   Mrs. Garrett R. Tucker, Jr.
1963–1965   Mrs. M. T. Launius, Jr.
1965–1967   Mrs. Thompson McCleary
1967–1969   Mrs. Theodore W. Cooper
1969–1970   Mrs. Allen H. Carruth
1971–   Mrs. David Hannah, Jr.

CONDUCTORS OF THE HOUSTON SYMPHONY ORCHESTRA

1913–1916   Julien Paul Blitz
1916–1918   Paul Bergé
1931–1932   Uriel Nespoli
1932–1935   Frank St. Leger
1936–1947   Ernst Hoffmann
1948–1954   Efrem Kurtz
1954–1955   Sir Thomas Beecham
1955–1961   Leopold Stokowski

1961–1967   Sir John Barbirolli[2]
1967–1969   André Previn
1971–   Lawrence Foster

Personnel of the Original Houston Symphony Orchestra
1913

Conductor: Julien Paul Blitz
Concertmaster: B. J. Steinfeldt

First violin: Anton Diehl, E. G. Saunders, M. Derdeyn, L. Arnouts (librarian), Eugene Diehl, Miss Rosetta Hirsch, Arthur Saft. *Second violin*: L. R. Smith, J. C. Willrich, J. A. Bruno, W. R. Patrick, F. H. Miller. *Viola*: E. P. Collins, O. M. Kendall, W. H. Dunlay. *Cello*: P. Gutierrez, Julio Galindo. *Contrabass*: J. Gutierrez. *Oboe*: Carlos Jakez. *Flute*: George N. Evans, A. Hussman. *Clarinet*: Ernest Hail, Clyde Fields. *Bassoon*: Francisco Anaya. *Trumpet*: S. J. Paul, C. V. Williams. *Trombone*: B. D. Boone, George Hughes, E. Kuhnel. *Horn*: E. F. Smith, William Diehl. *Timpani*: H. J. Weiss. *Drums*: E. E. Stokes. *Piano*: R. Guttman. *Organ*: Arthur J. H. Barbour.

Personnel of the Houston Symphony Orchestra
1970–1971

Conductor-in-chief: Lawrence Foster[3]
Associate Conductor: A. Clyde Roller
Concertmaster: Raphael Fliegel
Associate Concertmaster: Albert Muenzer
Assistant Concertmaster: David Chausow

FIRST VIOLIN

Marcella Boffa
Michael Wilkomirski
Joan Stanley
Irving Wadler
Doris Musgrave
John Oliveira
Eugene Settanni
Barbara Shook
Christine Louis

James Stephenson
Elizabeth Mosny
Theodore Mamlock
Mario Paglia

SECOND VIOLIN

George Bennett
Principal
Robert Perry
Ass't. Principal

[2] Conductor emeritus.
[3] Appointed March 10, 1971.

Mary Shelley McIntyre
Dorothe Robinson
Jan Karon
Mary LaMonaca
Johan Simonsen
Betty Stephenson
Vera Jelagin
Harry Cowan
Elena Diaz
Helen Furbay
Verna McIntyre

VIOLA

Wayne Crouse
Principal
Violeta Moncada
Ass't. Principal
William Welch
Thomas Molloy
Hugh Gibson
Joy Plesner
Kyla Bynum
Thomas Elliott
Peter Filerman
Sherman Shand
Shaler Moscovitz

CELLO

Shirley Trepel
Principal
Thomas Bay
Ass't. Principal
Stephen Gorisch
Dorothy Moyes
Frank Bruinsman
Fred Mazzari
Louis DeRudder
Marian Wilson
Hyunjin Cho
Bonnie King

CONTRA-BASS

William Black
Principal

Keith Robinson
Ass't. Principal
Philip Edley
Paul Ellison
Robert Pastorek
Kendrick Wauchope
Newell Dixon
Leonard Manno

FLUTE

Byron Hester
Principal
David Colvig
Carol Robertson

PICCOLO

Carol Robertson

OBOE

Raymond Weaver
Principal
Barbara Hester
Louis Ruttenberg
Ass't. Principal

ENGLISH HORN

Larry Thompson

CLARINET

Richard Pickar
Principal
Don G. Slocomb
Richard Nunemaker

BASS CLARINET

Richard Nunemaker

BASSOON

Paul R. Tucci
Principal
Richard Hall
Ralph Schulze

CONTRA-BASSOON

Ralph Schulze

240

HORN

James Tankersley
Principal
Caesar LaMonaca
Leo Sacchi
Jay L. Andrus
Jan Bures

TRUMPET

James Austin
Principal
Ned Battista
Richard Schaffer
Ass't. Principal

TROMBONE

Albert Lube
Principal
Ralph Liese
David Waters

TUBA

William Rose

TIMPANI

David Wuliger

PERCUSSION

James Simon
Principal
Henry Fulgham
Fraya Fineberg

HARP

Beatrice Schroeder Rose

PIANO AND CELESTE

Mary Elizabeth Lee

ORGAN

Robert Jones

INDEX